BAKED
OCCASIONS

BAKED
OCCASIONS

DESSERTS FOR LEISURE ACTIVITIES, HOLIDAYS,
AND INFORMAL CELEBRATIONS

BY **MATT LEWIS** AND **RENATO POLIAFITO**

PHOTOGRAPHY BY BRIAN KENNEDY

STEWART, TABORI & CHANG • NEW YORK

INTRODUCTION 11 | **A HANDY BAKED REFERENCE GUIDE** 15

••• JANUARY

BAKED'S BIRTHDAY | BAKED ULTIMATE BIRTHDAY CAKE 24

NEW YEAR'S DAY | HAIR OF THE DOG CAKE 28

LA BEFANA | BRUTTI MA BUONI (UGLY BUT GOOD) COOKIES 30

ELVIS'S BIRTHDAY | CARAMEL-Y BANANA, PEANUT BUTTER, AND CHOCOLATE BREAD PUDDING 32

DOLLY PARTON'S BIRTHDAY | DOLLY'S DOUGHNUT 36

CHINESE NEW YEAR | CHINESE FIVE-SPICE SESAME SCONES 41

••• FEBRUARY

GROUNDHOG DAY | TOFFEE COFFEE CAKE SURPRISE 44

WORLD NUTELLA DAY | NUTELLA CHIP COOKIES 48

VALENTINE'S DAY | CONVERSATION HEART CAKES 50

VALENTINE'S DAY | VANILLA BEAN ANGEL FOOD CAKE WITH MILK CHOCOLATE GLAZE 54

MARDI GRAS | THE NEW ORLEANS 56

SHROVE TUESDAY | KITCHEN-SINK DUTCH BABY 61

WASHINGTON'S BIRTHDAY / PRESIDENTS' DAY | CHERRY ALMOND CRISP 65

NATIONAL PISTACHIO DAY | PISTACHIO WHITE CHOCOLATE CHEESECAKE 67

••• MARCH

TEXAS INDEPENDENCE DAY | CHOCOLATE TEXAS SHEET CAKE WITH PEANUT BUTTER FROSTING 72

THE IDES OF MARCH | BLOOD ORANGE TIRAMISU 74

ST. PATRICK'S DAY | ST. PATRICK'S DRUNK BUNDT CAKE 77

VERNAL EQUINOX | LIGHT AND LEMONY JELLY ROLL WITH RASPBERRY CREAM FILLING 79

••• APRIL

EASTER | MEGA EASTER PIE: A MEAT AND CHEESE UTOPIA 84

EASTER | EASTER COCONUT SHEET CAKE 86

EARTH DAY | HIPPIE CAKE 90

SHAKESPEARE DAY | BUTTERY POUND CAKE WITH SALTY CARAMEL GLAZE 93

SECRETARY'S DAY (AKA ADMINISTRATIVE PROFESSIONALS' DAY) | CARAMEL CANDY POPCORN BALLS 96

••• MAY

MAY DAY | STRAWBERRY SUPREME CAKE 100

BLACK FOREST CAKE FESTIVAL | BLACK FOREST CUPCAKES 104

KENTUCKY DERBY | DERBY COOKIES 107

TEACHER APPRECIATION DAY / NATIONAL CHOCOLATE CHIP COOKIE DAY |
OLD-SCHOOL OATMEAL CHOCOLATE CHIP COOKIES 110

MOTHER'S DAY | ULTRALEMONY LEMON BUNDT CAKE WITH ALMOND GLAZE 113

NATIONAL WINE DAY | RED WINE CHOCOLATE CUPCAKES WITH CHOCOLATE GLAZE 117

••• JUNE

THE QUEEN'S BIRTHDAY | CHAI SPICE TRIFLE WITH MIXED BERRIES 120

GAY PRIDE | RAINBOW ICEBOX CAKE WITH HOMEMADE CHOCOLATE COOKIES 125

FLAG DAY | BROWN SUGAR SHORTCAKES WITH BROWN SUGAR SYRUP, MIXED BERRIES, AND WHIPPED CREAM 128

FATHER'S DAY | DAD'S BLACK COCOA BUNDT WITH BUTTER WHISKEY GLAZE 132

NATIONAL CHOCOLATE PUDDING DAY | HOT CHOCOLATE PUDDING CAKE 135

JULY

CANADA DAY | NANAIMO ICE CREAM BARS 138

INDEPENDENCE DAY | ORANGE BUTTERMILK PICNIC CAKE WITH CHOCOLATE CHIPS 142

BASTILLE DAY | CHEESY BASTILLE DAY BEER BREAD 144

HUNTER S. THOMPSON'S BIRTHDAY | GONZO CAKE 146

A LEISURELY CONVERSATION ABOUT HOLIDAYS, OCCASIONS, AND CHILDHOOD TRAUMA WITH MATT AND RENATO 150

AUGUST

MARTHA STEWART'S BIRTHDAY | EVERYONE'S FAVORITE BIRTHDAY CAKE 156

JULIA CHILD'S BIRTHDAY | SALTED CARAMEL SOUFFLÉ 158

FERRAGOSTO | BRIOCHE ICE CREAM SANDWICHES 161

BLUEBERRY MONTH | NONNIE'S BLUEBERRY BUCKLE 165

NATIONAL DOG DAY | CHOCOLATE CHIP HUSH PUPPIES 168

SEPTEMBER

NATIONAL GRANDPARENTS DAY | FROZEN SWISS CHOCOLATE PIE 172

ROSH HASHANAH | ORANGE PANCAKES WITH HONEY BUTTER 175

FIRST DAY OF SCHOOL | MINI CHOCOLATE BROWNIE CUPCAKES 178

MILDRED DAY'S BIRTHDAY | CHOCOLATE RICE CRISPY "CAKE" WITH HOMEMADE MARSHMALLOW "ICING" 181

OCTOBER

ELEANOR ROOSEVELT'S BIRTHDAY | PEANUT BUTTER AND JELLY CRUMB MORNING MUFFINS 186

COLUMBUS DAY | PUMPKIN SWIRL CHEESECAKE CHOCOLATE BROWNIES 189

ALASKA DAY | INDIVIDUAL BAKED ALASKAS WITH VANILLA AND COFFEE ICE CREAM 193

HALLOWEEN | MILK CHOCOLATE MALTED BROWNIES WITH CHOCOLATE GANACHE 195

HALLOWEEN | CHOCOLATE POP TARTS WITH PEANUT BUTTER AND JAM FILLING 199

••• NOVEMBER

DAY OF THE DEAD | CHOCOLATE CINNAMON CHIPOTLE SUGAR COOKIES 204

ELECTION DAY | ELECTION PALMIERS 208

THANKSGIVING | BROWN BUTTER APPLE CRANBERRY GALETTE 212

THANKSGIVING | SWEET POTATO TART WITH GINGERSNAP CRUST AND HEAVENLY MERINGUE 217

BLACK FRIDAY | CHOCOLATE ESPRESSO TAPIOCA PUDDING WITH KAHLÚA WHIPPED CREAM 220

••• DECEMBER

HOLIDAY BAKING INTERLUDE | TWELVE DAYS OF COOKIES 224-240

S COOKIES 227 | PEANUT BUTTER BLOSSOMS 228 | GINGERSNAPS WITH LEMON SUGAR 229 |
EXCEEDINGLY CHOCOLATY CRINKLES 230 | WHIPPED SHORTBREAD 231 | PEPPERMINT
CHOCOLATE CHIP MERINGUES 232 | PEANUT BUTTER BUTTERSCOTCH COOKIES 233 |
LEBKUCHEN 234 | MAE'S CRESCENT COOKIES 236 | CAMPFIRE COOKIES 237 |
TRADITIONAL LINZER COOKIES 238 | DATE SQUARES 240

NATIONAL MAPLE SYRUP DAY | BROWN SUGAR OATMEAL WHOOPIE PIES WITH MAPLE MARSHMALLOW FILLING 242

WINTER SOLSTICE | WINTERMINT CAKE 244

CHRISTMAS EVE | PINK PEPPERMINT STICK ICE CREAM WITH HOMEMADE HOT FUDGE 249

CHRISTMAS | TRICOLOR CAKE 252

CHRISTMAS | ORANGE PINEAPPLE WALNUT FRUITCAKE 257

BOXING DAY | SALTED CARAMEL CHOCOLATE CUPCAKE SHAKES 260

SOURCES 263 | ACKNOWLEDGMENTS 264 | BADASS RECIPE TESTERS 266 | INDEX 267

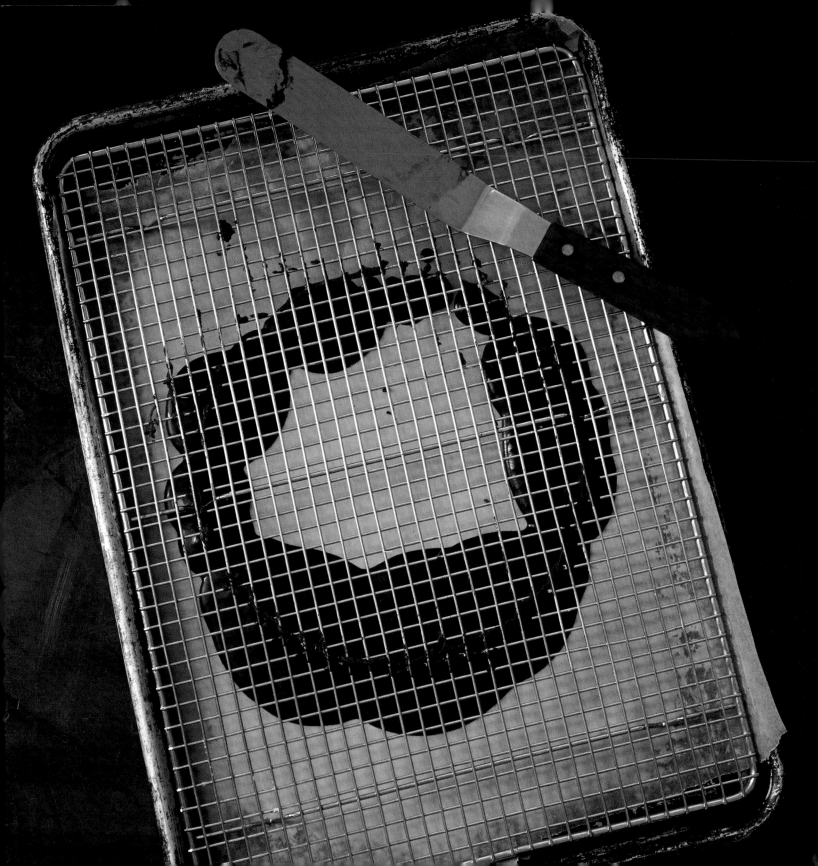

THIS BOOK IS DEDICATED
TO OUR FATHERS.

INTRODUCTION

●●● **THE THINGS WE DIDN'T KNOW: ALASKA AND NUTELLA**

There is an inherent madness required to own and operate a bakery. We knew this before we opened Baked. We knew owning a bakery was, by and large, a low-margin business with masochistic hours. We knew it was going to be a bumpy path marked with occasional recipe failures, oven malfunctions, employee tears, and achy, weary bones. We knew all these things and more. But we dove in regardless. We opened a bakery because it was inevitable. It was predestined. We opened a bakery because, well, we were young (or youngish) and naïve, and we both really like chocolate cake.

We opened our Brooklyn bakery in 2005. The entire first year of business was propelled by a combination of mania, fear (fear is a strong motivator), and pride (we really liked our chocolate cake). Each day was a mini life lesson. Each hour was a master class. It was a lot to absorb and disseminate. We made many of the classic freshman-year missteps. We never fully completed a business plan, and that business plan draft was short (one page, double spaced), full of adjectives and aspirations, and lacking substance and numbers and a healthy dose of reality. We also made many bad hiring decisions because we were wild-eyed with exhaustion and desperation. We hired random warm bodies without any reference checks and pretended to ignore their shortcomings and bizarre quirks.

We also learned a great deal. We absorbed things that can only be taught while in the midst of the madness, the trial by fire. This is the stuff that is absent from traditional "how to" books and sterile business classrooms. For instance, we learned that anything and everything sells better if you put salted caramel in it, on it, or next to it. Literally, anything! We also became aware, very quickly, that Brooklyn is a borough of lovely and sweet procrastinators (ourselves included). Our customers like to order birthday cakes last minute and Thanksgiving pies on, well . . . Thanksgiving. We adjusted our baking schedule accordingly.

But, in hindsight, it was the entirely unexpected customer devotion to all manner of holidays that surprised us most. Of course, we expected more orders from the traditional holidays. We anticipated an avalanche of pies for Thanksgiving and an assembly line of sugarplum dreams (and their assured profits) for the month of December. We even predicted (with a whiff of overconfidence) slight bumps for Valentine's Day, Easter, and Mother's Day. What we didn't anticipate—what we never could have anticipated—was the fascination and excitement surrounding seemingly inconsequential holidays. Simply put, before opening Baked, we were not aware of World Nutella Day or Alaska Day. Now, a few years in, not only do we celebrate them, but they are etched upon our subconscious. ●●●

●●● HOW WE LEARNED TO STOP WORRYING AND LOVE THE CALENDAR

As bakery owners and dessert Pied Pipers, we are (now) hyperaware of the calendar. It is a wild, thrashing, untamed beast spilling out and over. It is, at once, both a reminder of immense possibility and promises unfulfilled. So many holidays, so little time.

It wasn't always like this. There used to be fewer holidays. They used to be more genteel, more reflective, and they were generally based upon religion (Easter) or great national moments (adoption of the Declaration of Independence). Now, for better or worse, there are holidays commemorating polar bears, chocolate chip cookies (yes!), and candy corn.

Social media (hand in hand with widespread Internet access) has certainly propelled some of these less cerebral holidays beyond perfunctory status. For example, way back in 1984, President Ronald Reagan (yes, Ronald Reagan) proclaimed the third Sunday in July as National Ice Cream Day. We were blissfully unaware of this until recently. Actually, until recently, everyone was blissfully unaware of this, except for maybe a few members of some random dairy association. Now, on or near the end of July, National Ice Cream Day mentions clog our Twitter feed, and our smartphones are alive with images of banana splits. It's now a holiday, fully formed.

At first, we were cynical. We were typical Grinches anchored by a touch of arrogance. We felt a little bit above all of the various national "put your favorite foodstuff here" days. Then, eventually and slowly, we gave in. We joined the party. We loosened the belt and gained a waist size. We went to a birthday party for Elvis (without irony) and truly enjoyed it. True, we treat these less significant holidays with a lighter touch than Christmas or even Mother's Day, but we celebrate nonetheless. Bring us a holiday, we will bring the cake. ●●●

●●● ABOUT THIS BOOK

In the end, this is our holiday collection as shaped by our own perverse sentimentality. We felt it was our duty to make it wholly representative of us. These are the holidays and celebrations we enjoy; these are the dates highlighted and circled in red on our overflowing calendar. Obviously, we included several holidays shaped by family rituals and hazy nostalgia (Christmas, Halloween, and—in Renato's case—Ferragosto). We embraced many more (National Wine Day, Julia Child's Birthday) simply because we couldn't help ourselves. The calendar is awash in unusual, mundane, and campy holidays, and we cherry-picked at will.

You'll notice this book is not an all-inclusive everybody/everything holiday cookbook. Those books—and there are plenty of them—are overly bland, overly broad, uninspired, or worse (Google "Sandra Lee's Kwanzaa Cake"). If we skipped a big spiritual holiday, it is only because we were both brought up as twice-a-year Catholics. We felt uncomfortable and slightly disingenuous taking on major religious holidays we were unfamiliar with. To be sure, we are an entirely inclusive duo and aching to expand our horizons. (Won't somebody please invite us to take part in their family's special or religious holiday feast? We will bring dessert.) We will continue to experiment beyond the familiar, and we expect our holiday-baking repertoire to grow and change as we learn and research. By the by, we dropped a few big crowd-pleasers from the book as well. While we absolutely understand the groundswell of excitement generated by the Super Bowl, we would be lying if we told you we could identify any NFL team by its jersey. We also debated treats for an Oscar bash, but alas, it is an event that is too gay even for us. ●●●

●●● HOW TO USE THIS BOOK

These are our favorite holidays, but this is your book, and we hope you use it often. Perhaps we are naïve, but we have fanciful notions of expanding your holiday knowledge (we tried to include important, relevant tidbits in the recipe intros) and baking alongside you (at least virtually). We hope you will partake and rejoice in National Chocolate Pudding Day (see page 135) at least once, and we want to see photos of your Baked Ultimate Birthday Cake (page 24).

Of course, you can rebel. In fact, we encourage it. You can make Mega Easter Pie (page 84) on Labor Day and bake our Tricolor Cake (page 252) for a favorite aunt's birthday in July. The recipes in the book are organized by holiday starting with January (of course) and continuing all the way through the mega holiday month of December, but feel free to mix and match.

As with any cookbook, we ask only that you read through the entire recipe before gathering ingredients. Knowledge is power. It's better to know ahead of time that your cookie dough needs twenty-four hours to rest (Old-School Oatmeal Chocolate Chip Cookies, page 110) and your frosting has to be applied to the warm cake in order to fuse properly (Chocolate Texas Sheet Cake with Peanut Butter Frosting, page 72).

Finally, as of this writing, we are still quite easy to contact if you like. We have yet to reach the stratospheric level of fame that most assuredly awaits us. At the moment, we are without personal bodyguards, myriad handlers, and throngs of screaming fans. This is the perfect time to reach out to us with your baking question. Or holiday question. Or maybe you just want to contact us to say hello. We are accessible via all manner of social media (and snail mail). Feel free to drop by with a query or comment. As long as we haven't disappeared under the guise of the Witness Protection Program, we are mostly available.

Now go enjoy the holidays. Embrace the calendar. Eat well. Be sweet.

MATT + RENATO

A HANDY BAKED REFERENCE GUIDE

(AKA EVERYTHING YOU NEED TO KNOW TO GET BAKED)

We present the following handy reference guide to serve you in almost all of your baking needs (or at least your baking needs as they relate to this book).

● ● ●

KITCHEN TOOLS AND EQUIPMENT

GADGETS AND TOOLS

Bench Knife A bench knife (aka dough scraper) is incredibly useful in the baker's kitchen (i.e., if you don't own one, it is well worth the minimal investment). A bench knife is generally a 3-by-5-inch (7.5-by-12-cm) sheet of metal attached to a handle (we much prefer the wooden handle from a purely aesthetic point of view). They are perfect for cutting, portioning, and turning all sorts of doughs. I have also used my bench knife to aid in frosting cakes: They are perfect for creating smooth, even buttercreams. Additionally, they are great for scraping down and cleaning surfaces.

Cake Turntable If you are serious about cake decorating, you must invest in a heavy-duty (avoid the cheap plastic) cake turntable, basically a lazy Susan for cakes. Look for one with a cast-iron stand and aluminum top, and you will be able to achieve the classic Baked swirl décor—we finish almost all of our bakery cakes with a signature swirl of frosting, achieved using a cake turntable and icing spatula—with the flick of a wrist.

Cooling Racks Wire cooling racks are necessary. We use them to promote even cooling; it is just as important for air to circulate below the baked goods as it is above. Additionally, we use cooling racks to temporarily store hot-from-the-oven baking sheets and to glaze cakes. Buy something sturdy and easy to store (they make collapsible versions), and just make sure they are large enough to hold at least one 12-inch (30.5-cm) cake round or a tray full of cookies.

Ice-Cream Scoop An ice-cream scoop with a release mechanism will become your best friend. I use several different sizes to make perfectly portioned cookie dough balls. I also use them to portion and fill cupcake tins (the no-mess method) and evenly disperse cake batter among many pans.

Measuring Cups and Spoons Liquid and dry measuring cups are different animals:

Liquid I recommend two glass measuring cups: one 2-cup (480-ml) and one 4-cup (960-ml)—Anchor Hocking brand is our favorite—with both imperial and metric measurement labels on the side. These measuring cups also come in handy for melting butter (or butter and chocolate) in the microwave, and I often use them in place of small mixing bowls.

Dry Invest in a heavy-duty set of measuring cups and they should last you a lifetime. A complete set includes ¼ cup, ⅓ cup, ½ cup, and 1 cup, but I highly recommend you seek out the more elusive 2-cup measuring cup as well. It will come in handy. All dry measures in this book were tested using the spoon-and-sweep method (i.e., "spoon" the dry ingredients into the cup measure and then "sweep" with the back of a knife so that it is flush or level with the top of the measuring cup).

Spoons As with measuring cups, invest in a heavy-duty batch of metal measuring spoons and you will never have to replace them. They are usually sold as a set starting with ¼ teaspoon and going up to 1 tablespoon.

Microplane Microplane actually refers to a brand of long, thin graters commonly found in commercial and home kitchens alike. I use them exclusively. They will run circles around the old, more common box graters (we finally gave in and donated ours). I use one specifically for grating cheese and zesting citrus, and another separate one specifically for grating spices (you don't want the lingering fragrant spices to affect the taste of your zest and cheese).

Mixing Bowls For the mixing bowl purist, we recommend one simple set of glass nesting mixing bowls. They are easy to clean; they maneuver between microwave, oven, and tabletop with ease; and they are fairly lightweight. If you are like us and collect mixing bowls, you might want to add some vintage milk-glass or sleek, handmade ceramic bowls (that double as décor). Honestly, any bowls will do as long as they are food safe and simple to wash.

Parchment Paper Parchment paper is essential for the home baker. We use it exclusively to line cookie sheets (you can reuse a sheet of parchment at least once) and all manner of cake, brownie, bar, and loaf pans to aid in removing your baked goods in a clean manner. We do not recommend using Silpat liners in place of parchment. In our humble opinion, Silpat liners produce monotonous cookies without any of the delicious browning or crisping we so desire.

Pastry Cutter (aka Pastry Blender) A pastry cutter—a handheld tool made up of several metal tines (wires) connected to a wooden or steel handle—is a bit of a kitchen extravagance. In truth, a fork with long, thin tines is usually just as adept at blending fats (butter or shortening) into flour. However, if you are making loads of pie crusts or flaky pastry doughs, it might be worth the small indulgence.

Pie Weights Pie weights, or dried beans, help the pie dough hold its shape and prevent it from shrinking while baking. Inexpensive, forever-reusable pie weights can be found at most kitchen supply stores. I still just use beans at home (I've run out of storage), but if you make a lot of pies, you might want to purchase some pie weights.

Spatulas We have pared back our overwhelming rubber spatula collection from twenty-plus to just three (small, medium, large). Look for something heat resistant to 500°F (260°C). They are ideal for scraping down bowls, light mixing, and carefully folding egg whites into batters. We also have a random (but necessary) collection of offset metal spatulas with wooden handles. They are perfect for icing cakes, smoothing batters in pans, loosening cakes from the sides of pans, removing the first brownie, and swirling or marbling batters.

Thermometers Even if you're only a casual baker or candy maker, we think you will be genuinely pleased to have a couple of inexpensive thermometers at the ready:

Candy and/or Deep-Fry Thermometer Look for a double-duty candy and deep-fry thermometer (they are often sold as one and the same) with a temperature range of 100°F to 400°F (40°C to 205°C) to make buckets of caramel and fry to your heart's content.

Instant-Read Thermometer Bakers tend to use instant-read thermometers quite a bit for taking the internal temperature of cheesecake and testing the temperature of liquids (i.e., water temperature for bread baking and the like). Instant-reads look like large nails, wherein the head of the nail is the gauge.

Oven Thermometer I've baked in a lot of ovens, and it is rare to find one where the readout is reflective of the true temperature. Often, they are as much as 50°F (10°C) degrees cooler or warmer. Instead of overpaying a professional to recalibrate your oven (a difficult task at best), we suggest investing in a simple, cheap oven thermometer and adjusting the oven gauge accordingly. For baking, it is extremely important to have an accurate oven temperature, as baked goods can bomb spectacularly even if the oven is off by just a few degrees.

Whisks We exclusively use basic, sturdy, stainless-steel whisks for both our bakery and our kitchen. There are all manner of new-fangled and ridiculous whisks on the market (avoid the silicone versions at all costs), but for the purposes of the home baker, simpler is better. We recommend purchasing a few classic whisks in a few different sizes. Don't skimp on price here; they should feel "heavy duty" and hefty when you hold them in your hand. Whisks are necessary tools for blending dry ingredients; beating egg whites, egg yolks, and cream; and stirring together melted butter and chocolate. That said, do not use your whisk as an all-purpose stirring device. They are not to be used for folding batters—use a spatula for this—or agitating candy-making ingredients (best to use the handle of a wooden spoon). Have no fear: We call out which stirring tool to use throughout the book.

PANS AND BAKEWARE

Brownie and Bar Pan We have baked our brownies in literally every conceivable type of pan, including vessels that weren't exactly "baking pans" (desperate situations call for desperate measures), and all of them work reasonably well. Light-colored metal and glass are our current faves, and the only pan type we would dissuade you from is dark metal (to avoid crispy edges).

Bundt Pan I have a Bundt obsession (aka problem, aka addiction). I have baked in all manner of Bundt pans (including vintage finds from eBay and flea markets), and, generally speaking, all the heavy-duty cast-aluminum models work like a dream. Avoid the less expensive pressed aluminum; these are much lighter and less workhorsey. Our favorite model is still the classic Nordic Ware Anniversary Bundt. It provides a nice, even bake, and the nonstick interior is heavenly (Bundts are notoriously fussy to get out of pans). It might be more expensive, but it will be with your family for many generations. If you decide to invest in some of the more decorative Bundts (who can blame you?), make sure to really grease the hell out of all the nooks and crannies to prevent sticking and surface breakage.

Cake Pan As with almost all of our pan suggestions, simpler equals better. We use a variety of economical, professional aluminum cake pans (nothing fancy or convoluted) that are available from almost any kitchen supply store.

Cupcake and Muffin Pan The explosion in popularity of cupcakes has given way to a plethora of cupcake pans. We use the familiar light-metal twelve- and mini-cupcake/muffin pans in this book. We did not test any recipes in this book with a jumbo cupcake/muffin pan, though, in theory, there is no reason it wouldn't work well; just make sure to increase the bake time by about 50 percent, give or take.

Loaf Pan I am not even sure how I acquired my old, blackened, battered loaf pans (9-by-5-by-3-inches / 23-by-12-by-7.5-cm or thereabouts), but they appear very old and work very well (did I black out at a garage sale?). Regardless, again, no need to go fancy. Steer toward light metal or basic glass; they are classic and consistent. Just a side note, I tend to keep about four loaf pans lying around so I can double the recipes of quick breads and freeze the extras.

Pie Plates or Tins We love the look of ceramic pie dishes, but we tend to get better results with glass or metal. Whatever you do, do not use disposable tins as they generally produce soggier crusts. If you are feeling generous, bake a pie in an inexpensive glass pan and give the pie and pan to a friend, neighbor, or relative. Cute gift.

Soufflé Dishes, Molds, and Ramekins The ubiquitous white porcelain soufflé dish (or mold or ramekin) comes in a variety of sizes. We have large ones and small ones, and we use them for everything from bread pudding to soufflés to puddings and casseroles. In a pinch, they also make decent ice cream dishes. As they are rarely (if ever) marked for size on the vessel itself, it pays to be proactive and label (in permanent marker on the bottom of the pan) the dish yourself immediately after purchase. If you already own a soufflé dish and are trying to determine the size, the best way to do this is to fill a liquid measuring cup with water and pour it into the dish to figure out the corresponding measurement.

Springform Pan We have lived our entire baking lives with only one springform each. A high-sided, light-metal 9-inch (23-cm) springform is all you need to create beautiful cheesecakes, flourless cakes, and fancy tarts. While springform pans should hold their shape for a long time, sometimes they can warp ever so slightly. So we are overly cautious and wrap the sides and bottom of our springform pans (from the outside) in foil before adding batters so the pan does not leak while in the oven. Less mess.

Tart Pan A 9-inch (23-cm)—or thereabouts—tart pan is essential to the home-baking kitchen assortment. Preferably, look for one with a removable bottom, so that you can push it up to remove the tart (it is very difficult, if not impossible, to release a tart from a pan without a removable bottom). If you bake often, you might want to invest in a set of individual 4-inch (10-cm) mini tart pans; they produce really cute personal-size tarts. Just make sure to store them between layers of paper towels when stacking to avoid sticking.

Tube Pan A tube pan—in the shape of a massive doughnut but with straight edges—is essential to make most angel food–type cakes (and it comes in handy when making Nonnie's Blueberry Buckle, page 165). While most tube pans come with little feet to support the pan when it is turned upside down (a common instruction in most angel food cake recipes), they are not necessary; you can simply place the upturned pan on the neck of a large bottle.

It is often not a good idea to substitute a Bundt pan for a tube pan. While similar looking, tube pans are generally lighter, taller, and honed for super-light cakes—therefore you must bake tube-pan cakes in tube pans only.

APPLIANCES

Blender Though we don't usually indulge in luxury purchases, our life has changed since we were introduced to the Vitamix blender. In addition to producing the smoothest milk shakes (like our cupcake milk shakes, page 260), they make silky sauces and soups, and rivers of various nut butters. You don't need a Vitamix brand blender (we just think the world of them), but if you bake often and cook regularly, you will most certainly want some sort of blender.

Food Processor Yes, food processers are bulky, heavy, difficult to clean, and expensive, but they are a necessary kitchen extravagance. We use ours for everything. They chop nuts with aplomb. They pulverize graham crackers and cookies into perfect tart crusts. They help make the perfect pie dough a cinch (our recipe is on page 84), and we even use them on occasion to create quick but luscious frostings. Additionally, you will want to use them for all manner of savory kitchen recipes (they shred cheese like nobody's business).

Ice-Cream Maker I have been using/abusing a cheap fifty-dollar Cuisinart ice-cream maker for about ten years, and it makes some amazing ice cream (just remember to chill the bowl ahead of time). Though I am tempted to purchase a more expensive maker—one with a larger capacity and built-in compressor (to avoid that whole "freeze the bowl ahead of time" thing)—I am still blown away by the quality of ice cream that my inexpensive Cuisinart churns out.

Microwave Oven Here is the thing about microwave ovens: They are amazing for the home baker because they melt butter and chocolate quickly and efficiently and they can boil water—say for dissolving cocoa powder—in a matter of seconds (and, yes, we have been known to use them to reheat coffee). Are they a necessary appliance? Not really. Would I use them to heat up leftover pizza? Probably not. Would I miss it if someone removed my microwave from my kitchen? Absolutely.

Standing Mixer Regardless of your skill level or baking frequency, we implore you to splurge and invest in a good, solid standing mixer. They are essential to the baking kitchen (I have not made cookies or cake by hand since purchasing my KitchenAid model over fifteen years ago). We wholeheartedly recommend KitchenAid brand mixers (we personally like the 7-quart/6.6-L bowl model) as they are true kitchen workhorses.

Even if you opt for a different brand, be sure to choose one that has all the attachments: whisk, paddle, and dough hook (crucial for the brioche recipe on page 161).

● ● ●

TECHNIQUES

Double Boiler By and large, as bakers, we use the double-boiler method as a fail-safe way to melt chocolate (or chocolate and butter together) without burning the chocolate. It is also a great way to gently warm other ingredients, especially those that should not come into contact with direct heat. Do not be fooled into thinking you need a special device. All you need is one medium saucepan filled with water and one (preferably metal) heatproof bowl that sits partway inside the pan without touching the water. Bring the water to a gentle simmer and stir or agitate the ingredients in the metal bowl until melted (or heated through).

Folding Folding is an often-used baking technique, employed when you want to gently, very gently, combine two parts of a batter, usually one heavy and one light. We use a very large rubber spatula (never, ever use a whisk) to scrape the sides of the bowl, then sweep and turn the bottom part of one batter (often the heavier one) onto the top of the other batter. The entire concept of folding is one of gentleness; folding is often a slow and methodical process and should not be sped up.

Sifting Sifting is the act of adding air to the dry ingredients to produce lighter cakes and baked goods. Sifting also does a great job of distributing ingredients and removing lumps. We do not suggest using a specialty sifter (it's just one more kitchen knick-knack); instead, use a large, fine-mesh sieve (bonus: they are inexpensive and multipurpose).

Toasting Nuts For the purposes of freshness, we like to buy raw nuts and toast them as needed per recipe. It is super easy, and it makes your house smell dreamy. Simply spread your nuts across a rimmed baking sheet in an even layer and toast until fragrant, flipping the nuts with a spatula once or twice during the suggested bake time. Use the following chart to estimate baking temperatures and times. Allow nuts to cool completely (unless otherwise stated) before adding them to your recipe.

Type of Nut	Bake Time	Bake Temp
Pine nuts (pignoli)	5 mins	300°F (150°C)
Almonds, walnuts, and pecans	10 mins	300°F (150°C)
Hazelnuts and macadamias	12 mins	300°F (150°C)
Shelled peanuts	15–17 mins	350°F (175°C)
Peanuts in their shells	20–22 mins	350°F (175°C)

● ● ●

INGREDIENTS AND BRAND RECOMMENDATIONS

Black Cocoa Powder We have fallen in love with King Arthur Black Cocoa Powder. It is a super-dark Dutch-process cocoa, and it creates beautifully dark (yup, almost black) chocolate cakes, brownies, and cookies. We especially love the dramatic high contrast (dark-chocolate sponge, light-colored frosting) effect it creates in our Wintermint Cake (page 244). It's available online at KingArthurFlour.com.

Butter All of the recipes in this book were tested using unsalted butter. Salted butter is terrific—we love it on toast—but if you use salted butter in your baking recipes, it is impossible to control the final salt content of the recipe (and an overly salty cake is kind of hard to disguise). We also often suggest using cool but not cold butter. More specifically, remove your butter from the refrigerator 15 to 20 minutes prior to baking and cut it into cubes, if directed. Finally, in one or two instances, we suggest using a higher-fat European-style butter. The most common, easy-to-locate brands are Plugrá and Kerrygold.

Chocolate If you splurge on just one pantry item, splurge on a premium chocolate. Great-tasting (and baking) chocolate produces great-tasting desserts. Similarly, crappy chocolate produces crappy desserts.

Premium chocolate is often on the pricey side, so we encourage you to buy in bulk and buy in blocks. Block chocolate is always less expensive than chopped because you have to go the extra

OUR RECS FOR DARK CHOCOLATE

Callebaut Chocolate Block 60% and Callebaut Chocolate Block 70% are found in specialty shops, often chopped and repackaged by the store. Callebaut is a helluva chocolate workhorse: It tastes lovely and is easy to use across multiple applications.

Valrhona Grand Cru is expensive, but it melts like a dream and is delectable in ganaches and frostings. Often found in specialty stores.

Scharffen Berger's Home Baking Bars are far easier to find, and we are happy to use them in a pinch. Look for the 62% and 70% bars for all dark-chocolate applications.

OUR RECS FOR MILK CHOCOLATE

We're completely addicted to the TCHO Serious Milk 39% chocolate discs. We often chop them up and use them in place of semisweet chocolate chips for chocolate chip cookies and the like.

We have been friends with master chocolatier Jacques Torres for years and still use his Milk Chocolate Bar for all sorts of applications.

Again, we're happy to recommend Scharffen Berger Milk Chocolate Bar 41% as it has a wide distribution and, though it is less expensive, is quite good.

step and "chunk" or chop the chocolate yourself. It is super easy and will save you a significant amount.

At our bakery (like many specialty bakeries), we use different chocolate brands for different applications. For instance, we might use one brand for the chunks in our chocolate chunk cookie and another brand altogether for chocolate frostings. This is based solely on personal preference after years of experimentation. The one thing all these brands have in common, however, is that they have very "clean" ingredient decks. Premium chocolate should include only cocoa butter, cacao, sugar, milk solids/powder, vanilla (maybe), and often a natural emulsifier (soya lecithin is popular). It should not include anything unnatural. Read all chocolate labels.

And about those chocolate percentages you find on labels: The percentage label on a bar of chocolate is referring to the cocoa mass in the bar itself. The higher the cocoa mass, the darker the chocolate. But even if the cocoa percentage is the same across multiple brands, the proportions of sugar, milk solids, and other ingredients can be wildly different. Simply put, the content (and therefore the taste) of chocolate bars varies wildly from brand to brand.

Our chocolate recommendations here are simply guidelines. The world of chocolate is changing rapidly (and for the better), and new specialty brands are popping up virtually overnight. Feel free to use our recommendations as a springboard, but we also encourage you to experiment with other brands—new and local and organic and all that jazz—until you settle upon your favorites. (See Sources, page 263, for specifics.)

Dyes and Food Gels At Baked, we use a variety of food dyes and gels to achieve certain colors for our frostings and icings. We prefer gels as they add less "liquid" to the overall mix/batter. While we don't always use 100 percent vegetable colorants (the colors are lovely but muted), we would be remiss not to recommend India Tree decorating colors (found at Whole Foods stores and online at IndiaTree.com). Besides India Tree, we recommend Ateco gel colors (found at most specialty baking stores and online at Amazon.com). Though Ateco is made in the United States, and their gels produce terrific results, be aware they are not vegetable-based (i.e., not all-natural) colors.

Maple Syrup Please, whatever you do, do not use imitation maple syrup. We know real maple syrup is expensive. If you are baking with maple syrup (as in our Brown Sugar Oatmeal Whoopie Pies with Maple Marshmallow Filling, page 242), you can, in general, use any grade syrup (the grading system can be confusing, as it is not universal), but we tend to gravitate toward the darker maple syrups, which generally have a more robust maple flavor. The fake stuff is usually just food coloring and corn syrup—ugh. Lucky us, we live in the Northeast where many farmers' markets sell local maple syrup. We also recommend the Crown Maple brand, available online at CrownMaple.com.

Purple Yam / Ube Powder In order to make our Gonzo Cake (page 146), we use purple yam powder (literally, dehydrated purple yam) and reconstitute it with water before adding it to the batter. Purple yam (also known as *ube*) powder is used in some traditional Filipino desserts and, like pumpkin, has a very delicate flavor that is often overpowered by the other ingredients in the recipe. It can be found stateside in Asian specialty markets and also at Amazon.com and a few other online purveyors.

Salt / Sea Salt Unless otherwise stated, we use ordinary, average kosher salt in our recipes. More than likely, you can substitute table or iodized salt without fear of ruining any recipe—just reduce the amount by about one-third (or to taste). We do specifically call for sea salt or fleur de sel for some recipes and for finishing (sprinkling on top of cookie dough, etc.). We absolutely love the slightly chunky fleur de sel made by Le Saunier de Camargue (easily found on the Internet or at gourmet grocers).

Unsweetened Cocoa Powder All of the recipes in this book that use unsweetened cocoa powder (not black cocoa, detailed above) were tested with both Valrhona and a less expensive brand (sometimes Hershey's, sometimes Ghirardelli). Invariably, we preferred the Valrhona, though the less expensive brands performed admirably. If cost is a concern, use the good stuff when making cocoa-based frosting or brownies, as the taste is more discernable; quality is less discernable in cake sponges. In order to purchase Valrhona cocoa at a discount, buy in bulk from a local specialty store or online and split the costs with another baker friend. (Also, we've found some local Whole Foods stores carry and sell Valrhona at a decent price.)

Vanilla Bean Paste We use Nielsen-Massey Madagascar Bourbon Pure Vanilla Bean Paste nearly as much as we use pure vanilla extract. The paste is thick and fragrant and contains real vanilla bean seeds that give light-colored frostings, fillings, and sponges a fun, speckled appearance. Generally speaking, vanilla bean paste is slightly more concentrated than extract, but it can be substituted for pure vanilla extract in a one-to-one ratio. Or you could use slightly less paste than extract (but we don't).

JANUARY

● ● ●

JAN 1 | BAKED'S BIRTHDAY
BAKED ULTIMATE BIRTHDAY CAKE 24

JAN 1 | NEW YEAR'S DAY
HAIR OF THE DOG CAKE 28

JAN 5 | LA BEFANA
BRUTTI MA BUONI (UGLY BUT GOOD) COOKIES 30

JAN 8 | ELVIS'S BIRTHDAY
CARAMEL-Y BANANA, PEANUT BUTTER, AND CHOCOLATE BREAD PUDDING 32

JAN 19 | DOLLY PARTON'S BIRTHDAY
DOLLY'S DOUGHNUT 36

DATE FLUCTUATES | CHINESE NEW YEAR
CHINESE FIVE-SPICE SESAME SCONES 41

BAKED ULTIMATE BIRTHDAY CAKE

VERY VANILLA SPRINKLE CAKE

YIELD: 1 8-INCH (20-CM) THREE-LAYER CAKE • 10 TO 12 SERVINGS

AT FIRST, Baked was just an idea—a grand vision of thick cake slices, giant cups of coffee, and endless slabs of fudge-like brownies—gestating and evolving for several years in Renato's and my collective mind. It was a sweeping, swirling, and ambitious dream that lived inside us—alongside us. We ate a lot of cake. We drank a lot of coffee. By turns gradually and impulsively, we honed the concept. First, we fell in love with a neighborhood: Red Hook, Brooklyn. It is the kind of neighborhood that doesn't much exist in New York City anymore. It is the kind of neighborhood that still feels special, small, local, artistic, unusual, and, most important, neighborly. Then, we fell in love with a space that needed a lot of love. Thankfully it was in the heart of Red Hook, on the heart of Van Brunt Street. In the summer of 2004 we set about piecing together our physical bakery. Slowly (perhaps much too slowly), the form began to take shape. After several months of nonstop mania, tears, exhaustion, and small triumphs, we proudly birthed our baby. Baked opened to the public on January 1, 2005.

We mark the occasion of our store opening, aka Baked's Birthday, every year. We usually do so with a lot of cake. We hope you will celebrate this happy occasion with us by making this cake. This is a very happy cake. This is the kind of birthday cake that turns gray skies blue; it is also very, very tasty. Obviously, our Very Vanilla Sprinkle Cake is full of vanilla. Vanilla is often the more stately, less sinful sister to our beloved chocolate, but it is just as powerful and enchanting in larger-than-average doses. We liberally applied vanilla to both the light white sponge cake and the smooth, rich frosting. Then—because we absolutely couldn't help ourselves—we filled and covered the whole cake with a rainbow explosion of sprinkles. The visual effect is a bit ridiculous and absolutely necessary.

●●● **BAKED NOTE**
If you like to decorate cakes, you might want to invest in a sturdy cake turntable (see page 15). While you don't absolutely need one, it will certainly help to achieve smooth cakes, special swirls, and, well . . . it makes adding the sprinkles to this cake a whole lot more fun.

INGREDIENTS

For the Very Vanilla Cake

2½ cups (315 g) cake flour

¾ cup (90 g) all-purpose flour

1 tablespoon baking powder

1 teaspoon baking soda

¾ teaspoon kosher salt

4 ounces (1 stick/115 g) unsalted butter, softened, plus more for the pans

½ cup (100 g) vegetable shortening, at room temperature

1¾ cups (350 g) granulated sugar

2 tablespoons pure vanilla extract

1 large egg

1 cup (240 ml) ice-cold water

½ cup (120 ml) whole milk

½ cup (120 ml) well-shaken buttermilk

1 cup (190 g) rainbow sprinkles

3 large egg whites, at room temperature

¼ teaspoon cream of tartar

For the Very Vanilla Frosting

1½ cups (300 g) granulated sugar

⅓ cup (40 g) all-purpose flour

1½ cups (360 ml) whole milk

⅓ cup (75 ml) heavy cream

12 ounces (3 sticks/340 g) unsalted butter, softened but cool, cut into small pieces

1½ teaspoons vanilla paste

1 teaspoon pure vanilla extract

MAKE THE VERY VANILLA CAKE

1 Preheat the oven to 325°F (165°C). Butter three 8-inch (20-cm) round cake pans, line the bottoms with parchment paper, and butter the parchment. Dust with flour and knock out the excess flour.

2 Sift both flours, the baking powder, baking soda, and salt together into a large bowl. Set aside.

3 In the bowl of a standing mixer fitted with the paddle attachment, beat the butter and shortening on medium speed until creamy, 3 to 4 minutes. Add the sugar and vanilla and beat on medium speed until fluffy, about 3 minutes. Scrape down the bowl, add the egg, and beat until just combined.

4 In a small bowl, whisk together the ice-cold water, milk, and buttermilk.

5 Add the flour mixture to the mixer bowl in three separate additions, alternating with the water mixture, beginning and ending with the flour mixture; turn the mixer to low when you add the ingredients, then up to medium for a few seconds to incorporate. Scrape down the bowl, then mix on low speed for a few more seconds. Remove the bowl from the standing mixer, scatter the sprinkles across the top of the batter, and fold them in with a rubber spatula.

6 In a medium bowl, whisk the egg whites and cream of tartar just until soft peaks form; do not overbeat. Gently fold the egg whites into the batter with a rubber spatula.

7 Divide the batter among the prepared pans and smooth the tops. Bake for 40 to 45 minutes, rotating the pans halfway through the baking time, until a toothpick inserted in the center of each cake comes out clean. Transfer the cakes to a wire rack and let cool for 20 minutes. Invert the cakes onto the rack, remove from the pans, and let cool completely. Remove the parchment.

MAKE THE VERY VANILLA FROSTING

1 In a medium heavy-bottomed saucepan, whisk the sugar and flour together. Add the milk and cream and cook over medium heat, whisking occasionally, until the mixture comes to a boil and has thickened to the consistency of a light pudding, 10 to 15 minutes.

2 Transfer the mixture to the bowl of a standing mixer fitted with the paddle attachment. Beat on high speed until cool, at least 7 to 9 minutes (you can speed up the process by pressing bags of frozen berries or corn against the sides and bottom of the mixing bowl). Reduce the speed to low and add the butter a few chunks at a time, every 20 to 30 seconds, while the mixer is constantly stirring; mix until thoroughly incorporated. Increase the speed to medium-high and beat until the frosting is light and fluffy, 1 to 2 minutes. Add the vanilla paste and extract and mix until combined. If the frosting is too soft, place the bowl in the refrigerator to chill slightly, then beat again until it can hold its shape. If the frosting is too firm, set the bowl over a pot of simmering water and beat with a wooden spoon until it is spreadable.

INGREDIENTS (CONT.)

For Décor

**1 to 1¼ cups (190 to 240 g)
   rainbow sprinkles**

ASSEMBLE THE CAKE

1 Place one cooled cake layer on a cake turntable (or a serving platter if you don't own a cake turn-table). Trim the top to create a flat surface, and evenly spread about 1¼ cups (215 g) of the frosting on top. Add the next layer, trim it, and frost it as before, then add the third layer (trim the final layer for a completely flat top, or feel free to leave it domed for an old-school appearance). Spread a very thin layer of frosting over the sides and top of the cake and place it in the refrigerator for about 15 minutes to firm up. (This is known as crumb coating and will help to keep loose cake crumbs under control when you frost the outside of the cake).

2 Place the turntable on a parchment-lined baking sheet with raised sides. Frost the sides and top with the remaining frosting. Grab a fistful of sprinkles and turn the turntable with your free hand while tossing the sprinkles at the sides of the cake. Using the leftover sprinkles from the parchment (i.e., sprinkles that didn't stick), continue turning and throwing until the cake (including the top) is covered in sprinkles. Chill the cake for about 5 minutes to set before serving.

HOW TO STORE

This cake will keep beautifully in a cake saver at room temperature (cool and humidity-free) for up to 3 days. If your room is not cool, place the cake in a cake saver and refrigerate for up to 3 days, then let it sit at room temperature for at least 2 hours before serving.

HAIR OF THE DOG CAKE

RUM-FLAVORED HOT MILK CAKE WITH BROILED RUM BROWN SUGAR FROSTING

YIELD: 1 9-BY-13-INCH (23-BY-33 CM) CAKE • 24 SERVINGS

IF WE WERE MORE PHILOSOPHICAL and a tinge more optimistic, we would embrace New Year's Day with wide-open arms and beaming smiles. We would pop out of bed at daybreak. We would shed our old skin. Refocus. Renew. In reality, our New Year's Day is more or less about sleep and B movies. Hangovers and pajamas. Our enlightenment burns within, but it is dimly lit. Renewal is essential, but so is *Aliens*.

Traditional New Year's Day feasts are brunch-centric. Piles of pancakes, greasy egg sandwiches, bacon, and buckets of coffee. We absolutely subscribe to this tradition, but we wouldn't be completely fulfilled without some sort of cake to kick off the New Year. And our Hair of the Dog Cake is just that cake. It's a no-muss, stumble-to-the-kitchen kind of cake. It contains the perfectly calibrated amount of rum—enough to soothe the beasts (from an industrious New Year's Eve), but not enough to restart the party. This recipe is virtually foolproof (just remember to apply the frosting to the warm cake) and incredibly snacky. It reminds us of a high-octane coffee cake. And it goes well with afternoon movies and best intentions.

●●● BAKED NOTE

Rum has certainly undergone a renaissance since our youthful collegiate days. It used to be a fairly straightforward selection: light or dark (and cheap or expensive). Now there are artisanal rums, small-batch rums, spiced rums, and very expensive, precious rums. For this cake, we highly recommend a spicy dark rum—something with a lot of body and flavor, which will absolutely come through in the cake, and you will be glad you didn't use the cheap stuff.

MAKE THE HOT MILK CAKE

1 Preheat the oven to 350°F (175°C). Butter the sides and bottom of a 9-by-13-inch (23-by-33-cm) pan. Line the bottom with a sheet of parchment paper, and butter the parchment.
2 Sift the all-purpose flour, cake flour, baking powder, and salt together in a medium bowl. Set aside.

INGREDIENTS

For the Hot Milk Cake

2 cups (255 g) all-purpose flour

¼ cup plus 2 tablespoons (45 g) cake flour

2½ teaspoons baking powder

¼ teaspoon kosher salt

6 ounces (1½ sticks/170 g) unsalted butter, cut into chunks, plus more for the pan

1¼ cups (300 ml) whole milk

4 large eggs

1 large egg yolk

2¼ cups (450 g) granulated sugar

¼ cup (60 ml) dark rum

2 teaspoons pure vanilla extract

For the Broiled Frosting

4 ounces (1 stick/115 g) unsalted butter, cut into chunks

1 cup (220 g) firmly packed light brown sugar

¼ cup (60 ml) heavy cream

¼ cup plus 2 tablespoons (90 ml) dark rum

For the Rum-Flavored Whipped Cream (optional)

1¼ cups (300 ml) heavy cream

2 tablespoons superfine sugar

1 to 2 tablespoons dark rum

3 In a saucepan set over low heat, stir together the butter and milk until the butter is melted and the mixture is hot and begins to bead (small bubbles appear) around the edge of the pan. Keep the mixture on very low heat (avoid a rolling boil) and stir occasionally while you make the batter below.

4 In the bowl of a standing mixer fitted with the whisk attachment, beat the eggs, egg yolk, and granulated sugar on medium-high speed until thick and pale (the mixture will change color as it thickens). Replace the whisk attachment with the paddle attachment. Add the dry mixture all at once and beat the on the lowest speed until just incorporated.

5 Remove the hot milk mixture from the heat. Stir in the rum and vanilla extract. Pour the hot milk mixture into the batter and beat until just combined.

6 Pour the batter into the prepared pan and bake the cake for 30 to 35 minutes, until a toothpick inserted into the center of the cake comes out with just a few moist crumbs. Transfer the cake, still in its pan, to a cooling rack and cool for 10 minutes. Meanwhile, make the frosting, as it is important to apply it to a very warm cake.

MAKE THE BROILED FROSTING

1 Preheat the broiler.

2 Melt the butter in a medium saucepan over medium heat. Remove from the heat, add the brown sugar, and stir until combined. Add the cream and rum and whisk until incorporated.

3 Pour the frosting over the warm cake (still in its pan) and place in the oven directly under the broiler. Broil for 2 to 4 minutes, until the top of the frosting is just starting to brown and looks bubbly; we recommend keeping a close eye on it to prevent burning (you might even want to keep the oven door slightly ajar and watch the cake the entire time) Transfer the cake to a cooling rack.

MAKE THE RUM-FLAVORED WHIPPED CREAM (OPTIONAL)

1 Pour the cream into a chilled metal bowl and beat vigorously with a chilled whisk for about 1 minute, until soft peaks form (alternatively, you can use a standing mixer). Sprinkle the superfine sugar and rum over the cream and continue whisking vigorously until stiff peaks form.

2 Serve the cake warm or at room temperature; spoon a dollop of whipped cream on each slice, if you like.

HOW TO STORE

The cake can be stored in an airtight container at room temperature for up to 3 days.

BRUTTI MA BUONI (UGLY BUT GOOD) COOKIES
PISTACHIO–CHOCOLATE CHIP MERINGUE COOKIES

YIELD: 24 LARGE OR 48 MEDIUM COOKIES

ITALY WINS, hands down, for "most imaginative celebration we would like to adopt." La Befana—the legend of a soot-covered witch who delivers gifts (or lumps of coal) to the children of Italy on Epiphany Eve—is the world's greatest mash-up of Halloween and Christmas. It is the first, and perhaps only, post-hip holiday: creepy-cool and entirely unsentimental. Popular culture (e.g., Edward Gorey, Tim Burton) has been trying to capture the essence of La Befana for an eternity, yet the original fable is nearly impossible to improve upon.

Renato created the perfect cookie in honor of La Befana. His *Brutti ma Buoni* cookies (literal translation: ugly but good) are a riff on the classic version he discovered, and subsequently fell in love with, while in Rome. Traditionally, *Brutti ma Buoni* are made with meaty hazelnuts or toasted almonds (both are entirely delicious); however, this recipe is all about bright pistachios— and chocolate, of course. It is chewy yet crunchy in the best possible meringue-y way. The cookie, like La Befana, may be unattractive (and a little crackly) on the outside, but it is sweet and tender on the inside.

●●● BAKED NOTE

If you are not a pistachio fan (for shame), you can easily swap them out for another nut. Just make sure the nuts are chopped coarsely (or they will sink to the bottom while baking) and are toasted (to bring out the most flavor). In addition to the recipe as written, we are very fond of an almond/chocolate chip combo.

INGREDIENTS

3   tablespoons all-purpose flour
1   tablespoon unsweetened cocoa powder
¼   teaspoon ground cinnamon
4   large egg whites
1   cup (200 g) granulated sugar
1   teaspoon pure vanilla extract
1½ cups (185 g) shelled pistachios, coarsely chopped and toasted (see page 19)
6   ounces (170 g) mini dark chocolate chips or chunks (about 1 cup)

1 Preheat the oven to 350°F (175°C). Line two baking sheets with parchment.

2 In a small bowl, sift together the flour, cocoa, and cinnamon. Set aside.

3 In the bowl of a standing mixer fitted with the whisk attachment, combine the egg whites and sugar and whisk until just combined, about 15 seconds. Set the mixer bowl over a saucepan of simmering water (the bowl should not touch the water) and whisk by hand until the sugar is completely dissolved and the mixture is warm to the touch, 4 to 6 minutes.

4 Transfer the bowl back to the mixer and whisk on medium-high speed until the mixture is glossy and voluminous and slightly stiff peaks begin to form (when you pull out the whisk, a peak should form, then slowly flop over). Add the vanilla and beat until incorporated.

5 Switch to the paddle attachment of the mixer, then add the flour mixture, beating just until incorporated. Scrape down the sides and bottom of the bowl and mix for 5 more seconds. Remove the bowl from the mixer and use a rubber spatula to manually fold in the nuts and chocolate.

6 Using a small ice-cream scoop (about a scant tablespoon) with a release mechanism, drop the mixture onto the prepared baking sheets, leaving about 2 inches (5 cm) between all of the cookies. (Alternatively, for larger cookies, scoop and drop by heaping tablespoons.) Bake for 15 to 20 minutes (smaller cookies will bake faster), rotating the pans halfway through the baking time, until the cookies are hard and crackly on the surface.

7 Set the pans on a wire rack to cool for 5 minutes. Use a spatula to transfer the cookies to the racks to cool completely.

HOW TO STORE

These cookies taste best the day they are made; however, they are still quite good within 2 to 3 days if stored at room temperature in an airtight container.

CARAMEL-Y BANANA, PEANUT BUTTER, AND CHOCOLATE BREAD PUDDING

YIELD: 8 VERY LARGE AND SHAREABLE SERVINGS

WE HARDLY NEED to elaborate on Elvis. He is, in America at least, everywhere and everlasting. He transcends musical genres and spans nearly every demographic; he's popular with hipsters and housewives alike. Elvis, the King of Rock and Roll, may not be with us anymore, but he never really left the building. My Elvis fandom is mild—more admirer status than Graceland obsessive—so it is perhaps a little strange that within just a few months of moving to New York, I found myself celebrating his birthday with some hard-core fans. It was an Elvis sonic boom. *Viva Las Vegas* blared from the TV, while partiers howled the Elvis catalog through the karaoke machine. Sounds overlapped and combined, the volume suitable only for inebriated twentysomethings. I hardly noticed, though. I was, as I am wont to do at parties, hovering near the food table. Of course, it was laden with all manner of peanut butter and banana foodstuffs.

Few megastars are so associated with one food item as Elvis is associated with the fried peanut butter and banana sandwich. In fact, thousands of menu items across America feature some type of peanut butter and banana combination and are simply called "The Elvis" in homage. We ourselves have hundreds of Elvis-inspired desserts. We love most any banana–peanut butter combo. Our Caramel-y Banana, Peanut Butter, and Chocolate Bread Pudding is just the latest, if not greatest, inspiration to date. It is more custardy than bready, as far as bread puddings go, with a real peanut butter punch. The bananas are *caramel-y*, not caramelized (we didn't want an unexpected crunch here), and the chocolate provides just a little balance. At least as much balance as can be provided in a dessert made with almost three cups of heavy cream.

●●● **BAKED NOTE**

We are aware that the average home cook is far more likely to own a baking dish as opposed to eight 8-ounce soufflé dishes, but have no fear: This bread pudding bakes up just as wonderfully in a classic 9-by-13-inch (23-by-33-cm) dish (about 3 quarts/2.8 L). To adapt the recipe, follow the instructions, but increase the bake time to 50 to 55 minutes, until the middle of the pudding is set.

INGREDIENTS

- 3 tablespoons unsalted butter
- ¼ cup (55 g) firmly packed dark brown sugar
- 6 very ripe medium bananas, cut into ½-inch (12-mm) slices
- 5 large egg yolks
- 1 large egg
- 2½ cups (600 ml) heavy cream
- 1 cup (240 ml) whole milk
- 1 cup plus 2 tablespoons (290 g) smooth peanut butter
- ⅔ cup (150 g) firmly packed light brown sugar
- 1 tablespoon pure vanilla extract
- ½ teaspoon kosher salt
- 1 loaf day-old brioche (about 12 ounces/340 g; see recipe on page 161), cut into 1-inch (2.5 cm) cubes (see Note, opposite)
- 5 ounces (140 g) dark chocolate (60 to 72% cacao), coarsely chopped
- 3 tablespoons confectioners' sugar (optional)
- 1 pint (473 ml) premium vanilla ice cream (optional)

1 Lightly spray eight 8-ounce (240-ml) ramekins or soufflé dishes with nonstick cooking spray (alternatively, pour a little canola oil on a paper towel and apply to the bottom and sides of the ramekins). Place four of the prepared ramekins in a large roasting pan and set aside. If you are lucky enough to own two roasting pans, you can place the remaining four ramekins in the second roasting pan. If not, bake them in two batches.

2 In a medium skillet over medium-high heat, melt the butter and dark brown sugar together and cook until bubbly. Add the banana slices and cook until lightly browned and encased in a thick syrup, about 10 minutes, tossing frequently to ensure even caramelization. Use a spoon to transfer the bananas to a large parchment-lined platter in one layer (some of the liquid will transfer with the bananas; this is a good thing).

3 In a very large bowl, whisk together the egg yolks and egg until blended.

4 In a medium saucepan over medium-high heat, whisk together the heavy cream, milk, peanut butter, and light brown sugar. Cook the mixture, whisking constantly, until it is just about to boil, then remove from the heat. Whisking constantly, slowly stream about ¼ cup (60 ml) of the cream mixture into the egg mixture. Continue whisking until well combined, then in a slow, steady stream, continue to add the remaining cream mixture into the egg mixture, again whisking constantly, until completely blended. Add the vanilla and salt and whisk vigorously for about 1 minute to release excess heat. Let stand for 5 minutes, stirring occasionally.

5 Stir all of the cubed bread into the custard. Use a large spoon to stir and flip the mixture to make sure every piece of bread is coated completely in the custard; set aside for about 30 minutes to soak. During the soaking period, use the back of the spoon to push the bread back down into the custard every few minutes.

6 Preheat the oven to 350°F (175°C). Bring a pot or kettle of water to a boil.

7 Divide the chocolate equally among the prepared ramekins. On top of the chocolate, divide about half of the bread-and-custard mixture evenly among the ramekins. Add the bananas in an even layer to each ramekin. Top the banana layer with the remaining bread-and-custard mixture. Pour boiling water into the roasting pan until the water reaches about halfway up the sides of the ramekins. Bake for 25 to 30 minutes, until the custard is set: A toothpick inserted into the center of the custard should come out clean, the custard will start to pull away slightly from the sides of the ramekin, and the top will look baked, not wet. Remove the baking dish from the oven, remove the ramekins from the hot water with tongs, and allow the puddings to cool for 20 to 30 minutes. Dust the warm bread puddings with confectioners' sugar and serve with vanilla ice cream, if desired.

HOW TO STORE

To store bread pudding, cool to room temperature, cover, and refrigerate for up to 3 days. Reheat bread pudding in a 250°F (120°C) oven until warm throughout (and, yes, some people happily eat the pudding directly from the refrigerator). A surprising number of people firmly believe that bread pudding tastes even better on Day Two; we like Day One and Day Two equally.

HOW TO USE FRESH BRIOCHE IN BREAD PUDDING

You can use fresh brioche in this bread pudding recipe, but you need to toast it first so it absorbs the custard properly.

Here is how we do it:

1   Preheat the oven to 350°F (175°C).

2   Cut the loaf of brioche into 1-inch (2.5-cm) cubes.

3   Place the brioche cubes on a parchment-lined baking sheet and toast for 10 to 15 minutes, tossing every 5 minutes.

4   Remove from the oven and let cool on the baking sheet, then proceed as directed.

DOLLY'S DOUGHNUT

COCONUT BUNDT CAKE WITH A DARK CHOCOLATE AND COCONUT FILLING

YIELD: 1 BUNDT CAKE • 12 TO 16 SERVINGS

"When I was born my Daddy paid the doctor with a sack of cornmeal, so when I leave this place and am standing at the Pearly Gates, I'm paying for admission with this cake!"

DOLLY PARTON

IT WOULD BE EASY, almost lazy, to categorize our yearly birthday tribute to Dolly Parton (forever known far and wide as just "Dolly") as mere kitsch. While we are partially attracted to Dolly's camp factor (who isn't?), we are equally, if not more, fascinated by her business acumen and all-around talent. She is Martha Stewart with a banjo. She is Oprah with a country heart. Her musical accolades are well known and well deserved—"Jolene" might be the best scorned-lover song ever written—but she has also dabbled in TV and movie production (*Buffy the Vampire Slayer* and *Father of the Bride*), acting (see *9 to 5* if you haven't already), and cookbooks (we own *Dolly's Dixie Fixin's*), and her Imagination Library inspires children all over the world. And then there is Dollywood. Dolly, anointed from the heavens and blessed with all that is good, has her own theme park . . . and it is genius and better than it should be. It is the essence of Dolly encapsulated in thrill rides, musicals, and other amusements. We want to live there.

It is hard to create a cake that emulates all that is Dolly, but we did our damnedest. We started with coconut. Apparently she loves coconut desserts. Our Dolly Parton Bundt cake is coconut-y times three. It's the perfect alternative birthday cake for any coconut fanatic. We start with an ultramoist, light coconut cake, fill it with a dark chocolate coconut fudge-like filling, and then we ice the cake with a pink coconut frosting, in honor of Dolly's favorite color. For some strange reason, we have fashioned the final cake to resemble a doughnut. We are not even sure if Dolly loves doughnuts, but it seemed appropriate in ways that are indescribable. And Dolly's Doughnut has an impossibly happy ring about it.

●●● BAKED NOTE

We are thoroughly enamored of the ribbon of chocolate running throughout this cake—it is a tasty and fun surprise. However, if you are not a chocolate fan (the horror!), you can turn Dolly's Doughnut into a straight-up (and quite tasty) coconut-y Bundt. Simply omit the dark chocolate filling in its entirety, pour all of the coconut batter directly into the pan, and bake per the recipe. We leave it up to you whether you want to omit the white chocolate glaze (and whether you consider white chocolate to be chocolate, anyway).

INGREDIENTS

For the Coconut Bundt Cake

- 3 cups (385 g) all-purpose flour
- 1 tablespoon baking powder
- ½ teaspoon kosher salt
- 8 ounces (2 sticks/225 g) unsalted butter, softened, plus more for the pan
- 2½ cups (500 g) granulated sugar
- 2 large eggs
- 2 large egg yolks
- 2 tablespoons coconut extract
- 2 teaspoons pure vanilla extract
- 1⅓ cups (315 ml) unsweetened coconut milk

For the Dark Chocolate Coconut Filling

- 5 ounces (140 g) cream cheese, softened
- ½ cup (40 g) lightly packed unsweetened shredded coconut
- 6 ounces (170 g) dark chocolate (60 to 72% cacao), melted and cooled
- 1 large egg
- 3 tablespoons granulated sugar

MAKE THE COCONUT BUNDT CAKE

1 Preheat the oven to 350°F (175°C). Butter the inside of a 10- or 12-cup (2.4- or 2.8-L) Bundt pan, dust with flour, and knock out the excess flour. Alternatively, spray the pan with cooking spray. Either way, make sure the pan's nooks and crannies are all thoroughly coated.

2 In a medium bowl, whisk together the flour, baking powder, and salt.

3 In the bowl of a standing mixer fitted with the paddle attachment, beat the butter and sugar on medium speed until light and fluffy, about 3 minutes. Scrape down the sides and bottom of the bowl, then add the eggs and egg yolks one at a time, beating well after each addition. Scrape down the bowl again, add the coconut and vanilla extracts, and beat until just incorporated.

4 Add the flour mixture in three parts, alternating with the coconut milk, beginning and ending with the flour mixture, mixing after each addition until just combined, about 10 seconds; do not overmix. Remove the bowl from the standing mixer, transfer the batter to a large bowl, and clean and dry the mixing bowl.

MAKE THE DARK CHOCOLATE COCONUT FILLING

1 In the now-clean bowl of the standing mixer fitted with the paddle attachment, beat the cream cheese until creamy, about 1 minute. Add the unsweetened coconut, melted dark chocolate, egg, and granulated sugar and beat again until completely incorporated, about 1 minute. Scrape down the sides and bottom of the bowl and mix again for a few more seconds. Add ½ cup of the cake batter to the filling batter and fold until incorporated.

ASSEMBLE THE BUNDT

1 Spoon half of the cake batter into the prepared pan. Spoon the filling on top of the batter, keeping it in the center of the batter and away from the sides of the pan. Then pour the remaining half of the batter over the filling. Smooth the top with an offset spatula. Bake in the middle of the oven for 50 to 55 minutes, until a small sharp knife or toothpick inserted in the center of the cake comes out with just a few moist crumbs.

2 Transfer the pan to a wire rack to cool completely. Gently loosen the sides of the cake from the pan and turn it out onto the rack. Place a baking sheet (lined with parchment if you like, for easy cleanup) underneath the wire rack.

INGREDIENTS (CONT.)

For the Simple Coconut Glaze

4 to 6 tablespoons (60 to 90 ml) coconut milk

½ teaspoon coconut extract

½ teaspoon pure vanilla extract

2 cups (225 g) confectioners' sugar, sifted

6 ounces (170 g) good-quality white chocolate, melted but still warm

Red or pink food dye or gel

For Décor

Pink or rainbow sprinkles (optional)

MAKE THE SIMPLE COCONUT GLAZE

1 In a large bowl, whisk together 4 tablespoons (60 ml) of the coconut milk, the coconut extract, and vanilla extract. Add the confectioners' sugar and whisk until incorporated and smooth. Slowly stir in the warm white chocolate. We prefer a thick yet pourable glaze; if the glaze appears too thick, thin it out with additional coconut milk, a tablespoon at a time, until you reach the desired consistency. Stir in the food dye, a few drops at a time, until the desired color is reached.

2 Pour the glaze in large, thick ribbons over the crown of the Bundt, allowing the glaze to spread and drip down the sides of the cake. Top with sprinkles, if using. Allow the glaze to set before serving, about 5 minutes.

HOW TO STORE

The cake will keep in an airtight container at room temperature for up to 3 days.

CHINESE FIVE-SPICE SESAME SCONES

YIELD: 8 LARGE SCONES

I OCCASIONALLY HAPPEN UPON Chinese New Year festivities in the streets of New York by chance. Depending on my mood, this is either an inconvenience, as it interferes with traffic and schedules (I am possibly a type-A New Yorker), or thrilling (the costumes, the sounds, the air so fragrant with a thousand spices you could almost eat it), or both. On more than one occasion, I have eaten something off a nearby cart standing up—watching and waiting for the parade to pass me by.

That is the extent of my Chinese New Year life experience. However, I have a bizarre fascination with the interconnected Chinese zodiac and the twelve animal signs—only a few zodiac books hidden away for some sporadic life guidance can attest to my minor obsession. Incidentally, I was born during the Year of the Pig. Not wholly inappropriate, but the moniker could be more pleasing.

I have eaten my fair share of New York Chinese food (cold noodles with peanut sauce was a post-grad favorite), but I rarely venture into the dessert side of Chinese food. Though I appreciate the *truth* of black glutinous rice dessert, I am most certainly a slave to classic Americana (chocolate chip cookies, brownies, three-layer cakes). These Chinese Five-Spice Sesame Scones are not something you would find in China—more homage than authentic—but our love for five-spice powder and the interplay of sesame is fun nonetheless. This is a crumbly scone, slightly more English in texture than our typical Baked scone recipe. Its elegance is its subtle flavoring. Of course, we are prone to slather the whole thing in peanut butter. Elegance be damned.

●●● BAKED NOTE

We are not morning people. Nine times out of ten, we premix our scone ingredients the night prior. This makes for less grumpy breakfasts. We encourage you do the same. Simply mix up your dry ingredients, cover with a tea towel, and let sit at room temperature. Then cube your butter and place it in the refrigerator. The only thing you have to do in the morning is toast your sesame seeds and pull the wet and dry ingredients together.

INGREDIENTS

⅓ cup (45 g) sesame seeds
2 cups (255 g) all-purpose flour
¼ cup (50 g) granulated sugar
1 teaspoon baking soda
1 teaspoon baking powder
1 tablespoon plus 1 teaspoon Chinese five-spice powder
½ teaspoon kosher salt
4 ounces (1 stick/115 g) cold unsalted butter, cut into cubes
¼ cup plus 1 tablespoon (75 ml) well-shaken buttermilk, plus more as needed
1 large egg yolk
¼ cup (60 g) demerara sugar (optional)

1 Preheat the oven to 375°F (190°C). Line a baking sheet with parchment paper.

2 In a medium skillet, toast the sesame seeds over medium heat, stirring and flipping, until just starting to brown, about 4 minutes. Remove from the heat and keep stirring for another minute or so. Remove from the pan onto a small plate and set aside to cool.

3 In a large bowl, whisk together the flour, granulated sugar, baking soda, baking powder, five-spice powder, salt, and cooled sesame seeds. Add the butter and use your fingertips (or a pastry cutter) to rub (or cut) it into the flour until the butter pieces are pea-size and the overall mixture looks coarse and pebbly.

4 Place ¼ cup of the buttermilk into a glass measuring cup or bowl and whisk in the egg yolk. Make a well in the dry ingredients and slowly pour in the wet ingredients. Use a large wooden spoon and stir until just combined; do not overwork the dough. Gently and briefly knead the dough in the bowl with your hands until it just comes together. The dough should be dry but hold its shape. If it feels too dry (i.e., the dough is falling apart), knead in another tablespoon of buttermilk.

5 Transfer the dough to a very lightly floured surface and pat it into a rough circle slightly under 1 inch (2.5 cm) thick. Cut into 8 wedges and transfer them to the prepared baking sheet.

6 Brush the tops of the scones with a little bit of buttermilk, top each scone with a sprinkle of demerara sugar, if you like, and bake for 16 to 20 minutes, rotating the pan halfway through the baking time, until the scones just start to brown and a toothpick inserted into the center comes out clean.

7 Transfer the pan to a cooling rack and cool for 5 minutes. Serve the scones slightly warm, or let them cool completely directly on the cooling rack; regardless, we like them with a little bit of peanut butter or butter.

HOW TO STORE

The scones taste best when eaten within 12 to 24 hours.

FEBRUARY

FEB 2 | GROUNDHOG DAY
TOFFEE COFFEE CAKE SURPRISE 44

FEB 5 | WORLD NUTELLA DAY
NUTELLA CHIP COOKIES 48

FEB 14 | VALENTINE'S DAY
CONVERSATION HEART CAKES 50

FEB 14 | VALENTINE'S DAY
VANILLA BEAN ANGEL FOOD CAKE WITH MILK CHOCOLATE GLAZE 54

DATE FLUCTUATES | MARDI GRAS
THE NEW ORLEANS 56

DATE FLUCTUATES | SHROVE TUESDAY
KITCHEN-SINK DUTCH BABY 61

3RD MON IN FEB | WASHINGTON'S BIRTHDAY / PRESIDENTS' DAY
CHERRY ALMOND CRISP 65

FEB 26 | NATIONAL PISTACHIO DAY
PISTACHIO WHITE CHOCOLATE CHEESECAKE 67

TOFFEE COFFEE CAKE SURPRISE

YIELD: 1 BUNDT CAKE • 12 TO 16 SERVINGS

POSSIBLY, AS MOSTLY LIFELONG NEW YORKERS, we invest too much in the Groundhog Day myth. We desperately want to believe. As each February rolls around—dreary, wintry February—we pray the symbolic groundhog will grant us an early spring and a welcome reprieve from winter. The stakes are high: If the groundhog emerges from his burrow and glimpses his shadow, we are supposedly due for another six weeks of winter. That is not a good thing.

We celebrate Groundhog Day (and by extension the excellent, cult-classic Bill Murray movie of the same name) with a cake that is a little bit whimsical, if not a little bit literal: After all, there is a "burrow" of chocolate toffee running through the middle of the cake. The cake itself is the perfect coffee-cake base, golden and fragrant and an afternoon pleasure all its own. We added a ribbon of toffee bits for an added surprise and a contrasting crunch. It might be a silly holiday, but it is a serious cake.

●●● **BAKED NOTE**

Please note that if you make your own toffee (you can also use store-bought, if you prefer) you will have plenty of leftovers for yourself or for gifts. This is a very good thing. Also, when chopping the toffee for the cake, we suggest using only a knife (avoid using a mallet or rolling pin) so that the toffee does not get too powdery. Feel free to experiment with both coarse and fine textures. We prefer a mix; ideally you want a few coarse pieces to stand out, but you don't want so many that the toffee chunks are overbearing.

INGREDIENTS

**For the Toffee
(30 ounces/850 g,
approximately 4 cups)**

1   cup (150 g) whole
    almonds, darkly toasted
    (see page 19)
8   ounces (2 sticks/225 g)
    unsalted butter, plus
    more for the pan
½   cup plus 2 tablespoons
    (125 g) granulated sugar
½   cup plus 2 tablespoons
    (140 g) firmly packed dark
    brown sugar
3   tablespoons corn syrup
1   teaspoon pure vanilla
    extract
½   teaspoon kosher salt
8   ounces (225 g) good-
    quality dark chocolate
    (60 to 72% cacao),
    coarsely chopped

MAKE THE TOFFEE

1 Butter a 9-by-13-by-2-inch (23-by-33-by-5-cm) glass or metal baking pan (do not use nonstick spray).

2 In the bowl of a food processor, pulse the almonds until they are super finely chopped, almost but not quite powdery. Place in a bowl and set aside.

3 Place the butter in a medium pan over low heat. When the butter is halfway melted, add the granulated and brown sugars, the corn syrup, and 2 tablespoons water. Cook over low heat, stirring very gently with a silicone or rubber spatula, until completely combined. Stop stirring. Clip a candy thermometer onto the side of the pan and turn the heat up to medium-high. The mixture will start to bubble and turn brown. If the browning seems uneven, gently swirl the pan during the cooking process, but do not stir. After 10 to 15 minutes, when the mixture is just under 300°F (150°C), remove the pan from the heat and remove the candy thermometer. Stir in the vanilla and salt. Pour into the prepared pan. After the mixture has evened out, wait 1 minute, then sprinkle the chocolate pieces all over the toffee. Wait for the chocolate to melt, about 3 minutes, then use an offset spatula to spread the chocolate into an even layer. Sprinkle the ground almonds over the chocolate in an even layer and ever so gently press them into the chocolate. Freeze the pan for about 30 minutes.

4 Remove the pan from the freezer and break the toffee into pieces with a sharp knife. Measure out 4 ounces (115 g), chop it very finely, and set aside; save the remainder of the toffee for another use. Store for up to 1 week between layers of parchment in an airtight container at cool room temperature.

INGREDIENTS (CONT.)

For the Toffee Coffee Cake

6   ounces (1 ½ sticks/170 g) unsalted butter, cool but not cold, cubed
2   cups (255 g) all-purpose flour
1   cup (130 g) cake flour
1½ cups (330 g) firmly packed dark brown sugar
¾   cup (150 g) granulated sugar
1   tablespoon pure vanilla extract
¾   teaspoon kosher salt
4   ounces (115 g) home-made toffee (see above), or 3 Skor or Heath bars, chopped very finely (see Baked Note)
½   cup (75 g) coarsely chopped toasted almonds (see page 19)
2   teaspoons baking powder
¼   teaspoon baking soda
1   large egg
2   large egg yolks
1½ cups (345 g) sour cream
3   tablespoons confectioners' sugar, for dusting

MAKE THE TOFFEE COFFEE CAKE

1   Preheat the oven to 350°F (175°C). Generously spray the inside of a 10- or 12-cup (2.4- or 2.8-L) Bundt pan with nonstick cooking spray; alternatively, butter it thoroughly, dust it with flour, and knock out excess flour.

2   In the bowl of a standing mixer fitted with the paddle attachment, beat the butter, both flours, the brown and granulated sugars, the vanilla, and salt on medium speed until the mixture resembles sandy crumbs, 2 to 3 minutes.

3   Scoop out ⅔ cup (90 g) of this crumb mixture and place it in a large bowl. Stir in the reserved 4 ounces (115 g) toffee and the almonds and set aside.

4   Sprinkle the baking powder and baking soda over the remaining crumb mixture in the mixing bowl. Beat on medium speed for 15 seconds to incorporate. Add the egg and egg yolks and beat on medium speed until combined. Scrape down the sides and bottom of the bowl. Add the sour cream and beat until smooth. Scrape down the sides and bottom of the bowl and beat again for 10 seconds.

5   Spoon half the batter into the prepared pan. Smooth the surface with an offset spatula. Spoon the dry toffee/nut mixture on top of the batter in an even layer, keeping it in the center of the batter, away from the sides of the pan. (If some of the toffee mixture touches the sides, nudge it gently back toward the center as best you can.) Cover with the remaining batter and smooth the top with an offset spatula.

6   Bake, rotating the pan halfway through the baking time, until a toothpick inserted in the center comes out clean, 45 to 55 minutes, depending on your Bundt pan size or shape. Transfer the pan to a wire rack to cool for about 30 minutes. Use a small knife or very small spatula to loosen the sides of the cake from the pan. Turn the cake out onto the rack and let it cool completely. Sift confectioners' sugar over the cake and serve.

HOW TO STORE

The cake can be stored, tightly covered, at room temperature for up to 3 days.

NUTELLA CHIP COOKIES

YIELD: ABOUT 48 COOKIES

WE WERE INITIALY HESITANT to embrace the Nutella holiday because it felt a little bit like a public relations gambit by Nutella's corporate parent, Ferrero International S.A. But, lo and behold, World Nutella Day was actually established by a wild and avid Nutella fan, Sara Rosso, in 2007. In a rather short time, the holiday became a behemoth, and epic Nutella events began to pop up. Nutella fans are extraordinary and dedicated, and they celebrate heartily (i.e., they will put Nutella on anything). We completely understand their enthusiasm. We are them.

Nutella, the heavenly chocolate-hazelnut spread, is almost life changing, addictive, and, most important, multipurpose. In truth, you can replace peanut butter or almond butter with Nutella in almost any baking recipe (though you might want to reduce the sugar a tad to account for the sweetness of the Nutella). But we tend to err on the side of simplicity: We think Nutella shines best when left to its own devices (i.e., slathered on a piece of toast or fruit). These cookies are essentially Nutella in cookie form. The chocolate-and-hazelnut flavor is prominent and all encompassing, and that, in our opinion, is the only way to fully enjoy all that is wonderful about Nutella. What else do you need in life?

●●● BAKED NOTE
It's true: We have been known to use leftover Nutella to sandwich two of these cookies together. Worth a try.

INGREDIENTS

2   cups (255 g) all-purpose
     flour
1   teaspoon kosher salt
1   teaspoon baking soda
4   ounces (1 stick/115 g)
     cold unsalted butter,
     cubed
1   cup (220 g) firmly packed
     dark brown sugar
1   cup (280 g) Nutella
2   large eggs
1   teaspoon pure vanilla
     extract
8   ounces (225 g) semisweet
     chocolate chips (about
     1⅓ cups)
5   ounces (140 g) hazelnuts
     (about 1 cup), toasted
     (see page 19), husked, and
     coarsely chopped

1 In a medium bowl, whisk together the flour, salt, and baking soda. Set aside.

2 In the bowl of a standing mixer fitted with the paddle attachment, beat the butter on medium speed until creamy, about 2 minutes. Add the brown sugar and Nutella and beat until fully incorporated, about 2 minutes. Scrape down the sides and bottom of the bowl and add the eggs, one at a time, beating until each is incorporated. Add the vanilla and beat again for 5 seconds.

3 Add half of the flour mixture and mix on low speed for 15 seconds. Add the remaining flour mixture and beat until just incorporated.

4 Using a spatula or wooden spoon, fold in the chocolate chips and hazelnuts.

5 Cover the bowl tightly and refrigerate for at least 4 hours or up to 48 hours.

6 Preheat the oven to 350°F (175°C). Line two baking sheets with parchment paper.

7 Scoop out heaping tablespoons of dough; alternatively, use a small ice-cream scoop with a release mechanism to scoop. Using your hands, roll the dough into perfect balls and place them about 1 inch (2.5 cm) apart on the prepared baking sheets. Bake until the tops of the cookies are set and begin to show a few cracks, 11 to 13 minutes, rotating the pans once during the cooking time. Remove them from the oven and let them cool slightly, about 5 minutes, before transferring them to a cooling rack.

8 Serve warm (a great cookie is a warm cookie, and if eaten warm, these are perfectly crunchy on the outside and chewy on the inside) or at room temperature (they will still taste just as delicious).

HOW TO STORE

The cookies can be stored in an airtight container for up to 3 days.

CONVERSATION HEART CAKES

BLACK VELVET HEART CAKES WITH VANILLA CREAM CHEESE FROSTING

YIELD: 6 4-INCH (10-CM) INDIVIDUAL HEART-SHAPED CAKES

THE ONLY THING BETTER than a hulking, beastly, oversize, shareable cake is one that is crafted with romantic intent, individually portioned, and basically adorable. And there are very few cakes in this world that are more adorable than our tribute to conversation hearts (variously sold by the name Sweethearts or Love Hearts). We originally dreamed up these mini heart cakes as an antidote to the more traditional Valentine's Day dessert, a box of chocolates. We really like chocolates, but we love cake. Obviously.

Each heart consists of two layers of black velvet cake (we are rightly obsessed with black cocoa powder) slathered in a simple tangy vanilla cream cheese frosting dyed to replicate the colors of the classic candies (or just a serious red). The pièce de résistance, however, is the inscription. You can adhere to the classic phrasing (I Do, Hug Me, Kiss, Love) or you can take a decidedly more cheeky route (we prefer the cheekier route). Regardless, the recipe makes enough tender tasty cakes for six people. Either ply your loved one with six different cakes, or find six different loved ones.

●●● BAKED NOTE

As with any recipe in this book that lists black cocoa powder as an ingredient, you can substitute a regular dark cocoa powder (like Valrhona) in a one-to-one ratio. Also, black food gel is not necessary; actually, it is a bit of a messy extravagance, but we like the idea of a truly "black heart" because it seems so brazen.

INGREDIENTS

For the Black Velvet Cake

2 tablespoons unsweetened dark cocoa powder, such as Valrhona

2 tablespoons unsweetened black cocoa powder (see Baked Note)

¼ cup (60 ml) boiling water

1 tablespoon black food gel (optional)

2½ cups (315 g) cake flour (not self-rising)

1 teaspoon kosher salt

3 ounces (¾ stick/85 g) unsalted butter, softened, plus more for the pan

1 tablespoon plus 1½ teaspoons vegetable shortening, at room temperature

1⅔ cups (330 g) granulated sugar

3 large eggs

1 cup (240 ml) well-shaken buttermilk

1 teaspoon pure vanilla extract

1 tablespoon cider vinegar

1 teaspoon baking soda

MAKE THE BLACK VELVET CAKE

1 Preheat the oven to 325°F (165°C) and position a rack in the center of the oven. Butter an 18-by-13-inch (46-by-33-cm) rimmed baking sheet, line with parchment paper, butter the parchment, and set aside.

2 In a medium bowl, whisk together both cocoa powders, the water, and food gel, if using. Set aside to cool.

3 In another bowl, sift together the cake flour and salt.

4 In the bowl of a standing mixer fitted with the paddle attachment, beat the butter and shortening together on medium speed until light and smooth, about 5 minutes; the mixture will appear to string or ribbon throughout the bowl. Add the sugar and beat on medium speed until the mixture appears light and fluffy, about 5 minutes. Add the eggs, one at a time, beating well after each addition. Scrape down the sides and bottom of the bowl.

5 Stir the buttermilk and vanilla into the cocoa mixture.

6 Add the flour mixture to the mixer bowl in three parts, alternating with the cocoa mixture, and beginning and ending with the flour mixture. Scrape down the sides and bottom of the bowl and mix again for 10 seconds. In a small bowl, mix together the vinegar and baking soda until the baking soda dissolves; the mixture will fizz. Add to the batter and mix until just combined.

7 Pour the batter onto the prepared baking sheet, smoothing the top. Bake the cake, rotating the pan after 10 minutes, until a cake tester inserted into the center of the cake comes out clean, 20 to 30 minutes.

8 Cool the cake completely in the pan on a wire rack. If possible, place the pan and cooled cake in the freezer for another 45 minutes. (A chilled cake will often produce better, cleaner results when cutting out the shapes, though this step is not necessary.)

9 Line another baking sheet with clean parchment.

10 Use a 4-inch (10-cm) heart-shaped cookie cutter to cut out 12 cake hearts; cut them out as closely as possible to get 12 hearts out of the layer cake. Place the hearts on the clean parchment and place in the freezer while you make the frosting.

MAKE THE VANILLA CREAM CHEESE FROSTING

1 Sift the confectioners' sugar into a large bowl and set aside.

2 In the bowl of a standing mixer fitted with the paddle attachment, beat the butter until it is completely smooth. Add the cream cheese and beat until combined.

3 Add the confectioners' sugar, vanilla, and salt and beat until smooth. Be careful not to overbeat the filling, or it will lose structure. Add the food dye, if using, drop by drop and beat until the desired color is reached. Chill the frosting in the refrigerator for about 5 minutes so it is easier to work with. (The frosting can also be made 24 hours ahead; cover the bowl tightly and refrigerate, letting the frosting soften at room temperature before using.)

INGREDIENTS (CONT.)

For the Vanilla Cream Cheese Frosting

3   cups (340 g) confectioners' sugar
8   ounces (2 sticks/225 g) unsalted butter, softened
2   (8-ounce/226-g) packages cream cheese, softened
1   tablespoon plus 1 teaspoon pure vanilla extract
½   teaspoon kosher salt
Food dye or gel (optional)

For the Assembly

4   ounces (115 g) white chocolate, chopped
Food dye or gel (optional)

ASSEMBLE THE CONVERSATION HEART CAKES

1 Cut parchment into six squares, each slightly larger than the hearts, and place them on a baking sheet. Place the first cake heart on a parchment, spread a thin layer of frosting over just the top, and top with another heart, bottom side up. Using a small offset spatula, cover the entire heart cake with a thin layer of frosting (a crumb coat). Continue this process, making 6 two-layer cakes in total, then transfer the baking sheet with all of the crumb-coated cakes to the refrigerator to set, 5 to 10 minutes.

2 Remove all of the cakes from the refrigerator. Cover the heart cakes with a generous layer of frosting, slightly more than ½ cup (130 g) each, and use the offset spatula to accentuate the heart shape (i.e., make sure the sides and tops are flat so that they resemble the candy conversation hearts). Refrigerate all of the cakes to set, about 5 minutes.

3 Place the white chocolate in a microwave-proof bowl and heat on medium power for 10 seconds. Remove and stir the chocolate. Repeat this process until it is just melted. Stir in the food dye, if using. Scrape the warm mixture into a pastry bag fitted with the smallest plain round tip. The chocolate should be warm enough to write with, but not so warm that it oozes out.

4 Remove the cakes from the refrigerator. Working quickly, write your messages on the cakes. Refrigerate the cakes one more time to set, about 5 minutes.

5 Take the cakes from the refrigerator, gently remove the parchment from underneath each cake, transfer each to a clean serving plate, and serve to your sweetheart(s).

HOW TO STORE

The cakes can be stored, tightly covered, in the refrigerator for up to 2 days. Bring to room temperature before serving.

VANILLA BEAN ANGEL FOOD CAKE WITH MILK CHOCOLATE GLAZE

YIELD: 1 TUBE CAKE • 12 TO 16 SERVINGS

CHOCOLATE TRUFFLES are as integral to Valentine's Day as roasted turkey is to Thanksgiving. They are the default—and much desired—amorous, indulgent gift of choice. (And, just for the record, we are fond of truffles any time of year.) However, if you want to surprise someone you love—especially someone who is not a romantic partner—with something different, we strongly suggest cake. (We are big on cake for Valentine's Day—see page 50 for another Valentine's Day cake.) Our Vanilla Bean Angel Food Cake is the sort of thing you can bring to Grandma's house on February 14—something to slice and enjoy over coffee on a wintry afternoon. Or it might be the kind of cake you have with friends while watching a bad rom-com. Sure, if single, you might want to spend the day gorging on chocolate and red wine in your sweatpants (er, we have), but baking and sharing a cake is (maybe) slightly healthier. In our experience, it is at least better for your disposition.

Though we have been known to shy away from angel food cakes in the past, we are quite enamored of this simple, spongy beauty. The cake is pure vanilla bliss, speckled with just enough vanilla paste to put it over the edge (and, by the by, the flecks of vanilla make a nice presentation). Whereas most desserts these days push the healthier-seeming dark chocolate, we think this cake deserves the sweeter, milkier milk chocolate. We highly recommend serving it with coffee or tea and, well, love.

●●● BAKED NOTE

The measurements given here for the all-purpose flour, cake flour, confectioners' sugar, and super-fine sugar are for "sifted" amounts. This means you should sift all of the ingredients and then measure the amount listed in the ingredient list. To make your sifting life easy, we recommend sifting over a large sheet of parchment. Less mess. Also, if you don't have superfine sugar handy, you can always pulse regular sugar in your food processor until fine.

MAKE THE VANILLA BEAN ANGEL FOOD CAKE

1 Preheat the oven to 325°F (165°C) and position a rack in the center of the oven.
2 Sift together the confectioners' sugar and both flours into a medium bowl. Repeat the sifting process two more times.

INGREDIENTS

For the Vanilla Bean Angel Food Cake

¾ cup (75 g) sifted confectioners' sugar

¾ cup (90 g) sifted cake flour

½ cup (55 g) sifted all-purpose flour

1¾ cups (420 ml) egg whites (from about 12 to 15 eggs), at room temperature

2 teaspoons warm water

1½ teaspoons cream of tartar

½ teaspoon kosher salt

1 cup (200 g) sifted super-fine sugar

1 tablespoon vanilla paste

For the Milk Chocolate Glaze

6 ounces (170 g) milk chocolate, chopped

¼ cup plus 2 tablespoons (90 ml) heavy cream

1 tablespoon plus 1½ teaspoons corn syrup

3 In the bowl of a standing mixer fitted with the whisk attachment, beat the egg whites and water on medium speed until frothy. Sprinkle the cream of tartar and salt over the mixture and beat on medium-high speed until soft peaks form. Gradually add the sifted superfine sugar and beat until peaks are droopy (somewhere between medium and stiff). Add the vanilla paste and whisk on low speed until just combined, about 10 seconds.

4 Remove the bowl from the mixer and sprinkle one-third of the flour mixture over the egg whites. Fold it in very gently. Add half of the remaining flour and fold it in gently. Add the remaining flour and fold it in until just incorporated.

5 Transfer the batter to an ungreased 10-cup (2.4-L) tube pan with a removable bottom; do not use a nonstick pan. Run an offset spatula through the batter to pop air bubbles and smooth the top of the batter.

6 Bake the cake for 35 to 40 minutes, rotating the pan halfway through the baking time, until it is pale golden in color and a toothpick or skewer inserted near the center of the cake comes out clean. If the pan has feet, immediately invert it onto a work surface; if not, invert the pan and place the center of the tube onto the neck of a bottle or a metal funnel. Cool the cake completely.

7 Once cooled, use a long, thin knife to cut around the sides of the cake and the center tube to loosen. Lift out the center tube with the cake still attached; run the knife between the cake and the bottom of the pan to loosen. Remove the cake from the center tube and invert it onto a wire rack. Place the rack with the cake onto a rimmed baking sheet lined with parchment.

MAKE THE MILK CHOCOLATE GLAZE

1 Place the chocolate in a large heatproof bowl and set aside.

2 In a small saucepan over medium heat, combine the cream and corn syrup and bring just to a boil. Remove from the heat and pour the cream mixture over the chocolate. Let stand for 1 minute, then, starting in the center of the bowl and working your way out to the edges, slowly stir the chocolate and cream mixture in a circle until the chocolate is completely melted and the mixture is smooth.

3 Drizzle the glaze over the top of the cake in a zigzag pattern. Let the glaze set, about 10 minutes, before serving. For the best cut, dip a serrated knife into hot water and dry it completely, then cut, using a sawing motion and trying not to press down on the cake while cutting. You can use any extra warm glaze to decorate individual slices if you are feeling decadent.

HOW TO STORE

The cake can be stored, tightly covered, at room temperature for up to 3 days, though it is generally best served within 48 hours.

THE NEW ORLEANS

BROWN SUGAR PRALINE ICE CREAM CAKE

YIELD: 1 8-INCH (20-CM) ROUND CAKE • ABOUT 16 SERVINGS

DURING MY COLLEGE YEARS, I attended five consecutive Mardi Gras celebrations in New Orleans. A group of us would set out every February (or March, depending) from our perch in Tuscaloosa, Alabama, and drive through what seemed like a thousand miles of nothingness (according to Google, it is only 292 miles)—anticipation building—to seek out one of the world's largest parties. Truth be told, I don't remember much. I remember beads and Bourbon Street and floats (and, well, other unmentionable things), but only as fuzzy touchstones. A few unfortunate photos survive. I don't look at them often. It would be many years before I was able to truly appreciate New Orleans—the food, the architecture, the overall mood—through less rummy eyes.

Despite our best intentions, we could not dream up a cake resplendent in the Mardi Gras colors of purple, green, and gold. Instead, we crafted a great big lovingly sweet ice cream cake dedicated to a New Orleans mainstay: the praline. Though many Southern cities lay claim to the praline—the sticky, sweet confection of pecans and sugar and some sort of dairy—we happily associate them with New Orleans (believed to be the true birthplace of this candy in America). Our cake is a praline dream. The ice cream is rich and creamy, and the graham layers provide a lovely contrast.

●●● **BAKED NOTE**

We urge you not to be frightened of the many parts to this recipe. Each one is fairly simple to make, and each one is a great dessert in its own right (the recipes for both the pralines and sauce will yield extra—great for gifting/snacking). Make only one component, or make them all and assemble this cake. You can halve the praline recipe, but be aware that you will have to make it in a smaller pot to ensure that there is enough liquid at the bottom of the pan to read the temperature properly. Also, the cook time to reach soft-ball stage will most likely be shorter.

INGREDIENTS

**For the Classic Pralines
(20 ounces/560 g)**

1   cup (200 g) granulated
    sugar
1   cup (220 g) firmly packed
    dark brown sugar
¾   cup (180 ml) heavy cream
2   tablespoons corn syrup
¼   teaspoon kosher salt
1½ cups (150 g) pecans,
    toasted (see page 19) and
    roughly chopped
3   tablespoons unsalted
    butter
1   tablespoon pure vanilla
    extract

**For the Sweet and
Salty Caramel Sauce
(about 1⅓ cups/315 ml)**

1   cup (200 g) granulated
    sugar
2   tablespoons light corn
    syrup
½   cup (120 ml) heavy cream
1   teaspoon fleur de sel
¼   cup (55 g) sour cream

MAKE THE CLASSIC PRALINES

1   Line two baking sheets with parchment paper.

2   In a medium saucepan, combine both sugars, the heavy cream, corn syrup, and salt. Stir the mixture gently and continuously with a wooden spoon over low heat until the sugar dissolves; avoid splashing the sides of the pan. Once the sugar has dissolved, stop stirring, and clip a candy thermometer to the side of the pan (the candy thermometer should be suspended in the liquid and should not touch the bottom of the pan). Turn the heat up to medium-high and continue cooking the mixture until it reaches the soft-ball stage (235°F to 238°F / 112°C to 114°C), 5 to 10 minutes.

3   Remove the pan from the stove and stir vigorously for 2 minutes to release excess heat. Stir in the pecans, butter, and vanilla and continue stirring for 2 more minutes. Using a spoon or a small ice-cream scoop with a release mechanism, drop the mixture by heaping tablespoons onto the prepared baking sheets and allow the pralines to cool to room temperature.

4   Once cooled, place approximately 5 ounces (140 g) of the pralines in a large zip-tight plastic bag and crush with a rolling pin, or alternatively, chop into small chunks with a chef's knife. The crushed pralines should equal about ¾ cup. Set this amount aside for the ice cream. (The remaining pralines [15 ounces/420 g] make excellent gifts and snacks. We like to crush all of the pralines and use the praline powder for ice cream and cake décor.) The pralines can be made ahead and stored in an airtight container for up to 3 days.

MAKE THE SWEET AND SALTY CARAMEL SAUCE

1   In a medium saucepan, combine the granulated sugar and corn syrup with ¼ cup (60 ml) water. Cook over medium-high heat, stirring gently until the sugar dissolves, avoiding splashing any of it up on the sides of the pan. Increase the heat to high and cook, without stirring, over high heat until the mixture is dark amber, just shy of 350°F (175°C) on a candy thermometer, 6 to 8 minutes (keep a close eye on it, as it goes from golden brown to black very quickly). Remove from the heat and slowly add the cream (be careful, as it will bubble up) and then the fleur de sel. Whisk in the sour cream. Let cool completely.

2   Set aside ¼ cup (60 mg) of the sauce for the ice cream; excess sauce can be used to decorate the finished cake or reserved for another use. The caramel sauce can be made, covered tightly, and refrigerated up to 3 days ahead. Allow to come to room temperature before adding to the ice cream.

INGREDIENTS (CONT.)

For the Brown Sugar Praline Ice Cream (about 3 pints/1.4 L)

5 large egg yolks

2½ cups (600 ml) heavy cream

¾ cup (180 ml) milk

1 cup (220 g) firmly packed dark brown sugar

2 tablespoons unsalted butter

¼ teaspoon kosher salt

1 tablespoon pure vanilla extract

¼ cup (60 ml) Sweet and Salty Caramel Sauce (see opposite page) or your favorite store-bought caramel

¾ cup (75 g) crushed Classic Pralines (see opposite page, or you can substitute store-bought)

For the Graham Cracker Layers

15 (5-by-2¼-inch/12-by-5.5-cm) graham crackers

4 ounces (1 stick/115 g) unsalted butter, melted and cooled

2 tablespoons granulated sugar

For the Assembly

¾ cup (75 g) toasted pecans, chopped

MAKE THE BROWN SUGAR PRALINE ICE CREAM

1 Place the egg yolks in a large heatproof bowl and set aside.

2 In a medium saucepan over medium-high heat, stir together the cream, milk, brown sugar, butter, and salt. Slowly bring the mixture to a full simmer (but do not let it boil), and remove from the heat.

3 Whisk the egg yolks until just combined, then slowly stream in half of the hot cream mixture while whisking constantly. Transfer the egg mixture back to the saucepan containing the other half of the hot cream mixture. Heat the custard over medium-low heat, stirring constantly, until it is thick enough to coat the back of a spoon (about 175°F/80°C on an instant-read thermometer).

4 Remove from the heat and strain the mixture through a fine-mesh sieve into a bowl. Whisk in the vanilla, and let the custard cool to room temperature. Press a piece of plastic wrap directly onto the surface of the mixture to prevent a skin from forming. Refrigerate for 4 hours.

5 Pour the custard into an ice-cream maker and process according to the manufacturer's directions. About 2 minutes before the ice cream is done churning, stream in the caramel sauce, followed by the crushed pralines. Transfer the mixture to an airtight container and place in the freezer to completely firm up (about 3 hours) before assembling the cake. If you make the ice cream ahead of time (it will last in the freezer for up to 5 days; place a piece of parchment on top of the ice cream to prevent freezer burn), allow it to thaw until it is workable before assembling the cake.

MAKE THE GRAHAM CRACKER LAYERS

1 Just prior to assembling the cake (not ahead of time), place the graham crackers in a large zip-tight plastic bag and crush them with a rolling pin to create about 2 cups (230 g) of graham cracker crumbs.

2 In a large bowl, stir to combine the graham cracker crumbs, butter, and granulated sugar together. Set aside.

ASSEMBLE THE ICE CREAM CAKE

1 Lightly spray the sides and bottom of an 8-inch (20-cm) springform pan with cooking spray. (You can use a 9-inch/23-cm round springform instead, though the 8-inch/20-cm will give the cake a little more height and visual flair.)

2 Press one-third of the graham cracker mixture into the bottom of the prepared pan in an even layer, then place in the freezer for 10 minutes. Place the ice cream in a mixing bowl and stir with a spatula to make it workable. Scoop one-third of the ice cream over the graham mixture and smooth with an offset spatula to create an even layer. Add another third of the graham mixture over the ice cream and press it into an even layer with your hands. Place the cake and remaining ice cream in the freezer for 45 minutes. Remove the cake and the bowl of ice cream from the freezer and add another third of the ice cream, smoothing the top. Add the remaining graham mixture and press it into an even layer with your hands. Return the cake and ice cream to the freezer for another 45 minutes. Remove the cake and bowl of ice cream from the freezer and top the graham layer with the remaining ice cream. Cover loosely with plastic wrap and freeze until completely hardened, at least 4 to 6 hours, or overnight.

3 To serve, remove the cake from the freezer. Run hot water over the blade of a paring knife, dry it off, then run it between the cake and the sides of the pan. Release the sides of the pan and place the cake on a serving platter. Sprinkle the top of the cake with a handful of pecans and gently press the remaining pecans onto the sides of the cake. Again, use a hot knife to run between the bottom of the springform pan and the cake. Gently push or lift the cake off the springform bottom and set it back down on the serving platter. Slice and serve immediately with an extra drizzle of caramel, if you like.

HOW TO STORE

If you have leftovers, cover the cake with foil and freeze for up to 1 week.

KITCHEN-SINK DUTCH BABY

YIELD: 4 SERVINGS

SHROVE TUESDAY, the day preceding Ash Wednesday, is a less well-known, less celebrated name for Mardi Gras. The names are nearly interchangeable; the significance (feast before fast) is the same. Except in practice. Whereas Mardi Gras is often one giant rolling carnival party, Shrove Tuesday is basically all about pancakes, an entire, glorious day with an emphasis on pancakes. Though I grew up in a tangentially Catholic household (okay, very tangentially), I was completely unfamiliar with Shrove Tuesday. Had I known about it—and its pancake rituals—it is quite possible I would have had better church attendance (at least in the days leading up to it).

The beauty of Dutch baby–type pancakes is their simplicity. It is basically a blend, pour, and bake scenario. Typical household ingredients, limited mess, and no need to stand and flip at a griddle—it's a pancake for lazy days (people). And, as with most Dutch baby pancakes, this one looks impressive. It is a giant, golden, oven-baked pancake, bursting up the sides of the pan, full of bananas and oozing with chocolate. The texture is more akin to a great crepe than a traditional American-style pancake, but it should still be drizzled with pure maple syrup. Finally, we highly recommend you serve this pancake directly from the oven to the table, in the pan it is baked in. Gather your group around and dig in.

●●● BAKED NOTE

We love the nuttiness that whole-wheat flour adds to this pancake; however, you can substitute regular flour, one for one, if you like. Also, we really recommend a 10-inch (25-cm) skillet. A 12-inch (30.5-cm) skillet might stretch the pancake batter a tad too thin, while an 8-inch (20-cm) skillet might make the batter too heavy and thick.

INGREDIENTS

3 tablespoons unsalted
   butter
1 ripe medium banana,
   sliced into ¼- to ½-inch-
   (6- to 12-mm-) thick
   slices
2 large eggs, at room
   temperature
½ cup (120 ml) whole milk,
   at room temperature
½ teaspoon pure vanilla
   extract
¼ cup (30 g) whole-wheat
   flour
¼ cup (30 g) all-purpose
   flour
3 tablespoons firmly
   packed dark brown sugar
½ teaspoon kosher salt
1½ ounces (40 g) chocolate
   chips, mini chocolate
   chips, or chocolate
   chunks (slightly less than
   ¼ cup)
2 tablespoons confectioners'
   sugar
Pure maple syrup, warmed,
   for serving
Handful of toasted, chopped
   walnuts (optional; see
   page 19)

1 Preheat the oven to 425°F (220°C).

2 Melt the butter in a 10-inch (25-cm) ovenproof skillet (ideally cast iron) over low heat. Swirl the butter to coat the bottom and sides of the pan. Increase the heat to medium, add the banana slices all at once, and toss them with a nonmetal utensil to coat them with the butter. Cook for 1 to 2 minutes. Remove the pan from the heat and arrange bananas in a single layer in the skillet; set aside.

3 In a blender, blend the eggs, milk, and vanilla for about 45 seconds on high until foamy. Add both flours, the brown sugar, and salt, and blend for another 30 seconds on high until frothy. Wait about 5 minutes, then pour the batter over the bananas. Sprinkle the top of the batter with the chocolate chips. Bake until the Dutch baby has climbed up the sides of the pan and is brown and dry to the touch in the center, 17 to 20 minutes.

4 Remove the Dutch baby from the oven, sift confectioners' sugar over the entire thing, slice, and serve immediately. Our Dutch baby is wonderful as is, but even better with a drizzle of warm maple syrup and a few walnuts sprinkled on top, if you like.

CHERRY ALMOND CRISP

YIELD: 8 TO 10 SERVINGS

MAYBE IT'S JUST ME, but there is something about cherry cordials (single preserved cherries in a chocolate shell) that evokes memories of both pleather (yup, plastic made to look like leather) couches and Swanson's microwaved meals. It's a hazy remembrance of a box of cordials left wanting while all the other desserts have already been devoured. Not so for Renato. Renato is all about the cherry cordial. And that is precisely why there is a very important "suggestion" to use a chocolate-based cereal or granola in the crisp portion of our Cherry Almond Crisp recipe. In his opinion, chocolate and cherry is a no-brainer.

Hopefully you will forgive us for the overtly literal homage of using a cherry dessert to illustrate Washington's Birthday. (Yes, it is now celebrated as the all-inclusive Presidents' Day in the States.) True, the tale of George Washington chopping down his father's favorite cherry tree ("I cannot tell a lie") is just that, a tale, but it is a good one. And our Cherry Almond Crisp would taste perfect for just about anyone's birthday. This crisp is everything a crisp should be: crispy, tart (nothing worse than a too-sweet crisp), and simple. It's clearly begging for vanilla ice cream, and leftovers are kind of perfect for breakfast.

●●● **BAKED NOTE**

If you don't own an 8-inch (20-cm) round cake pan, you can use an 8-inch (20-cm) square pan (with 2-inch/5-cm sides) in a pinch. Also, you can use frozen cherries in this crisp, but first thaw them and drain off excess liquid.

INGREDIENTS

For the Crisp Topping

- ⅔ cup (85 g) all-purpose flour
- ¼ cup plus 2 tablespoons (85 g) firmly packed light brown sugar
- 2 tablespoons granulated sugar
- ¼ teaspoon kosher salt
- 3 ounces (¾ stick/85 g) cold unsalted butter, cubed, plus more for the pan
- ¼ teaspoon pure almond extract
- ⅔ cup (100 g) blanched almonds, toasted (see page 19)
- ¾ cup (30 g) of your favorite oat-based childhood cereal, chocolate-based granola, or Fruity or Cocoa Pebbles

For the Cherry Filling

- 5½ cups pitted cherries (about 2 pounds/910 g before pitting)
- 2 tablespoons instant tapioca
- 1 tablespoon plus 1 teaspoon fresh lemon juice (about ½ lemon)
- 1 tablespoon pure almond extract
- 2 teaspoons granulated sugar
- 1 teaspoon lemon zest

For the Assembly

Premium vanilla ice cream (optional)

MAKE THE CRISP TOPPING

1. Preheat the oven to 400°F (205°C).
2. Lightly butter the bottom and sides of an 8-inch (20-cm) round cake pan with at least 2-inch (5-cm) sides.
3. Place the flour, both sugars, and the salt in a food processor and pulse until combined. Add the butter and almond extract and pulse until sandy (8 to 12 quick pulses). Add the almonds and pulse until the nuts are chopped and incorporated but the mixture is still coarse and chunky, not powdery; do not overpulse. Add the cereal and pulse with the almonds for a few more seconds. Place the topping in the refrigerator for at least 15 minutes.

MAKE THE CHERRY FILLING

1. In a large bowl, gently toss together the cherries, tapioca, lemon juice, almond extract, sugar, and lemon zest.

ASSEMBLE THE CHERRY ALMOND CRISP

1. Place the cherry filling in the prepared pan. Evenly scatter the chilled crisp topping over the filling and bake until the top is browned and the fruit is bubbling, 25 to 35 minutes. If the top starts to brown too quickly (but the filling is not bubbling), tent the crisp with foil and continue baking until the filling is ready. Remove from the oven, place the pan on a cooling rack, and allow to cool slightly. Serve the crisp warm, with vanilla ice cream, if you like.

HOW TO STORE

Wrap and refrigerate any leftover crisp for up to 3 days. To reheat, let the crisp come to room temperature, then rewarm it in a 300°F (150°C) oven for 15 to 20 minutes. Leftovers can also be eaten straight from the fridge with a dollop of Greek yogurt.

PISTACHIO WHITE CHOCOLATE CHEESECAKE

YIELD: 1 9-INCH (23-CM) CHEESECAKE • 16 SERVINGS

THERE IS REALLY NO RHYME OR REASON for pegging National Pistachio Day to February 26. It appears to be completely random. Regardless, we love pistachios and, technically speaking, we celebrate National Pistachio Day every day. Almost. We bake with them constantly and snack on them often. Our Pistachio White Chocolate Cheesecake is basically a dream. It is the perfect amalgam of three beautiful things: cheesecake, white chocolate, and—of course—pistachios. The interplay of the flavors is seamless, nothing overpowers. Each bite fires up a different taste-related neuron so that your brain goes from sour cream cheese to sweet white chocolate to pistachio bliss to crunchy chocolate cookie in a heartbeat. Did we mention that it is beautiful? While you could wait until February to make this cheesecake, there isn't really a reason you shouldn't be making it year-round.

As with any Baked cheesecake, we dutifully refer to Grandma Boreali's cheesecake tips, seeing as how she made cheesecake (thankfully) for nearly every event (small and large, and even uneventful): She always added a thin layer of sour cream to the top of her cheesecakes for two reasons. First, she liked the slightly sour note. Second, she told me it was a great way to cover up any cracks (though Grandma's cheesecake never cracked). Obviously, if you don't like the taste or visual idea of sour cream on your cheesecake, you can leave it off. Also, Grandma never "water bathed" a cheesecake in her life. Too much effort. If you are hardy, like Grandma, you can bake as is. If you are more cautious, like me, feel free to place a 9-by-13-inch (23-by-33-cm) pan of water in the oven directly below the cheesecake (not bathing the cheesecake, mind you) to help prevent cracking.

●●● BAKED NOTE

As with most cheesecakes, you will need to refrigerate this after baking it—so just a heads up that this will require an 8-hour chill time before serving. Also, for full nostalgia effect, we have been known to dye the pistachio layer the nuclear color of pistachio ice cream of yore. You don't have to do this—the pale green is also lovely—but trust us, it is kind of visually fun.

INGREDIENTS

For the Chocolate Cookie Crust

2½ ounces (70 g) shelled pistachios (about ½ cup)

12 ounces (340 g) chocolate wafer cookies

3 tablespoons granulated sugar

½ teaspoon kosher salt

6 ounces (1½ sticks/170 g) unsalted butter, melted

For the Pistachio White Chocolate Cream Cheese Filling

5 ounces (140 g) shelled pistachios (about 1 cup)

4 (8-ounce/226-g) packages cream cheese, softened

1⅓ cups (265 g) granulated sugar

1 tablespoon all-purpose flour

4 large eggs

1 large egg yolk

3 tablespoons heavy cream

4 ounces (115 g) white chocolate, melted and cooled

Green food dye or gel (optional)

½ cup (115 g) sour cream

MAKE THE CHOCOLATE COOKIE CRUST

1 Preheat the oven to 325°F (165°C). Using nonstick cooking spray, lightly coat both the bottom and sides of a high-sided (2½ to 3 inches / 6 to 7.5 cm) 9-inch (23-cm) springform pan. Line the bottom of the pan with parchment and lightly spray the parchment. Wrap the outside of the pan in foil on the off chance that it leaks liquid during baking.

2 In a food processor, pulse the pistachios until finely ground, about five 5-second pulses. Add the cookies, sugar, and salt, and process until the ingredients are coarsely ground, 30 to 40 seconds. Drizzle the melted butter over the crumbs and pulse until the mixture has the consistency of wet sand. Transfer the crumb mixture to the prepared pan and press it into the bottom and up the sides. Use the bottom of a flat measuring cup to create a firm, even crust.

3 Bake the crust for 8 to 10 minutes to set. Transfer the pan to a wire rack to cool completely.

MAKE THE PISTACHIO WHITE CHOCOLATE CREAM CHEESE FILLING

1 Increase the oven temperature to 500°F (260°C) and position a rack in the center of the oven.

2 In a food processor, pulse the pistachios until finely ground, about 30 seconds. Set aside.

3 In the bowl of a standing mixer fitted with the paddle attachment, combine the cream cheese, sugar, and flour. Beat on medium speed until just combined, being careful not to overbeat. Add the eggs and egg yolk, one at a time, beating well after each addition. Add the ground pistachios and cream and mix until incorporated.

4 Pour half the batter into a bowl. Fold the white chocolate into the batter in the bowl until combined. Pour this batter over the top of the chocolate cookie crust, smooth it out, and place the pan in the refrigerator for 10 minutes.

5 If using, add the green food dye, a few drops at a time, to the remaining batter and stir to incorporate until the desired color is achieved. Pour this batter over the refrigerated white chocolate batter. Smooth the top.

6 Bake in the middle of the oven for 10 minutes. Open the oven door for a few seconds to let out some heat and lower the oven temperature to 350°F (175°C). Close the oven door. Bake until the cheesecake is set around the outside, but still slightly wobbly in the center, 45 minutes to 1 hour, rotating the pan every 15 minutes. Remove from the oven and spread the sour cream over the top of the cheesecake in a swirly, decorative pattern. Return to the oven until the sour cream browns slightly, about 5 more minutes. Turn off the heat, crack the oven door, and let the cheesecake cool completely in the oven (about 1 hour).

7 Chill the cheesecake, lightly covered, in the refrigerator for 8 hours or overnight. Loosen the sides of the crust from the pan with an offset spatula, then remove the springform sides and serve.

HOW TO STORE

This cheesecake will keep, tightly covered, in the refrigerator for up to 3 or 4 days.

MARCH

●●●

MAR 2 | **TEXAS INDEPENDENCE DAY**
CHOCOLATE TEXAS SHEET CAKE WITH PEANUT BUTTER FROSTING 72

MAR 15 | **THE IDES OF MARCH**
BLOOD ORANGE TIRAMISU 74

MAR 17 | **ST. PATRICK'S DAY**
ST. PATRICK'S DRUNK BUNDT CAKE 77

DATE FLUCTUATES | **VERNAL EQUINOX**
LIGHT AND LEMONY JELLY ROLL WITH RASPBERRY CREAM FILLING 79

CHOCOLATE TEXAS SHEET CAKE WITH PEANUT BUTTER FROSTING

YIELD: 1 HALF SHEET CAKE • ABOUT 24 SERVINGS

WE ARE NOT TERRIFIC CAKE DECORATORS. At Baked we employ a talented and magical decorating staff. However, if left on our own, we have been known to fuss over a robust, tall three-layer cake far longer than we should. Whole decades pass by. We scrape and pipe and tinker and mess up and start all over again and again until some sort of semiperfection is achieved. Texans are smarter than us. Texans make one hell of a cake in sheet form that is every bit as delicious as their layered cousins. It's a lot less hassle for a whole lot of cake.

We'd like to dedicate our Peanut Butter Texas Sheet Cake to all our Texan friends. Contrary to popular belief, there are many Texans in New York. They are about as common as bagel shops and skyscrapers, and they are often stereotypically taller and more well-mannered than the average New York citizen. While we don't personally celebrate Texas Independence Day, the day commemorating the territory's separation from Mexico with the adoption of the Texas Declaration of Independence, we can only assume that a peanut butter Texas sheet cake would be an appropriate celebration cake. This cake is just this side of bliss. We intend to start making it for many non-Texas holidays as well. The cake itself is surprisingly moist and flavorful for such a short (about 1-inch-/2-cm-high) layer, and the icing, like most Texans we know, is decidedly sweet. It's a ridiculously snacky cake. And we love everything about it.

●●● **BAKED NOTE**

A properly fused Texas sheet cake is a great cake, so start making your icing the moment your cake goes in the oven, and then pour it on the hot finished cake. By the by, the origins of Texas sheet cake are murky at best. It is not 100 percent possible to trace the creation of this cake back to a great Texan baker, but it is most definitely Southern. There are many mentions of cakes baked in a jelly-roll (shallow) pan in and around Texas in the later part of the 1930s, and many similar-sounding recipes started appearing a few years later. Whoever created it, Texas adopted it and ran with it. Thankfully.

INGREDIENTS

For the Chocolate Sheet Cake

- 2 cups (255 g) all-purpose flour
- 1¼ cups (250 g) granulated sugar
- 1 cup (220 g) firmly packed light brown sugar
- ¾ teaspoon kosher salt
- 2 large eggs
- 1 large egg yolk
- ½ cup (120 ml) well-shaken buttermilk
- 1 tablespoon pure vanilla extract
- 6 ounces (1½ sticks/170 g) unsalted butter, cut into 1-inch (2.5-cm) pieces
- 1 cup (240 ml) coffee
- ⅓ cup plus 1 tablespoon (35 g) unsweetened cocoa powder
- ¼ cup (50 g) vegetable shortening
- 1 teaspoon baking soda

For the Peanut Butter Frosting

- 14 ounces (395 g) confectioners' sugar (about 4 cups)
- ⅔ cup (165 ml) evaporated milk
- 4 ounces (1 stick/115 g) unsalted butter, cut into small pieces
- ½ cup (130 g) creamy natural peanut butter
- ¼ teaspoon kosher salt
- 1 teaspoon pure vanilla extract
- 1½ cups (225 g) salted roasted peanuts, finely chopped

MAKE THE CHOCOLATE SHEET CAKE

1. Preheat the oven to 350°F (175°C). Lightly spray a half sheet pan with nonstick cooking spray. Line the pan with parchment paper, then lightly spray the parchment and the sides of the pan. Alternatively, you can grease and lightly flour the parchment paper and the sides of the pan.

2. In a large bowl, whisk together the flour, both sugars, and the salt. Make a well in the center of the bowl. Set aside.

3. In a small bowl, whisk together the eggs, egg yolk, buttermilk, and vanilla. Set aside.

4. In a medium saucepan set over medium heat, stir together the butter, coffee, cocoa powder, shortening, and baking soda. Once the butter just begins to melt, increase the heat to medium-high and bring the mixture to a boil for 20 to 45 seconds, but no more. Pour the hot mixture into the well of the dry ingredients and fold it all together. The mixture should be nearly room temperature (if it is not, wait a few minutes). Add the buttermilk mixture to the chocolate mixture and whisk gently to combine.

5. Pour the batter into the prepared pan and place in the oven. Bake the sheet cake until a toothpick inserted in the center comes out clean, 15 to 18 minutes, rotating the pan halfway through the baking time. Do not overbake; err on the side of slightly underbaked if you must.

6. Start making the icing while the cake is baking (the icing must be applied to a hot cake to fuse properly).

MAKE THE PEANUT BUTTER FROSTING

1. Sift the confectioners' sugar into a large bowl. (If you want to make sure your frosting is extra smooth, sift the sugar twice.)

2. In a medium saucepan set over medium heat, stir together the evaporated milk, butter, peanut butter, and salt. Once the butter begins to melt, increase the heat to medium-high and bring the mixture just to a boil.

3. Pour the hot mixture over the sifted confectioners' sugar and whisk to combine. Add the vanilla and whisk again for 10 seconds.

4. Pour the frosting over the hot cake and spread it into a consistent layer with an offset spatula. Sprinkle the chopped peanuts over the frosting and allow the entire cake and frosting to come to room temperature. Place the cake in the refrigerator for about 45 minutes to fully set the frosting.

5. Slice and serve the cake cold (our preference), or bring it to room temperature first.

HOW TO STORE

The cake will keep in an airtight container at room temperature or in the refrigerator for up to 3 days.

BLOOD ORANGE TIRAMISU

YIELD: 1 9-BY-13-INCH (23-BY-33-CM) PAN • 16 TO 20 SERVINGS

RENATO, RIGHTLY OR WRONGLY (but mostly wrongly), has romanticized the Ides of March as one giant toga party—10 percent historical reverence, 90 percent excuse to wear a toga and imbibe. Unfortunately (at least for Renato), the fantasy of March 15 as degenerate frat party is just that—a fantasy. It doesn't exist yet. For whatever reason, the Ides of March is not exactly widely recognized, and rarely celebrated. If the day is acknowledged at all, it is widely due to Shakespeare's dramatization of what befell Julius Caesar (in the play of the same name) on that fateful day in 44 BCE. It was the day that Caesar was "stabbed in the back" by a coterie of friends, all of them presumably wearing togas.

Renato's notion of togas and beer is not exactly unreasonable in a world where we celebrate a great many unreasonable holidays. In case the urge strikes you, we have the perfect dessert. Our Blood Orange Tiramisu nods to Caesar's Roman heritage. It is also overtly—if not a little ridiculously—literal in that, well, we use blood oranges (which happen to be in season in March). Aside from the blood oranges, this is a straightforward interpretation of tiramisu—creamy and pudding-like. It comes together quickly, it is easy to make, and it yields a party-size amount. If you like tiramisu, you will love this recipe. If you don't like tiramisu, we still implore you to wear a toga on the Ides of March.

●●● BAKED NOTE
Our recipe for Blood Orange Tiramisu is the perfect "make-ahead" dessert. In fact, we encourage you to make the tiramisu the night before serving to allow it to fully set up. Also, this recipe is made with uncooked eggs, so please exercise caution.

INGREDIENTS

- 4 large eggs, separated, at room temperature
- ¾ cup (150 g) granulated sugar
- 1 pound (455 g) mascarpone cheese, at room temperature
- Zest of 1 blood orange (about 1½ tablespoons)
- 4 tablespoons (60 ml) Grand Marnier
- ¼ teaspoon kosher salt
- 6 blood oranges, juiced (about 2 cups/480 ml)
- 40 (4-by-1-inch/ 10-by-2.5 cm) ladyfinger cookies (we prefer Savoiardi)
- ⅓ cup (30 g) unsweetened dark cocoa powder
- Chocolate shavings (optional)

1 In the bowl of a standing mixer fitted with the whisk attachment, beat the egg yolks and sugar on medium-high speed until the mixture is light and starts to thicken, 3 to 6 minutes. Switch to the paddle attachment, add the mascarpone cheese, and beat until incorporated. Add the zest and 2 tablespoons of the Grand Marnier and beat until just combined. Transfer the mixture to a large bowl and clean and dry the mixer bowl.

2 Place the egg whites in the clean bowl and fit the mixer with the whisk attachment. Sprinkle the salt over the egg whites and beat on medium-high speed until soft peaks form, 4 to 5 minutes. Add half of the egg whites to the egg yolk mixture and gently fold together until almost incorporated; add the remaining egg whites and gently fold until completely incorporated.

3 Stir together the blood orange juice and the remaining 2 tablespoons Grand Marnier in a wide-mouthed shallow bowl.

4 Working quickly, dip the first 20 ladyfingers in the juice mixture, making sure to soak each cookie from top to bottom (a second or two on each side), then arrange the ladyfingers to cover the bottom of a 9-by-13-inch (23-by-33-cm) pan in a single layer (reserve any leftover ladyfingers for the next step). Dollop about half of the mascarpone mixture over the ladyfingers and spread it into an even layer. Sift half of the cocoa powder over the mascarpone mixture. Dip the next 20 ladyfingers in the juice mixture as above and arrange them in an even layer over the mascarpone layer. Cover the ladyfingers with the remaining mascarpone mixture and spread it into an even layer. Sift the remaining cocoa powder over the top.

5 Cover the pan tightly with plastic and refrigerate for at least 5 hours or up to overnight (most people prefer tiramisu that has been chilled for at least 10 hours—if you can wait that long). Sprinkle with a few chocolate shavings, if desired, slice, and serve.

HOW TO STORE

The tiramisu can be kept, tightly covered, in the refrigerator for up to 3 days.

ST. PATRICK'S DRUNK BUNDT CAKE

CHOCOLATE-STOUT BUNDT CAKE WITH WHISKEY-BAILEYS GLAZE

YIELD: 1 BUNDT CAKE • 12 TO 16 SERVINGS

MY FAMILY BLOODLINE is splintered. It veers toward Italy with substantial detours to Scotland and Great Britain. As far as I know, we do not have any direct Irish ancestors, but my family absolutely loves St. Patrick's Day nonetheless. They embrace it. The height of our collective St. Paddy's pandemonium occurred during our tenure in the suburbs of Chicago—my middle school years. Mom would make a concerted effort to dress in many shades of green. The sentiment was more fashion forward than kitsch, with a flow of interconnected green patterns all set off with a smart (albeit inexpensive) bright green purse. And my gracious father was kind enough to gather us all up and truck us off to the big parade in Chicago—a trek unto itself, considering the snarling traffic and biting, late-winter Chicago wind.

Originally, for our St. Patrick's Day recipe, I had wanted to follow mom's all-green initiative. Instead, we went a more sensible route. A more delicious route. Our Chocolate-Stout Bundt Cake is a fine specimen flavored with a full cup and a half of Guinness, a favorite of ours. It is rich without being overpowering, and distinct without being obnoxious. Naturally, we covered this cake in a glaze infused with both Irish whiskey and Baileys Irish Cream because it tastes supreme. And because we felt obligated to hit everyone over the head with the Irishness of it all.

●●● BAKED NOTE

You can make this cake with any rich, thick stout. While Guinness is certainly the most ubiquitous choice, you should feel free to experiment with local and small-batch stouts. And, if possible, seek out a good chocolate stout (both Young's and Rogue make a super-tasty version)—it is a natural, almost perfect fit for this cake.

INGREDIENTS

For the Chocolate-Stout Bundt Cake

2 cups (255 g) all-purpose flour
2 teaspoons baking powder
¾ teaspoon kosher salt
¼ teaspoon baking soda
1½ cups (12 ounces/360 ml) Guinness, or other dark stout, measured without foam
1 cup (85 g) unsweetened cocoa powder
6 ounces (1½ sticks/170 g) unsalted butter
4 ounces (115 g) good-quality dark chocolate, 60 to 72% cacao
1½ cups (330 g) firmly packed dark brown sugar
¾ cup (150 g) granulated sugar
¼ cup (60 ml) canola oil
1 tablespoon pure vanilla extract
2 large eggs
2 large egg yolks
½ cup (115 g) sour cream
½ cup (120 ml) heavy cream

For the Whiskey-Baileys Glaze

1 (8-ounce/226 g) package cream cheese, softened
1 cup (115 g) confectioners' sugar, sifted
½ cup (120 ml) heavy cream
2 tablespoons Irish whiskey, such as Jameson
1 tablespoon Baileys Irish Cream

MAKE THE CHOCOLATE-STOUT BUNDT CAKE

1 Preheat the oven to 350°F (175°C).

2 Generously spray the inside of a 10- or 12-cup (2.4- or 2.8-L) Bundt pan with nonstick cooking spray, dust with cocoa powder, and knock out the excess cocoa powder. Alternatively, you can use butter instead of spray. Either way, make sure the pan's nooks and crannies are all thoroughly coated.

3 Whisk together the flour, baking powder, salt, and baking soda.

4 Place the Guinness, cocoa powder, butter, and chocolate in a large saucepan. Stir the mixture together over low heat until the butter is melted, then increase the heat to high and bring just to a boil. Remove from the heat and add the brown and granulated sugars, the canola oil, and vanilla. Whisk until combined. Add the eggs, egg yolks, sour cream, and heavy cream and whisk vigorously until combined. Using a rubber spatula, fold the flour mixture into the Guinness mixture until combined. If the flour clumps, use a heatproof spatula or the back of a wooden spoon to smash the flour against the side of the pan until it breaks up. Pour the mixture into the prepared pan.

5 Bake for 45 to 55 minutes, rotating the pan halfway through the baking time, until a toothpick inserted in the center of the cake comes out with just a few moist crumbs clinging to it.

6 Transfer the pan to a wire rack and cool for 30 minutes. Gently loosen the sides of the cake from the pan and turn it out onto the rack; place the rack over a half sheet pan lined with parchment.

MAKE THE WHISKEY-BAILEYS GLAZE

1 In the bowl of a standing mixer fitted with a paddle attachment, beat the cream cheese until fluffy. Add the confectioners' sugar all at once and beat until combined. Add the cream, whiskey, and Baileys and beat until the icing completely comes together.

2 Spread the glaze over the crown of the Bundt, allowing the glaze to drip down the sides of the cake. Allow the glaze to set, about 20 minutes, before serving.

HOW TO STORE

The cake will keep in an airtight container at room temperature for up to 3 days.

LIGHT AND LEMONY JELLY ROLL WITH RASPBERRY CREAM FILLING

YIELD: 1 JELLY ROLL CAKE • 12 TO 16 PIECES

IN NEW YORK, spring is an ideal. It is a reason to be. It is an awakening from the deep winter doldrums and liberation from bulky winter jackets. It's blue skies, low humidity, open windows, crayon-colored farmers' markets, and lightweight hoodies. The streets are infused with a renewed vigor; random smiles are infectious and everywhere. Unfortunately, spring is relatively short in New York. Summer, brutal and ugly and fragrant (not in a good way), is always nipping at the heels of our precious spring. Though spring may be brief, and though it is sandwiched between two less desirable seasons, it is welcome and celebratory and reason enough to move to New York City.

There are a million ways to celebrate spring via dessert, but we prefer the light and lemony route. We also happen to think a little retro flair—here, a jelly roll—is always in order. This dessert is extraordinarily light and bright with lemon flavor. The raspberry cream filling is a superb cake companion (and, by the by, incredibly addictive, so much so that we often "accidentally" eat—in the name of testing—quite a bit of frosting before it makes it to the cake). This cake is crowd-pleasing in that "wow, you rolled up a cake" kind of way. Do not fear the jelly roll—practice does indeed make perfect.

●●● BAKED NOTE

When buying any extract (including lemon), use only brands marked pure and natural. If you have trouble locating pure and natural lemon extract, you can substitute a pure and natural lemon "flavor" (often the same size as most extract bottles and often more ubiquitous) for the extract in this recipe; just use ½ teaspoon instead.

INGREDIENTS

For the Lemon Cake

1   cup (130 g) cake flour
1   teaspoon baking powder
5   large eggs, at room
     temperature, separated
1   cup (200 g) granulated
     sugar
Zest of 5 lemons (about 5
     tablespoons)
1   teaspoon lemon extract
     (see Baked Note)
¼   teaspoon cream of tartar
¼   teaspoon kosher salt
2   tablespoons confection-
     ers' sugar

For the Raspberry Cream Filling

1¾ cups (225 g) fresh
     raspberries
1¾ cups (420 ml) heavy
     cream
3   tablespoons confectioners'
     sugar
1 to 2 tablespoons Chambord
     liqueur (optional)
1   teaspoon pure vanilla
     extract

For the Assembly

2   tablespoons confectioners'
     sugar, for dusting
Fresh raspberries, for garnish
     (optional)

MAKE THE LEMON CAKE

1 Preheat the oven to 400°F (205°C). Lightly coat the bottom and sides of a half sheet pan with nonstick cooking spray and line it with parchment paper. Lightly spray the parchment with the nonstick cooking spray.

2 Sift the flour and baking powder into a small bowl. Turn the sifted ingredients onto a piece of parchment paper and sift them together one more time into the bowl. Set aside.

3 Place the egg yolks in the bowl of a standing mixer fitted with the paddle attachment. Sprinkle ½ cup (100 g) granulated sugar over the yolks, and beat on high speed until the mixture ribbons and is very pale and thick, at least 5 minutes. Add the lemon zest and lemon extract. Beat until just combined, about 15 seconds. Transfer the mixture to a large bowl, and clean and dry the mixer bowl.

4 Place the egg whites in the clean bowl and fit the standing mixer with the whisk attachment; beat on medium-high speed for 1 minute. Sprinkle the cream of tartar and salt over the egg whites and continue beating on medium-high until soft peaks begin to form, 3 to 5 minutes. Reduce the speed to medium, then slowly stream in the remaining ½ cup (100 g) granulated sugar and continue beating until the whites are glossy and stiff but not dry.

5 Using a rubber spatula, gently fold one-third of the beaten egg whites into the yolk mixture. Gently fold half of the sifted flour mixture into the yolk mixture, then half of the remaining egg whites. Gently fold in the remaining flour mixture, followed by the remaining egg whites. Transfer the batter into the prepared pan and very gently smooth the top into an even layer with an offset spatula. Bake the cake until it begins to pull away from the sides, 5 to 8 minutes; keep a keen eye on it the whole time to avoid overbaking. You can also test for doneness by gently pressing in the center with your finger: If the cake springs back, it is done.

6 Transfer the pan to a cooling rack, cover the cake with a few damp (but not wet) paper towels, and cool for 10 minutes. Run a knife under hot water, wipe dry, then run the knife around the edges of the still-warm cake. Remove the paper towels and sift 1 tablespoon confectioners' sugar over the cake. Drape a very thin tea towel over the cake, then place a half sheet pan right side up on top of the tea towel. With a quick motion, invert the cake onto the back of the clean sheet pan, and remove the baking pan. Gently remove the parchment paper. Sift the remaining tablespoon of confectioners' sugar over the cake. Trim a scant ¼ inch (6 mm) off all sides of the cake. Starting with a short side of the cake, roll the cake up ever so gently, using the towel to support the cake as you go (it's almost like a lift and turn motion)—the towel itself will roll up in the cake. Let the cake cool all rolled up in the towel, seam side down.

MAKE THE RASPBERRY CREAM FILLING

1 Chill the bowl of the standing mixer.

2 Slice ¼ cup (roughly 1 ounce/28 g) of the raspberries in half and set aside.

3 Place the remaining raspberries in a food processor or blender and process or blend until completely pureed. Push the raspberry mixture through a fine-mesh sieve into a large bowl. Discard the seeds left behind.

4 Place the cream in the chilled mixer bowl and fit the mixer with the whisk attachment; whisk on medium speed for 1 minute. Sprinkle the confectioners' sugar over the cream, then continue to beat until soft peaks form, 3 to 5 minutes. Add the Chambord, if using, a tablespoon at a time, to taste, and the vanilla, and beat again until incorporated. Gently fold in the raspberry puree until the mixture is almost but not completely uniform (the striations in the mixture make it more visually interesting).

ASSEMBLE THE JELLY ROLL

1 Unroll the cake gently onto a sheet of parchment on a flat surface. Spread the raspberry filling over the cake in an even layer. Sprinkle the sliced raspberries over the cream. Gently roll the cake back up, as tightly as possible (use the towel to help guide the cake if needed, but do not roll the towel into the cake). Place the cake, seam side down, on a serving plate, sift confectioners' sugar over the top, cover gently with plastic wrap, and refrigerate for 1 hour to set.

2 To serve, garnish with more raspberries, if you like, slice, and serve immediately.

HOW TO STORE

The cake can be stored, tightly covered, in the refrigerator for 2 days (though it tastes best within 24 hours); allow it to sit out at room temperature for about 30 minutes before serving.

APRIL

●●●

DATE FLUCTUATES | EASTER
MEGA EASTER PIE: A MEAT AND CHEESE UTOPIA 84

DATE FLUCTUATES | EASTER
EASTER COCONUT SHEET CAKE 86

APR 22 | EARTH DAY
HIPPIE CAKE 90

APR 23 | SHAKESPEARE DAY
BUTTERY POUND CAKE WITH SALTY CARAMEL GLAZE 93

APR 23 | SECRETARY'S DAY (AKA ADMINISTRATIVE PROFESSIONALS' DAY)
CARAMEL CANDY POPCORN BALLS 96

MEGA EASTER PIE: A MEAT AND CHEESE UTOPIA

YIELD: 1 MEGA EASTER PIE • 10 TO 12 GENEROUS SERVINGS

CURIOUSLY, though all manner of traditional Italian foods moved in and around Renato's world—like the more familiar buckwheat cake (*torta di grano*)—a meaty Easter pie was conspicuously absent from his childhood. There is no specific reason. There is no unusual ingredient. His parents just disliked it. Easter pie was the crazy neighbor—best avoided and, if acknowledged at all, always briefly and always from afar. Naturally, that just made this mysterious pie all the more interesting to the young Renato.

Renato's version is supernatural. It's a beast with double the typical amount of filling and a well-rounded assortment of ingredients, including the lovable but unfortunately named basket cheese. This cheese is like the angelic offspring of ricotta and fresh mozzarella, placed in a basket (hence the not-so-clever name) and sold around Easter. It is perfectly fine to substitute a fresh ricotta if you are basket-cheese-less.

●●● BAKED NOTE

This is your Easter pie. Feel free to customize it by subbing equal amounts of one type of meat or cheese for another (be aware that the salt amount might shift considerably—i.e., extra salty cheeses with salty meats might be too much, so keep a watchful eye when subbing). However, Renato is fairly insistent on using smoked mozzarella. In his eyes, this pie would not be the same without it.

INGREDIENTS

For the Classic Pie Dough

3   cups (385 g) all-purpose flour, chilled

1   tablespoon granulated sugar

1   teaspoon fine sea salt

Ice cubes

8   ounces (2 sticks/225 g) cold unsalted butter, cut into ½-inch (12-mm) cubes

MAKE THE CLASSIC PIE DOUGH

1   In a medium bowl, whisk the flour, sugar, and salt together. In a measuring cup, stir ¾ cup (180 ml) water with several ice cubes until it is very cold, then discard the ice.

2   Toss the cold butter in the flour mixture to coat. Place the mixture in a food processor and pulse in short bursts until the butter pieces are the size of hazelnuts.

3   Pulsing in 4-second bursts, slowly drizzle the ice-cold water into the food processor through the feed tube. As soon as the dough comes together in a ball, stop adding water.

4   Remove the dough from the food processor and divide it in half. Flatten each piece into a disk, and wrap each disk first in parchment paper and then in plastic wrap. Refrigerate the dough until firm, about 1 hour. The dough can be stored in the refrigerator for up to 3 days or in the freezer for up to 3 months. Thaw it in the refrigerator before proceeding.

INGREDIENTS (CONT.)

For the Easter Pie

1	tablespoon olive oil
¼	teaspoon crushed red pepper
½	onion, diced
½	teaspoon fresh thyme
3	ounces (85 g) roasted red peppers, drained and diced (about ¾ cup)
3	large eggs
1	pound (455 g) basket cheese, or 1 pound (455 g) fresh ricotta, drained well
¾	pound (340 g) smoked mozzarella cheese, shredded
½	pound (225 g) cooked ham, cubed (we prefer Black Forest)
½	pound (225 g) prosciutto, diced or rolled and sliced into ½-inch (12-mm) slices
¼	cup (30 g) grated Romano cheese
¼	cup (30 g) grated Parmesan cheese
¼	cup (30 g) cubed soft provolone cheese
1	tablespoon chopped fresh parsley
½	teaspoon lemon zest
¼	teaspoon freshly ground pepper

MAKE THE EASTER PIE

1   In a medium skillet or sauté pan, heat the olive oil and crushed red pepper over medium-low heat until the oil begins to shimmer, 2 to 3 minutes. Add the onion and thyme. Cook, stirring, until the onion is translucent, about 5 minutes. Add the peppers and cook for another 3 to 4 minutes, or until all the liquid has evaporated. Remove from the heat and set aside to cool while you prepare the rest of the filling.

2   Preheat the oven to 375°F (190°C) and position a rack in the center of the oven.

3   Using nonstick cooking spray, coat the bottom and sides of a 9-inch (23-cm) springform pan. Line the bottom with parchment paper and lightly spray the parchment.

4   In a large bowl, whisk 2 of the eggs. Add the basket cheese, mozzarella cheese, ham, prosciutto, Romano cheese, Parmesan cheese, provolone cheese, parsley, lemon zest, and pepper and stir together. Add the cooled onion-and-pepper mixture. Use your hands to toss everything together until thoroughly mixed.

5   Dust a work surface with a sprinkling of flour and roll out the first disk of chilled dough into a 14-inch (35.5-cm) round, about ¼ inch (6 mm) thick. Transfer it to the prepared pan and carefully work it into the bottom and build it up the sides. There shouldn't be a lot of overhang, but if there is, trim it back to 1 inch (2.5 cm) at most. Add the meat-and-cheese mixture.

6   Adding more flour to the work surface as needed, roll out the second disk of chilled dough into a 12-inch (30.5-cm) round. Center it on top of the filling with about a 1-inch (2.5-cm) overhang over the sides of the pan. Working carefully, crimp the bottom and top doughs together. Try not to let the dough extend out over the lip of the pan, as this will make it difficult to remove from the pan without breaking.

7   Make an egg wash by whisking together the remaining egg with 1 tablespoon water. Brush the top crust with the egg wash. Cut 3 steam vents into the top crust.

8   Place the pie on a half sheet pan and bake, rotating halfway through the baking time, until the crust is golden brown, about 1 hour.

9   Cool the pie in its pan on a rack for about 2 hours. Unmold the pie from the springform pan, remove the metal bottom, and transfer the pie to a serving plate. Serve slightly warm or at room temperature.

HOW TO STORE

The pie can be stored, tightly covered, in the refrigerator for up to 4 days. We recommend reheating it until warm to serve, but you can slice and eat directly from the fridge.

EASTER COCONUT SHEET CAKE

YIELD: 1 9-BY-13-INCH (23-BY-33-CM) CAKE • ABOUT 24 SERVINGS

MY MOM WAS WONDERFUL. She understood my Easter basket requirements well and never asked me to deviate. Without fail, Mom (or the Easter Bunny) delivered a heaping bounty of hollow chocolate rabbits (the solid kind were too difficult to eat), Reese's peanut butter eggs, and assorted marshmallow chick-shaped Peeps. The basket itself was a little trashy—plastic and cheap and overflowing with fake green-grass filler. I loved it. Mom also made a coconut sheet cake (probably from box mix) for Easter. I did not love this. It was topped with shredded coconut dyed green to simulate grass and a scattering of mini foil-wrapped chocolate eggs. Shudder. When I told Mom I disliked the coconut portion of the cake, she told me not to eat it. I tried, but lacked willpower. After all, it was still cake. I spent many long nights picking off the shredded coconut with one hand and holding a headless chocolate bunny in the other.

The genius chefs at Baked (thank you, Molly and Veronika) reworked this classic. It is still very coconut friendly, but not overly so. The cake is moist yet light and infused with coconut flavor, but the garish (in my opinion) shredded coconut topping is gone. It has been replaced with a mild coconut frosting decked out in Easter colors. Mom would have enjoyed it all the same.

●●● **BAKED NOTE**

Do not let the semi-labor-intensive decoration keep you from making this cake. If you want to simplify things, simply spread one color of frosting across the cake in an even layer as you would with any regular cake. And if you want to go full-on "mom-style"—that is, with additional shredded coconut that is supposed to look like grass—place 1 cup (90 g) of shredded coconut in a zip-tight plastic bag with 3 or 4 drops of green food dye, shake, and then sprinkle on top of the frosting.

INGREDIENTS

For the Coconut Sheet Cake

2½ cups plus 2 tablespoons (330 g) cake flour

2¼ teaspoons baking powder

¾ teaspoon kosher salt

4½ ounces (9 tablespoons/ 125 g) unsalted butter, cool but not cold, cut into ½-inch (12-mm) cubes

1½ cups plus 2 tablespoons (325 g) granulated sugar

⅓ cup (75 ml) coconut oil

1 large egg

1 large egg yolk

1½ teaspoons pure coconut extract

1½ teaspoons pure vanilla extract

¾ cup (180 g) cream of coconut

¼ cup plus 2 tablespoons (90 ml) whole milk

2 cups (180 g) lightly packed sweetened shredded coconut

5 large egg whites

½ teaspoon cream of tartar

MAKE THE COCONUT SHEET CAKE

1 Preheat the oven to 350°F (175°C) if your pan is metal and 325°F (165°C) if it's glass. Lightly spray a 9-by-13-inch (23-by-33-cm) glass or light-metal pan with nonstick cooking spray. Line the pan with parchment paper so that the paper overhangs the pan on two sides. Lightly spray the parchment and the sides of the pan. Alternatively, you can butter and lightly flour the parchment paper and sides of the pan.

2 In a large bowl, sift together the flour, baking powder, and salt. Set aside.

3 In the bowl of a standing mixer fitted with the paddle attachment, beat the butter and sugar on medium speed until light and fluffy, about 3 minutes. Add the coconut oil and beat until incorporated. Scrape down the sides and bottom of the bowl, add the egg, egg yolk, coconut extract, and vanilla, and beat until thoroughly combined. Scrape down the sides and bottom of the bowl.

4 In a medium bowl, whisk together the cream of coconut and whole milk.

5 Add the flour mixture to the butter mixture in three parts, alternating with the coconut milk mixture, and beginning and ending with the flour mixture. After each addition, beat on medium speed until incorporated, 10 to 15 seconds. Fold in the shredded coconut with a rubber spatula.

6 In a separate bowl, whisk the egg whites vigorously for 1 minute. Sprinkle the cream of tartar over the whites and continue whisking until stiff peaks form. Gently fold one-quarter of the egg whites into the batter until almost combined. Fold another quarter of the egg white mixture into the batter until nearly combined. Finally, add the remaining egg white mixture to the batter and fold gently until completely combined.

7 Pour the batter into the prepared pan and place in the oven. Bake the cake, rotating the pan halfway through the baking time, until a toothpick inserted in the center comes out with just a few moist crumbs, 42 to 48 minutes (if you're baking in a glass pan, you might need a few extra minutes). Transfer the pan to a wire rack and cool completely. Once the cake has cooled, you can gently lift the cake out of the pan using the parchment paper, if you want to—or you can serve it straight out of the pan.

MAKE THE COCONUT FROSTING

1 In the bowl of a standing mixer fitted with the whisk attachment, whisk the egg whites and sugar together until combined. Set the bowl over a pan of simmering water (double-boiler method, see page 19), making sure the water does not touch the bottom of the bowl. Heat the mixture, stirring occasionally, until the sugar is completely dissolved and the color is a milky white, 2 to 3 minutes. The liquid should be warm to the touch.

2 Place the bowl back onto the mixer fitted with the whisk attachment and beat on medium-high speed (start slowly at first) until smooth and fluffy, about 5 minutes. Remove the whisk attachment and replace it with the paddle attachment. Add the cubed butter, a few chunks at a time, and beat on medium-high speed (again, start slowly at first) until smooth and fluffy, about 5 minutes. If the

INGREDIENTS (CONT.)

For the Coconut Frosting

5   large egg whites
1¼   cups (250 g) granulated sugar
12   ounces (3 sticks/340 g) unsalted butter, cool but not cold, cut into ½-inch (12-mm) cubes
3   tablespoons cream of coconut
1½   teaspoons coconut extract
⅛   teaspoon kosher salt
4   food dyes or gels

buttercream breaks (i.e., looks like it is curdling), keep beating until it comes back together. Add the cream of coconut, coconut extract, and salt and beat for 10 to 15 seconds to combine.

3 Divide the frosting evenly into four separate bowls. Add a drop or two of food dye to each bowl (a lighter touch is preferred here to emulate muted pastel colors), and fold until the color is uniform; you can leave one bowl white if you like. If you own four separate pastry bags, fit each of them with a round medium tip; if not, gather four zip-tight plastic bags and fit them with four round medium tips (if you do not have tips, just be prepared to cut a corner of each plastic bag). Fill each bag with a separate color of frosting; if using a zip-tight plastic bag, cut a small triangle from one of the bottom corners after filling it three-fourths with frosting and zipping the top. Hold the first bag about ¼ inch (6 mm) above the cake and apply pressure to pipe a dot or "egg" of frosting into the corner of the cake. Carefully pull the tip slightly up and off to the side to mimic the pattern of the cake in the photo on page 87. Choose the next color and pipe the next two or three dots or "eggs" diagonally underneath the first color dot (see photo 1). Pick up your third color and pipe four dots underneath the second row of dots. Then use the fourth and final color to pipe the 5 or 6 dots or "eggs" underneath the third row of dots (see photo 2). Continue this pattern across the top of the cake until the complete cake is covered (see photos 3 and 4).

4 Place the cake in the refrigerator for about 30 minutes to set the frosting. Serve immediately.

HOW TO STORE

The cake will keep in an airtight container at room temperature or in the refrigerator for up to 3 days. Bring to room temperature before slicing and serving.

HIPPIE CAKE

VEGAN CHOCOLATE CAKE WITH OLIVE OIL AND BALSAMIC VINEGAR

YIELD: 1 8-INCH (20-CM) SINGLE-LAYER CAKE • ABOUT 10 SERVINGS

WE ARE CHAMPIONS OF MOTHER EARTH. We believe in repurposing, recycling, and smaller footprints. We don't even like to use hotel mini soaps and shampoos because it seems so wasteful. So please forgive us if our younger, less-worldly selves imagined (quite stereotypically) Earth Day as one gigantic Grateful Dead concert: grilled cheese sandwiches in a vast public park, tie-dyes, and lots and lots of hippies. In reality, Earth Day was probably much less exciting in Oskaloosa, Iowa (me) or Boca Raton, Florida (Renato). It was probably a fourth-grade teacher explaining the importance of turning off the lights while we slumped in our ill-lit cafeteria.

You will have to forgive us again for prolonging or exaggerating the Earth Day stereotype even further by way of our Hippie Cake. We love this simple vegan cake—good for both the Earth and animals alike. In fact, this cake is so rich and chocolaty and exceedingly moist (thanks to olive oil) it might even become your go-to chocolate cake. It is easy to put together and works well with or without our vegan almond-butter frosting. Enjoy this cake and, in the words of fourth-grade teachers everywhere, make every day Earth Day. .

●●● **BAKED NOTE**

In theory, cocoa powder is vegan, but we encourage you to go full hippie and seek out an organic and sustainable brand. Also, use a good fruity olive oil—we like Paesano—to add an extra layer of depth to the cake. Finally, don't feel obligated to make the icing unless you are an icing person. The chocolate cake, with all its inherent flavors (chocolate, olive oil, and balsamic vinegar) is quite beautiful as is, dusted with confectioners' sugar just before serving.

INGREDIENTS

For the Vegan Chocolate Cake

2 ounces (55 g) vegan dark chocolate, coarsely chopped
½ cup plus 2 tablespoons (150 ml) olive oil
1 tablespoon balsamic vinegar
1 cup (240 ml) almost-boiling water
1¼ cups (250 g) vegan granulated sugar
1½ cups (170 g) all-purpose flour
½ cup (40 g) unsweetened dark cocoa powder, such as Valrhona
1 teaspoon baking powder
½ teaspoon kosher salt
¼ teaspoon baking soda

For the Almond Butter Frosting

1¼ to 1¾ cups (140 to 200 g) vegan confectioners' sugar, sifted
½ cup (130 g) almond butter (ideally without any added sugar, with or without flaxseeds)
2 ounces (55 g) vegan butter, such as Earth Balance, softened
2 to 4 tablespoons (30 to 60 ml) almond milk, at room temperature
1 teaspoon vanilla bean paste
½ teaspoon kosher salt

MAKE THE VEGAN CHOCOLATE CAKE

1 Preheat the oven to 350°F (175°C).

2 Lightly spray the bottom and sides of an 8-inch (20-cm) round cake pan with nonstick cooking spray. Line the bottom with parchment paper and lightly spray the top of the parchment.

3 Place the chocolate, olive oil, and vinegar in a large bowl. Add the hot water, let stand 1 minute, and whisk until the chocolate is completely melted; whisk for an additional minute to release extreme heat. Add the sugar and whisk to combine. Set aside.

4 In a medium bowl, whisk the flour, cocoa powder, baking powder, salt, and baking soda until well combined.

5 Gently fold half of the dry ingredients into the wet. Add the remaining half of the dry ingredients and continue to fold until just combined. Pour the batter into the prepared pan and bake until a toothpick inserted into the center of the cake comes out with just a few moist crumbs, 28 to 32 minutes.

6 Transfer the pan to a wire rack to cool for at least 30 minutes. Turn the cake out onto the rack, remove the parchment, and let cool completely. You can also pop the cake in the refrigerator for about 30 minutes to firm up, so the cake cuts cleanly and precisely.

MAKE THE ALMOND BUTTER FROSTING

1 Place 1¼ cups (140 g) confectioners' sugar, the almond butter, vegan butter, 2 tablespoons almond milk, the vanilla paste, and salt in a food processor. Pulse in short bursts until the frosting comes together and is shiny and smooth. If you prefer a slightly looser frosting, add 1 to 2 additional tablespoons almond milk; if you prefer a thicker frosting, add up to ½ cup (55 g) more confectioners' sugar.

2 Use an offset spatula to spread the frosting into an even layer on only the top of the cake. Refrigerate the cake for about 10 minutes to set the frosting.

HOW TO STORE

The cake can keep, tightly covered, at room temperature for up to 2 days.

BUTTERY POUND CAKE
WITH SALTY CARAMEL GLAZE

YIELD: 1 9-BY-5-INCH (23-BY-12-CM) LOAF • ABOUT 10 SERVINGS

I SUPPOSE MY JUNIOR-YEAR high school English teacher wasn't well. In fact, these many years later, I can safely say she was borderline mad. In the summer sandwiched between my junior and senior years of high school, she handpicked a few enthusiastic students, including me, and whisked us away for a "learning adventure" to Shakespeare's birthplace, Stratford-upon-Avon, and the surrounding environs. Though we fancied ourselves worldly literature buffs, we were really just teenagers excited about England's less stringent alcohol laws. We meant well but slept through the entirety of what felt like a four-hour production of *Hamlet*. We skipped garden and castle tours to nurse hangovers. Our poor teacher, eternally let down by us, distanced herself completely. Our only chaperone disengaged and started drinking and smoking with the locals. None of us told our parents about the personal downfall we caused.

Needless to say, I don't have many food memories (or, sadly, Shakespearean memories) from that trip. It was my lost summer. However, I distinctly remember breakfast at one of the inns outside of Stratford-upon-Avon. They served a tremendous pound cake—thickly sliced, hefty, and none too sweet. I imagine I looked very American dipping it in my tea (and to think I thought I looked so European). So I took all of the existing pound cake and discreetly stashed it in my bag. Our Buttery Pound Cake with Salty Caramel Glaze is an homage to that cake, but a bit improved with the addition of glaze. Often salted caramel is redundant in desserts, but not here; it is the perfect complement of salty sweet atop a hearty loaf. This is a must-make. It is, of course, buttery, but it's less heavy than what you remember pound cake to be. It is perfect for picnics and parties and especially well suited to snack on while studying *The Taming of the Shrew* (but much less suited for *Macbeth*, in our humble opinion).

●●● **BAKED NOTE**

Our testers made this cake with regular butter and European butter. Blind taste tests were unanimous: The high-fat European butter version always won by a wide margin. Normally you wouldn't notice a butter switch in cakes and cookies, but here the butter really shines. Like all great pound cakes, this one tastes better on Day Two.

INGREDIENTS

For the Buttery Pound Cake

1   cup (130 g) all-purpose flour
¾   cup (90 g) cake flour
½   teaspoon baking powder
½   teaspoon kosher salt
6   ounces (170 grams) unsalted high-fat/European-style (cultured) unsalted butter, softened, plus more for the pan
1¼   cups (250 g) granulated sugar
2   teaspoons pure vanilla extract
2   large eggs, at room temperature
2   large egg yolks, at room temperature
¾   cup (180 ml) heavy cream

For the Salty Caramel Glaze

½   cup (110 g) firmly packed dark brown sugar
½   cup (120 ml) heavy cream
2½   ounces (5 tablespoons/70 g) high-fat/European-style (cultured) unsalted butter
1¾   teaspoons fleur de sel
¼ to ½ cup (30 to 55 g) confectioners' sugar, sifted

MAKE THE BUTTERY POUND CAKE

1   Preheat the oven to 350°F (175°C) and position a rack in the center of the oven. Butter the bottom and sides of a 9-by-5-inch (23-by-12-cm) loaf pan. Place a long piece of parchment paper in the bottom of the pan, letting the parchment extend up the two long sides of the pan and overhang slightly. (This will make it easy to remove the pound cake from the pan after it is baked.) Butter the parchment paper, dust with flour, and knock out the excess flour.

2   In a medium bowl, sift together the all-purpose flour, cake flour, baking powder, and kosher salt.

3   In the bowl of a standing mixer fitted with the paddle attachment, beat the butter and sugar on high speed until fluffy, 4 to 5 minutes. Add the vanilla and beat again for about 15 seconds to incorporate. Scrape down the sides and bottom and turn the mixer to medium-low. Add the eggs and the egg yolks, one at a time, beating for about 1 minute after each addition. Scrape down the sides and bottom of the bowl again and beat for 10 seconds.

4   Turn the mixer to low and add the flour mixture in three parts, alternating with the cream, beginning and ending with the flour mixture.

5   Transfer the batter to the prepared pan, smooth the top with an offset spatula, and bake until a skewer inserted into the center of the loaf comes out with a few moist crumbs, 55 to 65 minutes. (If the top of your cake begins to darken too much before it is done in the middle, tent the pan with aluminum foil and continue baking.)

6   Place the pan on a cooling rack for 15 minutes. Using a small knife or offset spatula, gently loosen the cake from the sides of the pan, pull up on the parchment paper to lift the cake out of the pan, and place it directly on the cooling rack.

7   You can eat the cake the same day it's baked, but ideally you will want to wait 12 to 24 hours, as it tastes better on the second day. Glaze the cake the same day you plan on serving it. (This cake is also delicious sans glaze.)

MAKE THE SALTY CARAMEL GLAZE

1 In a medium saucepan over low heat, stir together the brown sugar, cream, and butter. When the butter is half melted, increase the heat to medium-high and bring the mixture to a boil. Whisking constantly, boil the mixture for 1½ minutes. Remove from the heat, whisk the mixture vigorously for 1 minute to release excess heat, and add ¾ teaspoon fleur de sel. Let cool for 5 minutes.

2 Add ¼ cup (30 g) confectioners' sugar and whisk until combined. Continue adding confectioners' sugar, a tablespoon at a time, until the mixture is pourable and slightly thick (it will thicken more as it cools); you may not use all of the confectioners' sugar.

3 Place the cake on a wire rack set over a half sheet pan covered in parchment (to catch the excess caramel and make cleanup easier). Use a bamboo skewer and poke several holes in the cake. Pour the warm caramel glaze over the cake to cover. If you are feeling generous, you can spoon any of the glaze that collected on the parchment below back over the cake one more time. Sprinkle evenly with the remaining 1 teaspoon fleur de sel. Cut off the very ends of the cake and discard. Slice and serve.

HOW TO STORE

Leftover pound cake, wrapped tightly at room temperature or in the refrigerator, keeps for up to 4 days. Some of us even prefer it cold.

CARAMEL CANDY POPCORN BALLS

YIELD: 12 TO 16 (2- TO 3-INCH / 5- TO 7.5-CM) POPCORN BALLS

Surprisingly, the impetus for this book was Secretary's Day. The allure of the holiday is that it is uncomfortably anachronistic. For us, "secretaries," as defined by the holiday, are mythical beings. They live only in 1970s workplace situation comedies and *Mad Men*. Their habitat is solely defined by typewriters and pencils, coffee and heels. The holiday itself feels slightly (and thankfully) aged out; it's almost passé without being vintage, like floppy disks and answering machines. It's kitschy without being retro or chic. True, the holiday has since been renamed Administrative Professionals' Day. Though the title is slightly less sexist, it still feels classist. Dark. We approach Secretary's Day, like so much of our lives, with a touch of campy humor.

If we had happened to be secretaries in the 1960s at a very important office, we would most certainly have made these amazing Caramel Candy Popcorn Balls for our coworkers. They are adorable—each ball chock-full of salty popcorn and sweet caramel. Nine times out of ten, we like to stud the popcorn balls with a few M&M's (we have a weakness for the candy), but feel free to sub a mix-in of your choice. And, though this recipe is slightly sweeter and goofier than your typical Baked recipe, we promise our Caramel Candy Popcorn Balls are almost impossible to resist.

●●● **BAKED NOTE**

This recipe is written assuming you are using salty popcorn (hence, no additional salt is listed in the ingredients); however, if you are using unsalted popcorn, we suggest adding 2 to 3 teaspoons kosher salt with the vanilla. Also, we love using M&M's for the mix-ins, but just be aware that they will melt a little. Last, enlisting a friend to assist with rolling the popcorn balls helps guarantee you'll form all the balls before the caramel starts to harden.

INGREDIENTS

- 18 cups (about 250 g, depending on the brand) lightly salted popped popcorn (about 2 to 3 microwave-popcorn bags' worth)
- 2 cups (440 g) firmly packed dark brown sugar
- ½ cup (100 g) granulated sugar
- ½ cup (120 ml) light corn syrup
- ½ cup (120 ml) heavy cream
- 2 ounces (½ stick/55 g) unsalted butter, cut into cubes, plus more for the bowl
- 1 tablespoon pure vanilla extract
- 1½ teaspoons baking soda
- 1 cup (210 g) M&M's, or any other mix-in (like salty peanuts, toffee bits, or coarsely chopped salted, toasted almonds)

1 Preheat the oven to 350°F (175°C). Line two baking sheets with parchment paper.

2 Divide the popcorn between the sheets and spread it in an even layer. Place the sheets in the oven for 5 minutes, then remove from the oven and use a metal spatula to flip the popcorn. Return the sheets to the oven and continue baking until the popcorn is very dry and crunchy, about 5 more minutes; bake longer if you can, but do not let it brown or burn. Remove the sheets from the oven and place them on a cooling rack.

3 Lightly grease a large (preferably shallow, wide, and metal) bowl—the largest bowl you have—with butter or nonstick spray.

4 In a medium heavy-bottomed saucepan, combine both sugars, the corn syrup, heavy cream, and butter. Cook the mixture over medium heat, gently stirring together with the handle of a wooden spoon until the sugar is almost dissolved. Clip a candy thermometer to the side of the pan, making sure the bulb of the thermometer is immersed in the syrup. Stop stirring and increase the heat to high. Boil the mixture until it reaches the soft-ball stage (238°F to 240°F / 114°C to 116°C), about 5 minutes.

5 Meanwhile, transfer the popcorn to the large prepared bowl. Lightly grease or spray a heatproof rubber spatula and the existing parchment paper on the sheet pans (you do not need to change it).

6 Once the sugar mixture has reached the soft-ball stage, remove it from the heat and add the vanilla and baking soda. The mixture will foam for a few seconds; when it subsides, stir gently to combine.

7 Pour the caramel over the popcorn and, working very quickly with the prepared spatula, coat the popcorn with the caramel. Add the M&M's and quickly distribute throughout the mixture (you can fully integrate the mix-ins while shaping the popcorn balls). Working quickly, use your hands to form the popcorn into 2- to 3-inch (5- to 7.5-cm) balls. Place them on the prepared baking sheets to set.

HOW TO STORE

The popcorn balls can be stored in an airtight container for up to 1 week.

MAY

MAY 1 | **MAY DAY**
STRAWBERRY SUPREME CAKE 100

DATE FLUCTUATES | **BLACK FOREST CAKE FESTIVAL**
BLACK FOREST CUPCAKES 104

1ST SAT IN MAY | **KENTUCKY DERBY**
DERBY COOKIES 107

DATE FLUCTUATES | **TEACHER APPRECIATION DAY / NATIONAL CHOCOLATE CHIP COOKIE DAY**
OLD-SCHOOL OATMEAL CHOCOLATE CHIP COOKIES 110

2ND SUN IN MAY | **MOTHER'S DAY**
ULTRALEMONY LEMON BUNDT CAKE WITH ALMOND GLAZE 113

MAY 25 | **NATIONAL WINE DAY**
RED WINE CHOCOLATE CUPCAKES WITH CHOCOLATE GLAZE 117

STRAWBERRY SUPREME CAKE

YIELD: 1 8-INCH (20-CM) THREE-LAYER CAKE • 10 TO 12 SERVINGS

IF LIFE WERE FAIR, there would be a holiday named in honor of our Strawberry Supreme Cake. It would be at least as worthy as National Sea Monkey Day, celebrated every May 15. In lieu of going through the mountains of red tape to create a new holiday (we imagine there is a lot of red tape, but we haven't actually investigated it yet), we believe May Day is perfectly suited for this cake. We have recently reacquainted ourselves (and subsequently fallen back in love) with May Day. It means many things to many cultures, but we are particularly smitten with the idea of celebrating spring fertility (yup, not just soil fertility but, according to lore, livestock and people fertility as well) and dancing around a Maypole (we have yet to dance around said Maypole, but the idea is enthralling). And, not for nothing, May Day nearly coincides with strawberry season and the kickoff to a zillion strawberry festivals. We can help you with dessert for this holiday, but you are going to have to find your own Maypole.

Our Strawberry Supreme Cake was born in the Baked kitchen after we received many customer requests for a strawberry-flavored cake. Fresh strawberries are folded into both the vanilla cake batter and the whipped-cream filling and there are two layers of strawberry preserves. The whipped cream is a playful but tasty nod to strawberry shortcake. The whole thing is then covered in a light-pink vanilla buttercream frosting. While we were tempted to use a strawberry frosting, it felt like too much of a good thing. Besides, the vanilla and strawberry interplay is awesome.

●●● **BAKED NOTE**

To make this cake with frozen strawberries, simply replace the fresh berries in the cake with the same amount of frozen berries, thawed completely and pureed with their juices. In the filling, replace the fresh berries with an equal amount of frozen berries, thawing, draining, and patting them dry before folding into the whipped cream. Do not use frozen berries for décor.

INGREDIENTS

For the Strawberry Cake

8 ounces (225 g) hulled strawberries (about 2 cups)

2½ cups (315 g) cake flour

¾ cup (90 g) all-purpose flour

1 tablespoon baking powder

1 teaspoon baking soda

¾ teaspoon kosher salt

1 cup (240 ml) ice water

½ cup (120 ml) whole milk

½ cup (120 ml) well-shaken buttermilk

4 ounces (1 stick/115 g) unsalted butter, softened, plus more for the pans

½ cup (100 g) vegetable shortening, at room temperature

1¾ cups (350 g) granulated sugar

1 tablespoon pure vanilla extract

1 large egg

3 large egg whites, at room temperature

¼ teaspoon cream of tartar

For the Vanilla Frosting

1½ cups (300 g) granulated sugar

⅓ cup (40 g) all-purpose flour

1½ cups (360 ml) whole milk

⅓ cup (75 ml) heavy cream

12 ounces (3 sticks/340 g) unsalted butter, softened but cool, cut into small pieces

1½ teaspoons pure vanilla extract

Red food dye or gel

MAKE THE STRAWBERRY CAKE

1 Preheat the oven to 325°F (165°C). Butter three 8-inch (20-cm) round cake pans, line the bottoms with parchment paper, and butter the parchment. Dust with flour and knock out the excess flour.

2 Place the strawberries in the bowl of a food processor. Pulse in short bursts until they are just short of a smooth puree (all the better if a few rough strawberry chunks are still evident). Set aside.

3 Sift both flours, the baking powder, baking soda, and salt together into a large bowl. Set aside.

4 In a small bowl, whisk together the ice water, milk, and buttermilk.

5 In the bowl of a standing mixer fitted with the paddle attachment, beat the butter and shortening on medium speed until creamy, 3 to 4 minutes. Add the sugar and vanilla and beat on medium speed until fluffy, about 3 minutes. Scrape down the bowl, add the egg, and beat until just combined. In three separate additions, turning the mixer to low to add the ingredients then up to medium for a few seconds to incorporate, add half the flour mixture, then the ice-water mixture, then the remaining flour mixture. Scrape down the bowl, then mix on low speed for a few more seconds.

6 In a medium bowl, whisk the egg whites and cream of tartar just until soft peaks form; do not overbeat. Gently fold the egg whites into the batter with a rubber spatula. Fold in the reserved strawberry puree.

7 Divide the batter among the prepared pans and smooth the tops. Bake for 40 to 45 minutes, rotating the pans halfway through the baking time, until a toothpick inserted in the center of each cake comes out clean. Transfer the cakes to a wire rack and let cool for 20 minutes. Invert the cakes onto the rack, remove the pans, and let cool completely. Remove the parchment.

MAKE THE VANILLA FROSTING

1 In a medium heavy-bottomed saucepan, whisk the sugar and flour together. Add the milk and cream and cook over medium heat, whisking occasionally, until the mixture comes to a boil and has thickened to the consistency of a light pudding, 10 to 15 minutes.

2 Transfer the mixture to the bowl of a standing mixer fitted with the paddle attachment. Beat on high speed until cool, at least 7 to 9 minutes (you can speed up the process by pressing bags of frozen berries or corn against the sides and bottom of the mixing bowl). Reduce the speed to low and add the butter, a few chunks at a time, every 20 to 30 seconds while the mixer is constantly stirring; mix until thoroughly incorporated. Increase the speed to medium-high and beat until the frosting is light and fluffy, 1 to 2 minutes. Add the vanilla. Mix until just combined. Add a few drops of red food dye or gel and mix until satisfied with the overall color; we suggest a pale pink—not a hot pink—because we think pale pink is supremely elegant. If the frosting is too soft (i.e., it doesn't seem like it will hold when applied), place the bowl in the refrigerator to chill slightly, then beat again until it is the proper consistency. If the frosting is too firm, set the bowl over a pot of simmering water and beat with a wooden spoon until it is the proper consistency.

INGREDIENTS (CONT.)

For the Strawberry Whipped-Cream Filling

½ cup (120 ml) heavy cream
1 tablespoon confectioners' sugar
1 teaspoon pure vanilla extract
¼ cup (60 g) finely chopped hulled strawberries

For the Assembly

½ cup (160 g) strawberry preserves
Whole strawberries

MAKE THE STRAWBERRY WHIPPED-CREAM FILLING

1 Put a metal bowl and whisk or, if you prefer, the clean bowl of a standing mixer and the whisk attachment into the freezer to chill for a few minutes.

2 Right before assembling the cake, pour the cream into the chilled bowl and beat with the whisk for about 1 minute (alternatively, beat on medium speed using a standing mixer). Sprinkle the confectioners' sugar on top of the cream and continue whisking vigorously (or on high speed in the bowl of a standing mixer) until soft peaks form. Add the vanilla and whisk until just incorporated. Using a rubber spatula, gently fold in the chopped strawberries.

ASSEMBLE THE CAKE

1 Place the strawberry preserves in a small bowl and stir or whisk to loosen them.

2 Scoop about 1 cup (170 g) of the frosting into a piping bag fitted with the largest tip. Place one cooled cake layer on a turntable (or a serving platter if you don't own a turntable). Trim the top to create a flat surface, and pipe a small border of frosting around the top perimeter of the cake. Spread half of the preserves into an even layer within the border, then top the frosting and preserves with half of the strawberry whipped cream. Spread into an even layer, top with the next cake layer, and refrigerate for about 5 minutes to set before proceeding.

3 Remove the cake from the refrigerator and trim the second cake layer, then add the frosting border, remaining preserves, and remaining whipped cream as before. Place the third layer on top and refrigerate for 5 to 10 minutes.

4 Remove the cake from the refrigerator. Trim the final layer for a completely flat top, or leave it domed for an old-school appearance. Spread a very thin layer of frosting over the sides and top of the cake and place it in the refrigerator for about 15 minutes to firm up. (This is known as crumb coating and will help to keep loose cake crumbs under control when you frost the outside of the cake.)

5 Frost the sides and top with the remaining frosting. Decorate the top border with the whole strawberries. Refrigerate the cake for about 5 minutes to set it before serving.

HOW TO STORE

This cake will keep beautifully in a cake saver in the refrigerator for up to 3 days. Let the chilled cake sit at room temperature for at least 2 hours before serving.

BLACK FOREST CUPCAKES

YIELD: 24 CUPCAKES

RENATO ASSEMBLED THESE Black Forest Cupcakes—Frankenstein-style—from the back catalogue of some of our more popular recipes. The careful stitching together of rich chocolate cake batter, melt-in-your-mouth frosting, and boozy cherries is an homage of sorts, created for a little-known festival held in Todtnauberg, Germany. The Schwarzwälder Kirschtortenfestival (aka Black Forest Cake Festival) is a festival devoted to this singular dessert.

Black Forest cake's origins are murky (and my dessert research suggests that most dessert origins are "murky" at best, often couched in three or four creationist myths, some sounding more logical than others). It seems that this cake came on the record around the 1930s and is probably so named for the famous double-distilled clear alcohol produced from cherries grown in the Black Forest region. The classic cake is almost always the same: four chocolate sponge layers soaked in kirsch (the infamous cherry brandy), filled and frosted with some combo of cherries and whipped cream, and decorated with chocolate shavings and maraschino cherries. Renato's cupcake version adheres very closely to the classic German dessert, with just a few tiny adjustments (for example, frosting for whipped cream, sprinkles for shavings, stemmed cherries for maraschinos). Naturally, these are very tasty. Just one bite will remind you why this cake gets a festival to call its own.

●●● **BAKED NOTE**

Remember, a good-quality jam can put this recipe over the top. And no, though the kirsch is part of the recipe lore, it is not necessary if you are averse to alcohol in desserts. Omit the kirsch completely and replace with additional preserves for a slightly sweeter take on Black Forest Cupcakes.

MAKE THE BLACK FOREST CUPCAKES

1   Preheat the oven to 325°F (165°C). Line two 12-cup cupcake pans with paper liners.
2   Place the chocolate and cocoa powder in a medium heatproof bowl. Pour the coffee directly over them, let sit for 1 minute, and whisk until combined. Add the milk and whisk until smooth.
3   In another bowl, sift together the flour, baking soda, and salt. Set aside.
4   In the bowl of a standing mixer fitted with the paddle attachment, beat the butter and both sugars on medium speed until fluffy, about 3 minutes. Add the eggs, one at a time, beating well after each addition, then add the vanilla and beat until incorporated. Scrape down the bowl and mix again

INGREDIENTS

For the Black Forest Cupcakes

1 ounce (28 g) good-quality dark chocolate (60 to 72% cacao), chopped

½ cup (40 g) unsweetened dark cocoa powder, such as Valrhona

⅔ cup (165 ml) hot coffee

⅓ cup (75 ml) whole milk

1⅓ cups (170 g) all-purpose flour

1 teaspoon baking soda

½ teaspoon kosher salt

5 ounces (1¼ sticks/140 g) unsalted butter, cool but not cold, cut into ½-inch (12-mm) cubes

1 cup (220 g) firmly packed dark brown sugar

½ cup (100 g) granulated sugar

3 large eggs, at room temperature

1 teaspoon pure vanilla extract

For the Filling

1 scant cup (7 ounces/ 200 g) cherry preserves

2 tablespoons kirsch

For the Frosting

5 large egg whites, at room temperature

1½ cups (300 g) granulated sugar

1 tablespoon light corn syrup

1 teaspoon pure vanilla extract

For the Assembly

Chocolate sprinkles

24 fresh cherries with stems

for 30 seconds. Add the flour mixture in three parts, alternating with the chocolate mixture, and beginning and ending with the flour mixture.

5 Fill the prepared cups about three-quarters full. Bake, rotating the pans halfway through the baking time, until a toothpick inserted in the center of a cupcake comes out clean, 15 to 20 minutes. Transfer the pans to a wire rack and let cool for 15 minutes. Turn the cupcakes out onto the rack, place them right side up, and let them cool completely.

MAKE THE FILLING

1 In a small bowl, combine the cherry preserves with 1 tablespoon kirsch. Mix and set aside.

MAKE THE FROSTING

1 Place the egg whites in the bowl of a standing mixer fitted with the whisk attachment. Set aside.

2 In a medium saucepan over low heat, stir together 1¼ cups (250 g) of the sugar, the corn syrup, and ¼ cup (60 ml) water. Once the sugar is dissolved, increase the heat to medium-high and clip a candy thermometer to the side of the pot. Without stirring, heat the mixture to almost 235°F (113°C; almost the soft-ball stage). Remove the pan from the heat and let the syrup fully reach 235°F (113°C), but not higher.

3 Sprinkle the remaining ¼ cup (50 g) sugar over the soft peaks of the egg whites and turn the mixer to low. Slowly stream in the hot sugar syrup. Once all the syrup has been added, increase the speed to medium-high and beat the icing until it is thick and shiny, about 7 minutes. Add the vanilla and beat again for 10 seconds. Set aside.

ASSEMBLE THE CUPCAKES

1 Line up the cupcakes on a sheet tray. Stick a large round pastry tip (the kind you usually use in tandem with a pastry bag) into the center of each cupcake, pressing it about halfway down, essentially coring the cupcake. (Alternatively, you can use a small paring knife.) Remove the excess cake.

2 Uasing a pastry brush, spread the remaining tablespoon of plain kirsch on each cupcake top. Spoon a teaspoon of the cherry preserves mixture into each cored cupcake.

3 Transfer the frosting to a large pastry bag using the same large round pastry tip you used to core the cupcakes. Generously pipe frosting onto each cupcake.

4 Sprinkle each with chocolate sprinkles and top with a cherry. Serve immediately.

HOW TO STORE

The frosting used on these cupcakes tastes best when eaten within 24 hours (even better within 12 hours); however, if you have leftovers, you can cover them tightly and store at room temperature for up to 2 days.

DERBY COOKIES

BUTTERY BROWN SUGAR BOURBON WALNUT BALLS

YIELD: 36 TO 40 COOKIES

WE HAVE YET TO ATTEND the Kentucky Derby in Louisville, though we feel we are well versed in the attendant pageantry and traditions. We imagine delicate, impeccably dressed ladies sipping mint juleps under cover of their wide-brimmed, fashionable hats. We envision a sea of buffets and bourbon and Southern manners. And, of course, horses. Beautiful creatures in colorful garb, the winner dripping with roses.

We still hope to attend the actual Derby one of these days. Until then, we celebrate from afar and always with bourbon (sometimes even in a mint julep). At Baked, we have a well-documented history of making bourbon cakes, bourbon-based pies, and bourbon-based ice creams, but we are rather fond of these bite-size bourbon cookies for large events, like a Derby Day party. They are simple to make, scale up easily, and will nearly melt in your mouth. They are nutty with just the right amount of sugar crunch. Not that you need another reason to make these cookies, but the delicious bourbon-vanilla sugar the cookies are rolled in is a lovely addition. It gives the cookies sweetness, of course, but also a light, lingering boozy note.

●●● BAKED NOTE

Though we Derby-obsessors would never make this recipe without bourbon or bourbon sugar, you could. Simply add another teaspoon of pure vanilla extract instead, and roll the cookies in plain, raw, or demerara sugar. Also, the bourbon flavor is more apparent on Days Two and Three of these cookies, but it requires a lot of willpower to wait. Last, the final roll in confectioners' sugar is optional; we think it makes the cookies easier to transport and handle, but it does dampen the visual effect of the bourbon sugar.

1   In the bowl of a food processor, process the walnuts until almost all are finely ground but some remain coarse.
2   In a medium bowl, whisk the flour and salt. Set aside.
3   In the bowl of a standing mixer fitted with the paddle attachment, mix together the butter, bourbon, and vanilla on medium speed until smooth and combined. Add the brown sugar and beat again until the mixture is well combined and light, 3 to 4 minutes. Add the flour mixture and beat on low

INGREDIENTS

3½ ounces (100 g) walnuts
   (about 1 cup), toasted
   (see page 19)

2 cups plus 2 tablespoons
   (270 g) all-purpose flour

½ teaspoon kosher salt

8 ounces (2 sticks/225 g)
   unsalted butter, softened,
   cut into cubes

2 tablespoons good-quality
   Kentucky bourbon

1 tablespoon pure vanilla
   extract

½ cup (110 g) firmly packed
   dark brown sugar

½ cup (120 g) bourbon
   sugar (see sidebar) or raw
   or demerara sugar

¾ cup (85 g) confectioners'
   sugar (optional)

speed until just combined. Turn the mixer to the lowest speed and add the nuts; mix for 15 seconds. Remove the mixing bowl from the mixer and finish incorporating the nuts with a wooden spoon.

4 Line a baking sheet with parchment paper.

5 Using a small ice-cream scoop with a release mechanism (or a small spoon and your hands), form balls from tablespoons of dough and place them on the prepared baking sheet about ½ inch (12 mm) apart. More than likely, you should be able to fit all of the balls on one half sheet baking pan; the dough does not really spread during baking. Freeze the balls until firm, about 30 minutes.

6 Preheat the oven to 350°F (175°C).

7 Remove the balls from the freezer and let sit for 5 minutes. Place the bourbon sugar in a wide shallow bowl. Roll the balls in the sugar to coat them completely, applying pressure as needed to make the sugar stick, and place them back on the baking sheet. Bake just until the balls start to color, 12 to 14 minutes. Remove the baking sheet from the oven and let them cool for about 10 minutes.

8 If using, sift the confectioners' sugar into a wide shallow bowl. Roll the balls in the sugar and place then on a cool surface. Let the balls cool completely and sprinkle them again with more of the confectioners' sugar right before serving.

HOW TO STORE

The cookies will keep in an airtight container for up to 5 days.

BOURBON SUGAR TWO WAYS

Vainlla bourbon sugar is addictive. Use the leftovers to finsih other desserts, to stir into coffee, and to make assorted fancy cocktails.

- Quick and Dirty Bourbon Sugar: Place ½ cup (120 g) raw or demerara sugar in a ceramic canister that has an accompanying lid (or use a small bowl covered with a small plate). Add ½ teaspoon bourbon, cover with the lid, and shake vigorously until well combined. Wait at least 30 minutes for the flavor to develop before using.

- Slow and Steady Vanilla Bourbon Sugar: Place 1 cup (240 g) raw or demerara sugar in a canister that has an accompanying lid. Split a vanilla bean lengthwise and stick the vanilla bean halves into the sugar. Drizzle the sugar with 2 teaspoons of bourbon, and top with 1 more cup (240 g) raw or demerara sugar. Cover the canister and shake like crazy. Place the canister in a dark, cool place and wait about a week for the flavors to fully develop.

OLD-SCHOOL OATMEAL CHOCOLATE CHIP COOKIES

YIELD: 40 TO 48 COOKIES

IT IS MOST LIKELY mere coincidence that Teacher Appreciation Day (usually in the first week of May) very nearly intersects with National Chocolate Chip or Chocolate Cookie Day (usually in mid-May). However, conspiracy theorists (namely, Renato and I) believe teachers finagled the timing of these two holidays. We think teachers, at least on some subliminal level, really want these chocolate chip cookies for Teacher Appreciation Day. We think they will appreciate (er . . . deserve/need) the small addition of bourbon.

Obviously, we feel that chocolate chips (mainly in the form of chocolate chip cookies) do not need a holiday, as we tend to celebrate them (i.e., eat a few) daily. This recipe is a riff on our favorite oatmeal chocolate chip cookie. It has a whiff of old-school sensibility. It is the kind of cookie that made its way into our lunch boxes, if we were lucky. The kind of cookie that is full of rich, molasses-y flavor and overflowing with chocolate chips (yup, we added more chips than usual). The various-size oats provide a pleasing and memorable bite. Oh, and don't fear the tiny bit of shortening; it really helps the cookie keep a pleasant shape.

●●● **BAKED NOTE**

If you happen to have a convection setting on your oven, use it for these cookies. No need to adjust the time or temperature, though—just keep a close eye on them as they pass the 8-minute mark. The convection setting will create a puffier, more evenly browned cookie, and it should be crunchy on the outside, moist on the inside. Also, please note that this dough needs to rest for at least 8 hours before baking.

INGREDIENTS

3   cups (480 g) rolled oats
¾   cup (90 g) all-purpose flour
¾   cup (105 g) bread flour
1½ teaspoons kosher salt
1   teaspoon baking soda
1   teaspoon baking powder
1   teaspoon ground cinnamon
¼   cup (50 g) vegetable shortening, cold
6   ounces (1½ sticks/170 g) unsalted butter, cold and cubed
1½ cups (330 g) firmly packed dark brown sugar
½   cup (100 g) granulated sugar
2   tablespoons (30 ml) bourbon
1   tablespoon pure vanilla extract
1   tablespoon molasses
2   tablespoons heavy cream
1   large egg
1   large egg yolk
12 ounces (340 g) semisweet chocolate chunks (about 2 cups)
Fleur de sel, for sprinkling

1   In the bowl of a food processor, process 2¼ cups (360 g) of the oats until they are a mix of fine and coarsely ground pieces.

2   In a large bowl, whisk together the flour, bread flour, salt, baking soda, baking powder, and cinnamon. Stir in the processed oats and the remaining ¾ cup (120 g) whole oats.

3   In the bowl of a standing mixer fitted with the paddle attachment, mix the shortening and butter on medium speed until blended (do not worry about eliminating all the lumps at this point). Add both sugars, the bourbon, vanilla, and molasses, and beat again until the mixture is well combined, about 1 minute. Add the cream, egg, and egg yolk, beating until the mixture looks light and fluffy. Turn the mixer to the lowest speed and slowly stream in the oat mixture. Scrape down the sides and bottom of the bowl and mix until just combined (you might need to use your hands to fully incorporate). Using a wooden spoon, fold in the chocolate chunks. Refrigerate the dough for at least 8 hours or overnight. (Making the cookie dough 2 days in advance lets the flavors develop fully, but it's not necessary.)

4   Preheat the oven to 350°F (175°C). Line two baking sheets with parchment paper.

5   Using a small ice-cream scoop with a release mechanism (or a small spoon and your hands), form balls from heaping tablespoons of dough and place them about 1½ inches (4 cm) apart on the prepared baking sheet. Sprinkle the top of each cookie with a little fleur de sel.

6   Place the sheet pan in the oven and bake, rotating the pans halfway through the baking time, until the edges of the cookies are golden brown or just start to darken, 11 to 13 minutes.

7   Set the pan on a wire rack for 10 minutes to cool. Use a spatula to transfer the cookies to the rack to cool completely.

HOW TO STORE

These cookies can be stored in an airtight container for up to 3 days.

ULTRALEMONY LEMON BUNDT CAKE WITH ALMOND GLAZE

YIELD: 1 BUNDT CAKE • 12 TO 16 SERVINGS

IN AN ALTERNATE UNIVERSE, where the sky is deep blue and the grass is a rarefied green, I am giving my mom a whole stable of Arabian horses for Mom's Day. I am not even sure if she likes Arabian horses, but the gesture is grand and Mom is so deserving. Truth is, Mother's Day (or Mom's Day or, er . . . Mothering Day in the UK) is an underplayed holiday—one of the few. It's not brash or loud or overmarketed. For this, I am thankful. Yet I wish it were more than the quiet, elegant brunch holiday it has become. Moms are incredible, and (mostly) patient, and wise, and funny, and sweet. They deserve Arabian horses. Or, at the very least, a full day (not just a quick brunch) of attention and extra love.

In theory, most moms would be happy with any baking gesture (box mixes included). However, this Bundt is a true dazzler. The lemon flavor is clean and deep and bright, and it is as citrusy fragrant (ten lemons, thank you very much) as any centerpiece. Mom will appreciate the light (not overly dense) crumb, pleasing texture, and sweet lemon glaze. In the service of upending Mother's Day norms, we suggest you invite Mom over for some Ultralemony Lemon Bundt Cake with Almond Glaze and a midnight movie. Brunch is nice. Surprises are better.

●●● **BAKED NOTE**

While we are both fanatics for lemons and all things tart, we realize there is a lot of lemon going on in this recipe. One tester suggested an easy way to dial back the lemon in this cake without radically changing it: Simply replace some of the lemon juice with a little milk in both the syrup and the glaze.

MAKE THE LEMON BUNDT CAKE

1 Preheat the oven to 350°F (175°C). Generously spray the inside of a 10-cup (2.4-L) Bundt pan with nonstick cooking spray, dust with flour, and knock out the excess flour. Alternatively, you can butter and flour the pan. Either way, make sure the pan's nooks and crannies are all thoroughly coated.

2 Sift both flours, the baking powder, and salt into a medium bowl. Set aside.

INGREDIENTS

For the Lemon Bundt Cake

1½ cups (170 g) cake flour
1½ cups (170 g) all-purpose flour
1 tablespoon baking powder
1 teaspoon kosher salt
2¾ cups (550 g) granulated sugar
Zest of 10 lemons (approximately 10 tablespoons/60 g)
8 ounces (2 sticks/225 g) unsalted butter, melted and cooled
½ cup (120 ml) canola oil
3 tablespoons dark rum
2 tablespoons pure lemon extract
3 large eggs
3 large yolks
¾ cup (180 ml) heavy cream

For the Lemon Syrup

⅓ cup (65 g) granulated sugar
⅓ cup (75 ml) fresh lemon juice
2 tablespoons dark rum, or more to taste

For the Almond Glaze

2 to 4 tablespoons (30 to 60 ml) fresh lemon juice
2 teaspoons pure almond extract
2½ to 3 cups (250 to 300 g) sifted confectioners' sugar
¼ cup (25 g) slivered almonds, toasted (see page 19)

3   Place the sugar in the bowl of a standing mixer fitted with the paddle attachment. Sprinkle the lemon zest over the sugar and use the tips of your fingers to rub the zest in until the mixture is uniformly pale yellow.

4   Pour the melted butter and canola oil into the bowl of lemon sugar and beat on medium speed until well combined. Add the rum, lemon extract, eggs, and egg yolks and beat again on medium speed until just combined. Add the flour mixture in three parts, alternating with the cream, beginning and ending with the flour mixture. Scrape down the bowl, then mix on low speed for a few more seconds.

5   Pour the mixture into the prepared pan. Bake for 50 to 60 minutes, rotating the pan halfway through the baking time, until a toothpick inserted in the center of the cake comes out clean.

6   Transfer the pan to a wire rack and cool for 30 minutes. Place the wire rack over a half sheet pan lined with parchment paper.

MAKE THE LEMON SYRUP

1   In a small saucepan over very low heat, whisk together the sugar, lemon juice, and rum until the sugar starts to melt. Increase the heat to medium-high and bring to a boil. Then reduce the heat to a simmer for a minute or two, until the sugar is completely dissolved. Remove from the heat.

2   Gently loosen the sides of the somewhat cooled cake from the pan and turn it out onto the rack. Poke the cake with several holes (on the crown and sides) in preparation for the syrup. Use a pastry brush to gently brush the top and sides of the cake with the syrup. Allow the syrup to soak into the cake. Brush at least two more times. (You might have some syrup left over.) Continue to let the cake cool completely.

MAKE THE ALMOND GLAZE

1   In a medium bowl, whisk together 2 tablespoons of the lemon juice and the almond extract. Add 2½ cups (250 g) of the confectioners' sugar and continue whisking until the mixture is pourable. A fairly sturdy, thick glaze will give you the best visual result. If the mixture is too thick, add more lemon juice, a tablespoon at a time, until the desired consistency is reached. If the mixture is too thin, keep adding confectioners' sugar, ¼ cup (25 g) at a time, until the desired consistency is reached; this will make the glaze sweeter, of course.

2   Pour the glaze in large thick ribbons over the crown of the Bundt, allowing the glaze to spread and drip down the sides of the cake. Sprinkle the almonds over the glaze and allow the glaze to set (for about 20 minutes) before serving.

HOW TO STORE

The cake will keep in an airtight container at room temperature for up to 3 days.

RED WINE CHOCOLATE CUPCAKES WITH CHOCOLATE GLAZE

YIELD: 18 TO 20 CUPCAKES

I TEND TO SPEND MANY (MANY) NIGHTS post-dinner with a book, a glass (or two) of red wine, and a decent dark chocolate bar. True, it's a slightly decadent routine, but it is my only surviving vice. I suppose I need more exciting vices. Until then, the perfect pairing of hearty red and smoky chocolate will always be part of my nightly ritual. Besides, the combined flavors can improve even a mediocre read.

It is only natural, then, that I think the best way to celebrate National Wine Day (is this still a holiday if I celebrate it every day?) is to combine my two favorite flavors in this rich, adult-style cupcake. A full-bodied red is the way to go in this recipe—think Italian Super Tuscan or an intense California Cabernet. The moist cupcake itself is much less sweet than your average chocolate cupcake, allowing the flavor of the wine to really shine through. And the combination of dark cocoa powder and dark chocolate really provides an intense flavor—a double punch of chocolate.

●●● **BAKED NOTE**

Are you having dome issues? These cupcakes (like most cupcakes) do not have a massive dome. It is slight but noticeable. In general, to get a slightly more pronounced dome in any cupcake recipe, try preheating your oven to 375°F (190°C), then reducing the oven temperature to 350°F (175°C) as soon as you put the cupcakes in.

INGREDIENTS

For the Red Wine Chocolate Cupcakes

½ cup (40 g) unsweetened dark cocoa powder, such as Valrhona

2 ounces (55 g) dark chocolate (60 to 72% cacao), coarsely chopped

1¼ cups (300 ml) hearty red wine

2 cups (255 g) all-purpose flour

1¼ teaspoons baking soda

¾ teaspoon baking powder

½ teaspoon kosher salt

8 ounces (2 sticks/225 g) unsalted butter, cool but not cold

1 cup (200 g) granulated sugar

¾ cup (165 g) firmly packed dark brown sugar

2 large eggs, at room temperature

1 large egg yolk, at room temperature

1 teaspoon pure vanilla extract (optional)

For the Chocolate Glaze

4 ounces (115 g) dark chocolate (60 to 72% cacao), chopped

1 tablespoon corn syrup

½ cup (120 ml) heavy cream

For Décor

White sprinkles (optional)

MAKE THE RED WINE CHOCOLATE CUPCAKES

1 Preheat the oven to 350°F (175°C). Line one 12-cup cupcake pan with paper liners and another with only 6 to 8 paper liners (or bake in batches with one pan).

2 Place the cocoa powder and chocolate in a medium heatproof bowl. Heat the wine in the microwave in a glass measuring cup (or on the stovetop in a pan) until almost boiling. Pour the hot wine directly over the cocoa powder and chocolate and whisk until the chocolate is melted and completely combined with the wine.

3 In another bowl, whisk together the flour, baking soda, baking powder, and salt. Set aside.

4 In the bowl of a standing mixer fitted with the paddle attachment, beat the butter until smooth. Add both sugars and mix on medium-high speed until the mixture is light and fluffy, about 3 minutes. Add the eggs and egg yolk, one at a time, beating well after each addition, then add the vanilla, if using. Scrape down the sides and bottom of the bowl and beat again for 30 seconds.

5 Remove the bowl from the mixer and, using a rubber spatula, fold in the flour mixture in three parts, alternating with the wine mixture in three parts, beginning with flour and ending with wine.

6 Fill the cupcake liners about three-quarters full with the batter. Bake, rotating the pan halfway through, until a toothpick inserted in the center of a cupcake comes out clean, 20 to 24 minutes.

7 Allow the cupcakes to cool for 20 minutes in the pan, then turn them out onto a cooling rack to cool completely.

MAKE THE CHOCOLATE GLAZE

1 Place the chocolate in a shallow, heatproof bowl. Drizzle the corn syrup on top of the chocolate.

2 Heat the cream in small saucepan over medium heat until it just begins to bubble along the edges. Pour the hot cream over the chocolate and wait 30 seconds. Whisk from the center out until the mixture is completely smooth.

ASSEMBLE THE CUPCAKES

1 Dip the top of each cupcake into the glaze. Allow the excess glaze to run off back into the bowl and return each cupcake, right side up, to the cooling rack. Add a stripe of white sprinkles, if using, right along the center top of each cupcake, and allow to set for at least 30 minutes before serving.

HOW TO STORE

The cupcakes can be stored in an airtight container in the refrigerator for up to 3 days. Allow to come to room temperature before serving.

JUNE

● ● ●

DATE FLUCTUATES | THE QUEEN'S BIRTHDAY
CHAI SPICE TRIFLE WITH MIXED BERRIES 120

DATE FLUCTUATES | GAY PRIDE
RAINBOW ICEBOX CAKE WITH HOMEMADE CHOCOLATE COOKIES 125

JUN 14 | FLAG DAY
BROWN SUGAR SHORTCAKES WITH BROWN SUGAR SYRUP, MIXED BERRIES, AND WHIPPED CREAM 128

3RD SUN IN JUN | FATHER'S DAY
DAD'S BLACK COCOA BUNDT WITH BUTTER WHISKEY GLAZE 132

JUN 26 | NATIONAL CHOCOLATE PUDDING DAY
HOT CHOCOLATE PUDDING CAKE 135

CHAI SPICE TRIFLE WITH MIXED BERRIES

YIELD: 1 MEGA TRIFLE • ABOUT 24 LARGE SERVINGS

LONG BEFORE AMERICAN CELEBRITIES started adopting British accents for their everyday speaking voices (we are looking at you, Madonna), I was a part-time Anglophile. This preoccupation of mine, not so coincidentally, occurred during the intersecting years I spent in strip-mall Florida and small-town Alabama. I was that person in Tuscaloosa who insisted on spelling *color* as *colour*. Oddly, while I briefly immersed myself (via magazines) in British fashion, music, and food (bangers and mash, anyone?), I never quite caught the royal bug. I enjoyed the pomp and circumstance, but was never obsessed with it. Perhaps if Prince Philip had been more ruggedly handsome, I would have paid more attention. Regardless, there is something enthralling about watching the Queen.

We celebrate the Queen's birthday with camp fascination and a big bowl of trifle. And some of you true Anglophiles may be wondering why we put this recipe in June, given that the Queen's actual birthday is April 21—we'll respond that the official celebration is a Saturday in June. You can celebrate it whenever you like; just do it with our Chai Spice Trifle. We must admit, trifle is not often on our list of must-have desserts, but every so often, we crave one. Here, we present you with our trifle jackpot: a tremendous lovely mix of buttery pound cake, chai-spiced pastry cream, and fresh mixed berries. The recipe may seem intimidating, but don't let the many steps frighten you. It may take some time to put together (see recipe for details about various resting times), but each step is easy (er, easy peasy), and the "wow" factor is impressive.

●●● **BAKED NOTE**

We recommend fresh berries, but frozen are fine. Just defrost them and reserve the liquid. Testers tell us that the frozen berry juice is delicious poured over the servings of trifle. Also, if you can find whole cardamom pods (to grind the seeds yourself) you will be rewarded by a fresher, more fragrant cardamom experience. And it is a lot less expensive to purchase this way.

INGREDIENTS

For the Pound Cake

1   Buttery Pound Cake (page 93) without the Salty Caramel Glaze, made 1 day ahead, or 1 store-bought pound cake

For the Chai Spice Mix

1   tablespoon ground cinnamon
2½ teaspoons ground cardamom
2   teaspoons ground ginger
½   teaspoon ground white pepper
¼   teaspoon ground allspice
¼   teaspoon ground nutmeg
⅛   teaspoon ground cloves

For the Chai Pastry Cream

12 large egg yolks
1   cup (200 g) granulated sugar
¼   cup (30 g) cornstarch
2 to 3 tablespoons Chai Spice Mix (recipe above)
½   teaspoon kosher salt
4   cups (960 ml) whole milk
5   tablespoons (70 g) unsalted butter, cut into cubes
¼   cup (60 ml) dark rum
2   tablespoons heavy cream
2   tablespoons pure vanilla extract

For the Rum Syrup

1   tablespoon plus 1½ teaspoons granulated sugar
2   tablespoons dark rum

For the Whipped Cream

2   cups (480 ml) heavy cream
2   teaspoons pure vanilla extract

MAKE THE CHAI SPICE MIX

1   Place the cinnamon, cardamom, ginger, white pepper, allspice, nutmeg, and cloves in a small bowl and whisk to combine. Set aside.

MAKE THE CHAI PASTRY CREAM

1   In a large bowl, whisk together the egg yolks, ½ cup (100 g) of the sugar, the cornstarch, 2 tablespoons of the Chai Spice Mix, and the salt until the mixture is thick and smooth. (The flavors of the spices will lose some pungency once incorporated fully into the other pastry cream ingredients; for a stronger flavor, add all of the spice mix.)

2   In a medium saucepan over medium heat, stir together the milk and the remaining ½ cup (100 g) sugar. Increase the heat to medium-high, and continue stirring slowly until the mixture boils. Remove the pan from the heat, and slowly pour a scant third of the liquid into the egg mixture, whisking constantly. Transfer the tempered egg mixture back to the saucepan with the remaining milk mixture, still whisking constantly, and bring to a boil over medium-high heat. Boil for 2 minutes.

3   Remove the pan from the heat and strain the mixture through a fine-mesh sieve into a large bowl. Stir in the butter, rum, cream, and vanilla. Let the pastry cream cool for about 15 minutes, then cover the top with plastic wrap (pressing the plastic directly onto the top of the cream to prevent a skin from forming). Refrigerate until firm, about 5 hours or overnight.

MAKE THE RUM SYRUP

1   On the day of the trifle's assembly, in your smallest saucepan, stir together 2 tablespoons water and the sugar and cook over medium heat until the sugar melts. Remove from the heat and let cool for 5 minutes. Add the rum, whisk to combine, and set aside.

MAKE THE WHIPPED CREAM

1   Immediately before putting the trifle together, place a metal bowl and whisk or, if you prefer, the bowl of a standing mixer and the whisk attachment into the freezer to chill for a few minutes.

2   Pour the cream into the chilled bowl and beat with the whisk for about 1 minute, until the cream begins to thicken (alternatively, beat on medium-high speed in the bowl of a standing mixer fitted with the whisk attachment). Add the vanilla and keep whipping until medium-firm peaks form. Set aside.

ASSEMBLE THE TRIFLE

1   In a medium bowl, toss the berries together with your hands.

2   Cut the pound cake into twelve approximately ¾-inch (2-cm) slices, discarding the ends. The skinnier the slice, the better the absorption. Cover the bottom of a 2- or 2½-quart (2- or 2.4-L)

INGREDIENTS (CONT.)

For the Assembly

4   cups (500 g) fresh raspberries (or frozen, see Baked Note)

2   cups (290 g) fresh blackberries (or frozen, see Baked Note)

trifle dish with approximately 4 slices in a single layer, cutting as needed to fill in the gaps. Brush the rum syrup on top of the cake—be generous with it, as you want the syrup to soften the cake. Scatter about one-third of the mixed berries over the rum-soaked cake. Stir the pastry cream to loosen. Place a heaping 1½ cups (360 ml) of pastry cream over the berries and use an offset spatula to spread into an even layer. Cover the pastry cream with a heaping 1½ cups (360 ml) of whipped cream. Spread into an even layer. Repeat these layers two more times, ending with a glorious, oversize mound of whipped cream.

3   Refrigerate the trifle for at least 2 hours, and up to 6 hours. Before serving, garnish with a few berries and a sprinkling of leftover Chai Spice Mix, if you have any.

HOW TO STORE

Leftover trifle can be kept, tightly covered, in the refrigerator for up to 2 days, though the optimum eating time is usually within 24 hours.

RAINBOW ICEBOX CAKE WITH HOMEMADE CHOCOLATE COOKIES

YIELD: 1 ICEBOX CAKE • 12 TO 16 SERVINGS

AS ONE CAN IMAGINE, there is a lot of gay pride at Baked. It is practically bursting with rainbows during the month of June, a symphony of colors and cakes and cookies. Politically, the month is about equal rights, about hard-won victories. Equally as important, the month is about fun, about celebration. Balance between the two is essential. Thankfully the largest Gay Pride Parade in the United States, here in New York City, has somehow figured out a way to meld them. Though it's packaged as pageantry—big, busted drag queens sashaying down Fifth Avenue or dykes on bikes (quite literally, lesbians on motorcycles)—there is a message within: simply, marriage and rights for everyone regardless of sexual orientation.

The symbol of gay pride, the rainbow, lends itself to a million baked-good possibilities, but we are rather in love with our Rainbow Icebox Cake. It is a little goofy and a little perfect, like the parade itself. The base is built with some sturdy homemade chocolate wafers because (a) they are delicious, and (b) it sometimes requires a bit of a scavenger hunt to find the Nabisco-brand chocolate cookies most commonly used in icebox cakes. The taste and texture are exactly as you imagine—somewhere between a semifreddo and a mousse, all chocolaty, whipped-cream heaven—only 100 percent gayer.

●●● BAKED NOTE

If you live in a small urban apartment like both of us and do not have room for six separate mixing bowls (to mix the six rainbow colors), we recommend reserving pint and quart yogurt containers. They come in handy for all sorts of storage and mixing situations, and they stack and store easily. Also, a heads up: This cake must be refrigerated overnight before serving so that the cookies absorb some moisture from the whipped cream and take on that perfect cakey texture.

INGREDIENTS

For the Rainbow Whipped Cream

3   cups (720 ml) heavy whipping cream, very cold
¾   cup (170 g) crème fraîche
¾   cup (150 g) granulated sugar
2   teaspoons pure vanilla paste
6   rainbow colors of food gel

For the Chocolate Cookies

10½ ounces (2⅔ sticks/300 g) unsalted butter, softened
1½ cups (300 g) granulated sugar
1   large egg yolk
1   tablespoon pure vanilla extract
1⅓ cups (115 g) unsweetened cocoa powder
½   teaspoon kosher salt
¼   teaspoon baking powder
2½ cups (315 g) all-purpose flour

For the Assembly

1   cup (240 ml) heavy whipping cream, very cold
1   tablespoon granulated sugar
Rainbow sprinkles (optional)

MAKE THE RAINBOW WHIPPED CREAM

1   Chill the bowl and whisk attachment of a standing mixer in the refrigerator for 10 minutes.

2   Put the cream and crème fraîche into the chilled bowl of the stand mixer and whisk on low for 1 minute. With the mixer running, stream in the sugar and vanilla paste. Increase the speed to medium-high and continue whisking. Stop the mixer before soft peaks form; it's important not to overwhip the cream at this stage. (The thickened cream should stream off the whisk but still pile softly back into the bowl; the whisk will leave faint streaks in the cream that will smooth out fairly quickly.)

3   Line a colander with one layer of cheesecloth and place the colander in a bowl. Pour the partially whipped cream into the colander and place the bowl in the refrigerator for at least 3 hours. The cream should be thick enough to remain in the colander, but not so thick that any additional whipping will take it past soft peaks.

MAKE THE CHOCOLATE COOKIES

1   In the bowl of a standing mixer fitted with the paddle attachment, beat the butter and sugar at low speed until smooth. Beat in the egg yolk and vanilla. Scrape down the sides of the bowl and the paddle. Add the cocoa powder, salt, and baking powder and beat until combined. Scrape down the bowl again. Add the flour and beat just until combined. Form the cookie dough into four disks, wrap each in plastic wrap, and refrigerate for about 1 hour, or until firm.

2   Preheat the oven to 350°F (175°C). Line two baking sheets with parchment paper.

3   On a lightly floured board, roll out a disk of chilled cookie dough into a 12-inch (30.5-cm) round, ⅛ inch (3 mm) thick. Using a 2-inch (6-cm) round biscuit cutter, stamp out as many rounds of dough as you can; transfer the rounds to the prepared baking sheets. Repeat with a second disk. Quickly gather the dough scraps, reroll, and stamp out more cookies. Bake the chocolate cookies until they are dry and set, 8 to 10 minutes. Transfer the pans to a wire rack to cool for 10 minutes, then transfer the chocolate cookies directly to the rack to cool completely. Repeat the rolling, stamping, and baking process with the remaining dough disks. You should have 60 to 75 finished cookies in total.

FINISH THE RAINBOW WHIPPED CREAM

1   Put ¼ cup of the refrigerated whipped cream into a small bowl and set aside. Evenly divide the remaining whipped cream into six medium bowls. Add a different food gel, a drop or two at a time, to each of the six bowls, then fold each with a rubber spatula until incorporated and the desired color is reached. (As you fold the whipped cream, it will get stiffer; do not fold too much or it could become overwhipped.)

2   If needed, whisk each bowl of colored whipped cream a few more times by hand to reach soft peaks. Do not overwhip.

ASSEMBLE THE RAINBOW ICEBOX CAKE

1 Arrange 7 cookies on a platter in a 7- to 8-inch (17- to 20-cm) circle (side by side, with one cookie in the middle—do not overlap). Dollop the first color of whipped cream (in this case, red) gently over the cookie layer. Spread the whipped cream with an offset spatula to the very edge of the cookies. Top the whipped cream with another layer of cookies, offset from the first layer. Repeat the process, filling in any blank spots in the layers with broken cookie pieces and using the whipped cream in rainbow order. Top the last layer of cookies with the reserved ¼ cup of plain whipped cream, spreading in a thin layer to help soften the top layer of cookies. Place the cake, loosely covered, in the refrigerator overnight to set.

2 The next day, chill the bowl and whisk attachment of a standing mixer in the refrigerator for 5 minutes.

3 Put the cream in the chilled bowl of the stand mixer and whisk on low speed for 1 minute. With the mixer running, stream in the sugar. Increase the speed to medium-high and continue whisking just until soft peaks form.

4 Remove the cake from the refrigerator and top it with a big pile of the white whipped cream, completely covering the thin layer of whipped cream. Cover loosely in plastic wrap or invert a glass or plastic container over the cake and refrigerate for at least 30 minutes. Sprinkle with rainbow sprinkles just before serving, if desired.

HOW TO STORE

Store leftovers in the refrigerator, covered, for up to 1 day. You might have leftover cookies—we always like to have a few extra on hand in case a few crumble or break; you can snack on the rest or store, tightly covered, for up to 4 days.

BROWN SUGAR SHORTCAKES WITH BROWN SUGAR SYRUP, MIXED BERRIES, AND WHIPPED CREAM

YIELD: 6 SERVINGS

ON JUNE 14, 1777, Congress adopted the Stars and Stripes as the flag of the United States. Just under 140 years later, President Woodrow Wilson issued a proclamation for a nationwide observance of Flag Day to be held annually on that day. Then in 1949, an act of Congress established National Flag Day, though it is not an official federal holiday. That is the history of the day in miniature. However, the history of the flag (and the Betsy Ross legend) is quite interesting and more voluminous than we originally imagined. We shouldn't have slept through history class. If you have a moment, a little American flag research is well worth your efforts. It will make you proud all over again.

This is a rather literal dessert for Flag Day. Red, white, and blue are proudly represented, but—we make no bones—it is delicious. After all, it is a terrific mash-up of whipped cream, berries in a brown sugar syrup, and biscuits (brown sugar shortcakes, no less). When crafted carefully, the dessert is a photogenic darling. Then, as you (or your guests) begin to dig in, it becomes messy—flavors and textures clanging around with abandon. And while we think this is the ultimate Flag Day dessert, we would not be sorry to eat this for our birthday or July Fourth or any spring or summer day for that matter, especially if the berries are ripe.

●●● **BAKED NOTE**

Obviously, this is not a super-easy-to-transport dessert; however, the shortcakes (aka biscuits) are divine in their own right and, might we add, transport quite nicely. Simply toss them in the picnic basket and serve them with a schmear of high-fat butter for a quick snack.

INGREDIENTS

For the Brown Sugar Shortcakes

2   ounces (½ stick/55 g) unsalted butter, cold, cut into small cubes, plus more for the pan
4   tablespoons (50 g) shortening, cold
1   cup plus 2 tablespoons (145 g) all-purpose flour
1   cup plus 2 tablespoons (145 g) cake flour
½   cup (110 g) firmly packed light brown sugar
1   tablespoon baking powder
1   teaspoon baking soda
½   teaspoon kosher salt
½   cup (120 ml) plus 2 tablespoons heavy cream, divided
1   large egg yolk
1   teaspoon pure vanilla extract
1   large egg white
2   tablespoons raw sugar

For the Brown Sugar Syrup and Berries

8   ounces (225 g) strawberries, hulled and sliced (about 1½ cups)
8   ounces (225 g) blueberries (about 1½ cups)
2   tablespoons firmly packed dark brown sugar
1   teaspoon orange zest
¼   cup (60 ml) Grand Marnier (optional)

MAKE THE BROWN SUGAR SHORTCAKES

1   Place the cubed butter and shortening in a small bowl, give a quick stir, cover the bowl, and place in the freezer for 15 minutes.

2   Line a baking sheet with parchment paper.

3   In a large bowl, whisk together both flours, the brown sugar, baking powder, baking soda, and salt. Set aside.

4   Pour ½ cup (120 ml) of the cream into a glass measuring cup. Add the egg yolk and vanilla and whisk until combined. Place in the refrigerator.

5   Remove the butter and shortening from the freezer and drop the cubes over the flour mixture. Use your fingers to rub the butter and shortening into the flour until the mixture is coarse and pebbly. Add the cream mixture. Working quickly, use a fork to cut the wet ingredients into the dry until just a few dry streaks remain; do not overmix the dough.

6   Dust a work surface with a sprinkling of flour, place the dough on it, and dust the top of the dough with a little more flour. Gently knead the dough until it is uniform and smooth, only about 1 minute; the dough should hold its shape without falling apart.

7   Roll the dough into about a 9-inch (23-cm) round (if anything it should be slightly less than that, not larger), about 1 inch (2.5 cm) thick. Using a 2½-inch (6-cm) round cutter, cut out 6 shortcakes. You might need to gather the scraps and reroll one time to get all 6 cakes.

8   Transfer the cakes to the parchment-lined baking sheet and freeze for at least 15 minutes and up to 30 minutes. (Meanwhile, you can make your brown sugar syrup and berries, if you want to serve the shortcakes warm.)

9   Preheat the oven to 400°F (205°C). Whisk together the remaining 2 tablespoons cream with the egg white.

10 Remove the baking sheet from the freezer and brush the top of each cake with the egg wash, sprinkle with raw sugar, and bake until the cakes are evenly browned and a toothpick inserted into the center of a cake comes out clean, 12 to 16 minutes; do not overbake. Allow the cakes to cool for at least 10 minutes. The cakes taste just as good warm as they do at room temperature.

MAKE THE BROWN SUGAR SYRUP AND BERRIES

1   Place the berries in a large bowl. Sprinkle them with the brown sugar and orange zest. Gently toss a few times with your hand, then add the Grand Marnier, if using, and toss again. Let the berries macerate for at least 30 minutes and up to 2 hours, tossing the mixture every 10 minutes until ready to use.

INGREDIENTS (CONT.)

For the Whipped Cream

1½ cups (360 ml) heavy
   cream
2 tablespoons firmly
   packed light brown sugar
1 teaspoon pure vanilla
   extract

For the Assembly

Confectioners' sugar
  (optional)

MAKE THE WHIPPED CREAM

1 Place a metal bowl and whisk or, if you prefer, the bowl of a standing mixer and the whisk attach-ment into the freezer to chill for a few minutes.

2 Right before assembling, pour the cream into the chilled bowl and beat with the whisk for about 1 minute; alternatively, beat on medium speed in the bowl of a standing mixer fitted with the whisk attachment. Sprinkle the brown sugar on top of the cream and continue whisking vigorously until soft peaks form. Add the vanilla and whisk until just incorporated.

ASSEMBLE THE SHORTCAKES

1 Using a slotted spoon, remove the berries from their syrup and place them in a separate bowl. Do not discard the syrup.

2 Gently slice a shortcake in half horizontally (a serrated knife works well here). Place the bottom section (sliced side facing up) on a serving plate. Spoon a few tablespoons of syrup over the cake to cover. Add about ½ cup (75 g) of berries to cover the bottom of the cake, spoon with a few dollops of whipped cream, and top with the other half of the cake (sliced side facing down). Repeat with the remaining shortcakes, syrup, berries, and cream. Dust the shortcakes with confectioners' sugar, if you like, and serve immediately.

DAD'S BLACK COCOA BUNDT
WITH BUTTER WHISKEY GLAZE

YIELD: 1 BUNDT CAKE • 12 TO 16 SERVINGS

IT WAS ONLY AFTER MOTHER'S DAY was deemed a smashingly successful holiday that Dad got his official due, albeit fifty-eight years later. Richard Nixon—of all people—signed the proclamation turning Father's Day into a federally recognized June holiday in 1972. Tie salesmen everywhere rejoiced.

But I was lucky. My dad was not a tie person, and he never wore the cheap, commonly gifted colognes of his day (Drakkar Noir, English Leather, Brut, Stetson, etc.). For him, Father's Day was about food. His obsession with his battered charcoal grill was boundless (he didn't switch to gas until long after I left for college), and our family almost always celebrated the day with one long, hazy backyard barbeque. Dad was also a pie and cake man. Preferably à la mode. And after the last burger left the grill and the final beer was guzzled, we moved on to a makeshift Father's Day cake. Mom made the cake from whatever Betty Crocker mix we had lying around. I decorated it (just barely). Dad always ate two slices.

This cake is perfect for Dad and perfect for backyard barbeques. It is lighter than the average Bundt, courtesy of the whipped cream, and full of smoky cocoa-chocolate flavor. And it is dark. It is spectacularly, almost otherworldly, black. Though the cake would be welcome on its own, we do suggest covering it in our butter whiskey glaze. It provides a welcome sweet contrast, and just enough whiskey to make Dad feel special.

●●● **BAKED NOTE**

If you can get your hands on black cocoa powder (see page 19), use it in this cake per the recipe, though we don't recommend subbing it for all the unsweetened cocoa powder here or in other baked goods, as it can be overpowering. It makes a stunningly deep, dark cake without any bitter notes. However, this cake is also wonderful when made completely with regular dark (Dutch-process) cocoa powder, such as Valrhona. The cake might not be as beautifully black, but it will be equally delicious.

INGREDIENTS

For the Black Cocoa Bundt

½ cup (40 g) unsweetened dark cocoa powder, such as Valrhona

¼ cup (20 g) unsweetened black cocoa powder (see Baked Note and page 19)

1 tablespoon instant espresso powder

1 cup (240 ml) hot coffee

2¼ cups (285 g) all-purpose flour

2 teaspoons baking powder

1¼ teaspoons kosher salt

¼ teaspoon baking soda

2¼ cups (495 g) firmly packed dark brown sugar

¾ cup plus 2 tablespoons (210 ml) canola oil

1 tablespoon pure vanilla extract

2 large eggs

2 large egg yolks

1½ cups (360 ml) heavy cream

For the Butter Whiskey Glaze

3 tablespoons unsalted butter

2 tablespoons heavy cream

2½ to 3 cups (280 to 340 g) confectioners' sugar, sifted

3 tablespoons good-quality whiskey

For Décor

Chocolate sprinkles (optional)

MAKE THE BLACK COCOA BUNDT

1 Preheat the oven to 350°F (175°C). Butter the inside of a 12-cup Bundt pan, dust with cocoa powder, and knock out the excess. Alternatively, liberally apply a nonstick cooking spray, dust with cocoa, and knock out the excess. Either way, make sure the pan's nooks and crannies are all thoroughly coated.

2 Place both cocoa powders and the instant espresso powder in a medium heatproof bowl. Pour the hot coffee directly over the powders and whisk until combined. Set aside to cool.

3 In a large bowl, whisk together the flour, baking powder, salt, and baking soda.

4 In another large bowl, whisk the brown sugar, oil, and vanilla until combined. Add the eggs and egg yolks and whisk again until just combined. Add the flour mixture in three parts, alternating with the chocolate mixture, beginning and ending with the flour mixture. Whisk each addition gently to combine.

5 Whip the cream (either by hand or with a standing mixer) just until medium peaks form. Fold one-third of the whipped cream into the batter to lighten it. Fold in half of the remaining whipped cream until just incorporated, then fold in the rest until no streaks remain.

6 Pour the batter into the prepared pan and bake in the middle of the oven until a small sharp knife or toothpick comes out with just a few moist crumbs, 50 to 55 minutes. Transfer the pan to a wire rack to cool completely. Then gently loosen the sides of the cake from the pan and turn it out onto the rack so that the crown is facing up. Place a baking sheet (lined with parchment paper, if you like, for ease of cleaning) underneath the wire rack.

MAKE THE BUTTER WHISKEY GLAZE

1 In a saucepan, melt the butter over low heat. Remove from the heat and whisk in the cream. In three parts, add 2½ cups (280 g) confectioners' sugar, whisking to combine after each addition. Add the whiskey and whisk until uniform. The glaze should be thick and ropy, but pourable—not runny and thin. If the glaze looks too thin, add the remaining ½ cup (60 g) confectioners' sugar and whisk to combine.

ASSEMBLE THE BLACK COCOA BUNDT

1 Pour the glaze over the room-temperature cake in thick ribbons; it will slowly drip down the sides. Add a few sprinkles to the top, if you like. Let set for about 15 minutes before serving.

HOW TO STORE

The cake will keep in an airtight container at room temperature for up to 3 days.

HOT CHOCOLATE PUDDING CAKE

YIELD: 9 TO 12 SERVINGS

THE CALENDAR, rightly or wrongly, is overflowing with national [insert favorite flavor here] pudding days. It is an embarrassment of custard riches. Whole separate days are dedicated to different pudding varieties and flavors like plum, Indian, vanilla, rice, butterscotch, and even the oft-derided tapioca. We appreciate each and every one of these days (okay, perhaps we aren't as enthralled with Indian pudding as we could be), but it is the chocolate variety that makes our hearts beat a little faster and our smiles beam a little brighter.

There are myriad ways to celebrate National Chocolate Pudding Day. The simplest would be to prepare and serve a basic chocolate pudding (actually, buying a premade chocolate pudding would be the simplest, but wholly unsatisfying). Or, if you are feeling particularly Gatsby, you could fill a backyard swimming pool with chocolate custard and invite everyone over for a hedonistic swim. In the middle of the celebration spectrum is our Hot Chocolate Pudding Cake. True, it is not a traditional pudding. That would be boring. This is a cake that nearly turns into a pudding, or something like it. It is the blessed union of chocolate cake and chocolate pudding, and there is no turning back after one bite. The cake itself is humble. In theory you are baking a "pudding" underneath a "cake" layer (although you can invert the slices when serving so the pudding is on top). It will not replace a three-tiered occasion cake anytime soon, but it more than makes up for its basic appearance (the top of the cake resembles Jupiter's surface) with a complex chocolate flavor. In a nutshell: Imagine dunking a good slice of chocolate cake in chocolate milk. Bliss.

●●● BAKED NOTE

Forgive us for using the words *custard* and *pudding* almost interchangeably. Traditionally speaking, *custard* is defined as being thickened with eggs, and *pudding* is defined as being thickened with cornstarch (or another starch), but the line is very blurry. There is endless overlap. And, we happen to like our pudding a little more on the custardy (eggy) side.

INGREDIENTS

For the Hot Chocolate Pudding Cake

- ¾ cup plus 2 tablespoons (105 g) all-purpose flour
- 1 teaspoon baking powder
- ¼ teaspoon baking soda
- ½ teaspoon kosher salt
- 2 large egg yolks
- ½ cup (120 ml) well-shaken buttermilk
- 2 tablespoons canola oil
- 2 ounces (½ stick/55 g) unsalted butter
- 1½ ounces (40 g) dark chocolate (60 to 72% cacao), coarsely chopped
- ⅓ cup (30 g) unsweetened dark cocoa powder, such as Valrhona
- ¾ cup (165 g) firmly packed dark brown sugar
- 1 tablespoon pure vanilla extract

For the Chocolate Topping

- ⅓ cup (65 g) granulated sugar
- ⅓ cup (75 g) firmly packed dark brown sugar
- ¼ cup plus 1 tablespoon (25 g) unsweetened dark cocoa powder, such as Valrhona
- 1¼ cups (300 ml) boiling water
- 1½ teaspoons instant espresso powder
- 2 ounces (55 g) dark chocolate (60 to 72% cacao), coarsely chopped (about ⅓ cup)

For the Assembly

Vanilla ice cream (optional, but highly recommended)

MAKE THE HOT CHOCOLATE PUDDING CAKE

1 Preheat the oven to 350°F (175°C). Lightly spray the sides and bottom of an 8-by-8-by-2-inch (20-by-20-by-5-cm) baking dish with nonstick cooking spray.

2 In a small bowl, whisk together the flour, baking powder, baking soda, and salt. Set aside.

3 In another small bowl or glass measuring cup, whisk together the egg yolks, buttermilk, and oil. Set aside.

4 Melt the butter and chocolate in a large heatproof bowl placed over simmering water (double-boiler method, see page 19) set over low heat until almost completely melted. Add the cocoa powder and whisk until the mixture is combined and completely melted. Remove it from the heat and continue whisking gently for about 1 minute to cool the mixture slightly. Add the brown sugar and vanilla and continue whisking until completely combined. Whisk in the buttermilk mixture until incorporated, then, using a rubber spatula, gently fold in the flour mixture. Transfer the batter to the prepared pan, and set aside.

MAKE THE CHOCOLATE TOPPING

1 In a medium bowl, stir together both sugars and the cocoa powder. You might need to use your fingers to rub the clumps of brown sugar into the rest of the mix.

2 Stir the boiling water and instant espresso powder together in a small bowl.

3 Sprinkle the chocolate chunks over the cake batter. Then sprinkle the sugar mixture over the chocolate chips and batter, covering it completely. Pour the hot espresso liquid evenly over the top of the sugar mixture. Bake the cake in the center of the oven until the cake looks set but still feels jiggly in the center, 35 to 40 minutes.

4 Remove the cake from the oven and let it rest about 20 minutes, then slice and serve warm. Slices can be served upside down (with pudding on top), or serve each slice on a plate and spoon the pudding (the batter in the bottom of the pan) alongside the cake. Serve with vanilla ice cream, if you like.

HOW TO STORE

Leftover cake can be stored in the refrigerator, wrapped tightly in plastic, for up to 3 days. To reheat, cook individual portions in the microwave for 20- to 30-second bursts, until warmed through.

JULY

●●●

JUL 1 | **CANADA DAY**

NANAIMO ICE CREAM BARS 138

JUL 4 | **INDEPENDENCE DAY**

ORANGE BUTTERMILK PICNIC CAKE WITH CHOCOLATE CHIPS 142

JUL 14 | **BASTILLE DAY**

CHEESY BASTILLE DAY BEER BREAD 144

JUL 18 | **HUNTER S. THOMPSON'S BIRTHDAY**

GONZO CAKE 146

NANAIMO ICE CREAM BARS

YIELD: 40 (1-BY-1½-INCH / 2.5-BY-4-CM) BARS

WE ARE FAIRLY CERTAIN that the famed Nanaimo bar originated in Nanaimo, British Columbia. We are also (mostly) convinced that the original bar consisted of a chocolate-wafer crumb base topped with vanilla custard that itself was doused in a chocolate icing or ganache. Beyond that, it is hard to distinguish fact from fiction and folklore. Did local housewife Mabel Jenkins from Cowichan Bay, British Columbia, really invent the recipe in the early 1950s? Or, as some conspiracy theorists insist, did it come into being in the early nineteenth century in Nanaimo? Regardless of where the original recipe came from, we are completely baffled that Nanaimo bars are not more prevalent throughout the United States (and the world). After all, despite being born in Canada, the recipe skews very American in flavor. And, might we add, they are delicious. It is the kind of treat you want to see more often in heavy rotation.

Our version of the Nanaimo, the distinctly Canadian dessert, is our ode to Canada Day, of course. Canada Day, by the by, is often referred to as Canada's birthday, the day three British North American colonies joined together to create the new "kingdom" of Canada. We love Canada. It is like a clean and polite version of the United States, and we visit often (their cooler summers are a great antidote to sticky, stinky August in NYC). These Nanaimo Ice Cream Bars are everything you'd want in July. They are cool, crisp, textured, salty (thanks to the pretzels), and sweet without being obnoxious. True, they are not 100 percent Nanaimo, but we think you will love the ice cream variation.

●●● BAKED NOTE

While we kind of have an addiction to the digestive biscuits—they sound so healthy—often found clustered near other British-type foods in American grocery stores, you can replace them (one for one) with graham crackers. (We find the average digestive biscuits to be slightly less dry than grahams, that is, slightly more pleasing.) Obviously, you can swap ice cream flavors at will, though we prefer salted caramel, mint, vanilla, or coffee; chocolate ice cream on top of all of that other chocolate is a bit much. This recipe includes an uncooked egg, so please exercise caution.

INGREDIENTS

For the Cocoa Pretzel Crust

2 ounces (55 g) toasted walnuts (about ½ cup; see page 19), coarsely chopped

5¼ ounces (150 g) digestive biscuits or graham crackers (approximately 15 biscuits)

2½ ounces (70 g) thin, salty pretzel sticks

2 ounces (½ stick/55 g) unsalted butter, cut into cubes

¼ cup (55 g) firmly packed light brown sugar

¼ cup (20 g) unsweetened dark cocoa powder, such as Valrhona

1 large egg, beaten

1 teaspoon pure vanilla extract

For the Ice Cream Layer

2 pints (946 ml) homemade or store-bought premium vanilla or salted caramel ice cream

MAKE THE COCOA PRETZEL CRUST

1 Line an ungreased 8-inch (20-cm) square pan with parchment paper so that it overhangs by approximately 2 inches (5 cm) on two opposite sides.

2 Place the walnuts in a large bowl.

3 Place the digestive biscuits in a food processor and pulse in three or four short 2-second bursts until the biscuits are finely ground, with a few coarsely ground pieces for texture. Sprinkle the biscuit crumbs over the walnuts. Put the pretzel sticks in the same food processor (no need to wash in between) and pulse five or six times in 1-second bursts to create small sticklike chunks. Alternatively, place the pretzels in a zip-tight plastic bag and crush them with a rolling pin. Do not overprocess the pretzels; the pieces should be peanut size, not powdery. Sprinkle the pretzel chunks over the biscuit crumbs and use your hands to toss them together.

4 Place the butter in a large bowl and set it over a saucepan of simmering water (double-boiler method, see page 19), stirring until the butter is completely melted. Remove the bowl from the pan of simmering water, add the brown sugar and cocoa, and stir until combined. Add the egg in a slow stream while whisking. Return the bowl to the pan of simmering water and whisk slowly and constantly until the mixture thickens slightly, 60 to 90 seconds. It won't thicken up like a pudding, but it should be a smooth mixture that shows whisk marks. Remove it from the heat and whisk in the vanilla. Stir in the dry ingredients until just combined; try to ensure that the dry ingredients are covered by the wet. Turn the crumb mixture out into the prepared pan and firmly press it into an even layer on only the bottom of the pan, not the sides; if you like, use the back of a metal measuring cup to help even it out. Refrigerate the pan for 30 minutes.

ASSEMBLE THE ICE CREAM LAYER

1 Remove the ice cream from your freezer and let it soften, about 15 minutes. Place the ice cream in a large bowl and use a rubber spatula to beat it until it is slightly malleable. Alternatively, beat the ice cream in a standing mixer fitted with the paddle attachment (a chilled bowl and paddle are preferable) until almost smooth but not melty, about 10 seconds. Remove the crust from the refrigerator.

2 Spread the ice cream over the cocoa pretzel crust in an even layer. Cover with plastic wrap and freeze for 2 hours.

MAKE THE FUDGE TOPPING

1 In a small saucepan over low heat, heat the cream, butter, and corn syrup together until just simmering. Remove the pan from the heat and add the chocolate. Whisk until the fudge is smooth. If you have a few stray unmelted chocolate chunks, reheat the mixture over very low heat until completely melted.

INGREDIENTS (CONT.)

For the Fudge Topping

2   tablespoons heavy cream
2   tablespoons unsalted butter
1   tablespoon light corn syrup
5   ounces (140 g) dark chocolate (60 to 72% cacao), chopped

ASSEMBLE THE BARS

1   Whisk the fudge topping vigorously for 1 minute to release excessive heat or until it reaches room temperature. Remove the bars from the freezer and pour the fudge over the ice cream layer. Working quickly, use an offset spatula to spread the fudge topping into an even layer. Again, cover with plastic wrap and freeze until the bars are solid, at least 2 hours and up to 24 hours.

2   Once the bars are completely frozen, remove from the freezer. Dip a knife in hot water and wipe it dry. Using the hot knife, go around the edges of the pan. Gently pull up on both sides of the parchment overhang to release the bars from the pan and place the bars with the parchment on a large cutting board. Freeze the bars on the cutting board for 10 minutes.

3   Remove the bars from the freezer. Dip a knife in hot water and wipe it dry. Using a hot knife, score and slice the bars into 1-by-1½-inch (2.5-by-4-cm) rectangles. (Freeze the bars in between scoring and slicing if the ice cream gets too soft.) Serve immediately.

HOW TO STORE

The bars will keep, tightly wrapped in foil, in the freezer for up to 5 days. Let the bars sit at room temperature for a few minutes before serving.

ORANGE BUTTERMILK PICNIC CAKE WITH CHOCOLATE CHIPS

YIELD: 1 9-INCH (23-CM) SINGLE-LAYER CAKE • 8 TO 12 SERVINGS

EVERY YEAR, as summer begins its slow and steady approach on the calendar, I begin to romanticize a June and July full of picnics. This is odd, because I am not a picnic person. In my gossamer-filtered Fourth of July picnic fantasies, I am running through tall grass with a lightweight vintage picnic basket in one hand and an icy bottle of Lambrusco in the other. Somewhere in this fiction, someone is playing guitar, firecrackers paint the faraway sky, and I am eating crackly fried chicken. Unfortunately, the reality is my picnics are hot and buggy. I am almost always thirsty and embarrassingly sweaty. The food is inappropriately lukewarm. But I still fantasize. And I still make this amazing Orange Buttermilk Picnic Cake with Chocolate Chips. Even if I plan on devouring it indoors, fully air-conditioned, in front of my television. This is a perfect, delicious, and uncomplicated summer cake. It's low fuss, single-layer, and pleasingly citrusy. Since there is no messy frosting involved, you can cart it nearly anywhere, picnics included. And the best part: The cake smells like heavenly pancakes (I don't know why) while baking.

●●● BAKED NOTE

We roll our chocolate chips in flour to help suspend them in the batter and keep them from sinking to the bottom of the cake. You can use smaller (mini) chocolate chips or chop regular-size chocolate chips. Smaller chips weigh less and suspend more easily.

INGREDIENTS

For the Buttermilk Cake

1 orange
½ cup (120 ml) well-shaken buttermilk
½ cup plus 2 tablespoons (70 g), plus 1 teaspoon all-purpose flour
½ cup plus 2 tablespoons (85 g) cake flour
½ teaspoon kosher salt
¼ teaspoon baking soda
¼ teaspoon baking powder
¾ cup (165 g) firmly packed light brown sugar
3 ounces (¾ stick/85 g) unsalted butter, softened, plus more for the pan
1 large egg
1 large egg yolk
¾ teaspoon pure orange extract
½ teaspoon pure vanilla extract
4 ounces (115 g) semisweet mini chocolate chips or coarsely chopped regular-size chocolate chips (about ¾ cup)
1 tablespoon orange liqueur or canola oil

For the Orange Syrup

3 tablespoons freshly squeezed orange juice
3 tablespoons granulated sugar
1 to 2 tablespoons Grand Marnier (optional)

For the Assembly

2 tablespoons confectioners' sugar

MAKE THE BUTTERMILK CAKE

1 Preheat the oven to 325°F (165°C).

2 Butter one 9-inch (23-cm) round cake pan, line the bottom with parchment paper, and butter the parchment. Dust the parchment with flour and knock out the excess.

3 Zest and juice the orange. Set aside the zest. Place ¼ cup (60 ml) of the juice into a glass measuring cup and reserve the rest for the orange syrup (below). Add the buttermilk to the orange juice in the measuring cup and whisk until combined. Set aside.

4 Sift ½ cup plus 2 tablespoons (70 g) all-purpose flour, the cake flour, salt, baking soda, and baking powder into a small bowl.

5 In the bowl of a standing mixer fitted with the paddle attachment, cream the brown sugar and butter on medium speed until fluffy, about 3 minutes. Add the egg and egg yolk and beat well, then add the orange extract, vanilla, and orange zest until incorporated. Scrape down the sides and bottom of the bowl, and mix again for 15 seconds. Add the flour mixture in three parts, alternating with the buttermilk mixture, beginning and ending with the flour mixture.

6 Toss the chocolate chips in the liqueur and sprinkle them with 1 teaspoon all-purpose flour. Toss to coat the chips in the flour. Fold the chocolate chips into the batter and pour the batter into the prepared pan. Smooth the top. Bake, rotating the pan halfway through the baking time, until a toothpick inserted in the center of the cake comes out clean, plus another minute or two, 32 to 37 minutes. (Since this is a picnic cake, you should bake it a tiny bit more than you are normally comfortable with. This cake will still be moist—you just don't want it "falling-apart moist.")

7 Transfer the pan to a wire rack and cool for 15 minutes.

MAKE THE ORANGE SYRUP

1 Meanwhile, in a small saucepan over very low heat, whisk together the orange juice, sugar, and Grand Marnier, a tablespoon at a time (to taste), until combined. Once the sugar is melted, increase the heat to medium-low and simmer until the syrup is slightly thickened, about 2 minutes. Remove it from the heat.

2 Turn the still-warm cake out of the pan onto the rack, remove the parchment paper, and flip the cake right side up. Place the wire rack over a baking sheet. Using a toothpick or wooden skewer, poke holes evenly all over the cake. Brush the cake with the orange syrup and allow it to sink in and set, about 15 minutes. Dust it with the confectioners' sugar immediately before serving (or before packing up for your picnic).

HOW TO STORE

The cake will keep in an airtight container at room temperature for up to 3 days.

CHEESY BASTILLE DAY BEER BREAD

YIELD: 1 9-BY-5-INCH (23-BY-12-CM) LOAF • 12 SERVINGS

A FAIR NUMBER OF BROOKLYNITES are Francophiles at heart. And though the adoration for all things French (chic French, country French, coastal French) is not always bubbling on the surface, we have witnessed plenty of unironic beret-wearing hipsters sipping their morning lattes, scuffed Voltaire paperbacks in hand. Needless to say, Bastille Day is big in Brooklyn (and Manhattan). Despite its origin as the day the Bastille prison was stormed in 1789, which is considered to be the beginning of the French Revolution, here it is celebrated with a raucous, convivial, and charming street party. There are crepes and wine, éclairs and *macarons*, and lots and lots of cheese. It is one of the few foreign holidays so expertly co-opted and celebrated by New Yorkers that it almost feels . . . American.

As part-time Francophiles ourselves, we celebrate the day with loads of French cheese. Actually, we celebrate as many days as possible with as many cheeses as possible. But Bastille Day is a particularly great time to focus on and enjoy the cheeses of France. While we might occasionally indulge in the stinkier varieties, we are particularly obsessed with Comté these days. And when you pair that with a lovely sheep's-milk cheese from the Pyrenees region (we love Brebis) in a simple quick bread, you have the makings for a perfect cheesy loaf. The base of this recipe is the stalwart and omnipresent (at least in the 1980s) beer cheese bread. It is beyond simple—no yeast, no rising—and we did our best to make sure the flavors of the cheese shine. While, like all quick breads, this isn't as complex tasting as a sourdough, it is absurdly good as morning toast.

●●● BAKED NOTE

We have been making cheesy quick breads for years, but the method of sprinkling the bottom of the pan with some cheese before baking was a revelation. Much credit to America's Test Kitchen for the brilliant idea; it adds a wonderful dimension: a crispy, cheesy top to an already wonderful bread.

INGREDIENTS

- **4** ounces (115 g) Comté cheese, shredded
- **3** cups (385 g) all-purpose flour
- **1** tablespoon baking powder
- **1** teaspoon kosher salt
- **¼** teaspoon freshly ground black pepper
- **¼** teaspoon ancho chile powder (optional)
- **4** ounces (115 g) Pyrenees Brebis cheese or other semisoft sheep's-milk cheese, cut into ½-inch (12-mm) cubes
- **1¼** cups (10 ounces/300 ml) beer
- **1** large egg, beaten lightly
- **¼** cup (55 g) sour cream
- **2** tablespoons unsalted butter, melted

1 Preheat the oven to 350°F (175°C) and position a rack in the center. Spray a 9-by-5-inch (23-by-12-cm) loaf pan with nonstick cooking spray.

2 Sprinkle approximately 1 ounce (30 g) of the Comté over the bottom of the pan in an even layer.

3 In a large bowl, whisk together the flour, baking powder, salt, black pepper, and the ancho chile powder, if using. Stir in the Brebis and 2 ounces (55 g) of the Comté, making sure each piece is completely coated in flour. Set aside.

4 In a medium bowl, whisk together the beer, egg, sour cream, and butter.

5 Add the wet ingredients to the flour mixture, using a rubber spatula to fold together until they are completely combined. Do not overmix.

6 Transfer the batter to the prepared pan. Smooth the top and sprinkle with the remaining 1 ounce (30 g) Comté. Bake, rotating the pan halfway through the baking time, until the top is browned and the loaf is cooked all the way through, 45 to 55 minutes; insert a toothpick into the center of the bread to check for doneness—it should come out clean (except perhaps for some melted cheese). Remove from the oven and place the loaf on a cooling rack for 20 minutes. Then turn it out onto a wire rack to cool completely.

7 Slice and serve; the bread can also be toasted before serving.

HOW TO STORE

The bread will keep, tightly wrapped, at room temperature for up to 2 days. It also freezes really well—wrap tightly in plastic wrap, then foil, before freezing.

GONZO CAKE

PURPLE VELVET CAKE WITH CREAM CHEESE FROSTING

YIELD: 1 8-INCH (20-CM) THREE-LAYER CAKE • 10 TO 12 SERVINGS

I INSTANTLY, OVERWHELMINGLY fell in love with Hunter S. Thompson's *Fear and Loathing in Las Vegas* from the first few pages. It's a slim volume, and I finished it in one sitting. I have since read it, or parts of it, many more times. The novel (or fictionalized nonfiction) has since taken on the weight of implied stereotypes. If the oft-imagined (oft-maligned) reader of Kerouac's *On the Road* is an angsty teen from a prosperous family pretending to slum it with cheap cigarettes and dirty clothes, the clichéd reader of *Fear and Loathing in Las Vegas* is often portrayed as a counterculture hippie with a penchant for drugs. This is unfortunate. It is a boring surface mentality. Hunter S. Thompson invented a new journalistic medium, *gonzo* journalism (essentially objective, stream-of-consciousness journalism), and his writing is lyrical, smart, and, well . . . literary. That the word *gonzo* also happens to be the name of my favorite underdog Muppet is serendipitous. It is cause for celebration.

Our Gonzo Cake is a many-wondered thing. For starters, it is purple. The color comes from purple yam powder (aka *ube*, often used in the Philippines to make all manner of desserts and ice creams) gently augmented with a few drops of natural color gels. And though the yam flavor is not particularly strong—it's sweet and sort of wine-like—we love the idea of infusing a cake with a nutritional and unexpected ingredient, a welcome sneak attack. Regardless, the layers bake up into a perfect moist sponge, and we cover the whole thing with a simple cream cheese frosting. It is the kind of cake you might crave in the middle of the night for no apparent reason. It is the kind of cake you should make for Hunter S. Thompson's birthday.

●●● **BAKED NOTE**

Purple yam powder is not always easy to find locally, though it is readily available via the Internet and in some Asian grocery stores. If you don't feel like chasing down this ingredient, you can try substituting mashed sweet potatoes (see sidebar, page 149). It may not be a purple cake, but it will be a delicious one. Also, per our testers' suggestions, we made the vanilla optional, as a vanilla-free frosting is pure white and very striking against a purple cake. We are vanilla freaks, so we might encourage keeping it, but ultimately it is up to you.

INGREDIENTS

For the Purple Velvet Cake

1   (4-ounce/115-g) package purple yam powder (about ½ cup plus 2 tablespoons; see Baked Note)

¼   cup (60 ml) canola oil or other vegetable oil

2¼ cups (285 g) cake flour

¾   cup (90 g) all-purpose flour

1   tablespoon baking powder

1   teaspoon baking soda

¾   teaspoon kosher salt

4   ounces (1 stick/115 g) unsalted butter, softened, plus more for the pans

¼   cup (50 g) vegetable shortening, at room temperature

2   cups (400 g) granulated sugar

1   tablespoon pure vanilla extract

Blue and red food dyes or gels

4   large egg whites, at room temperature

For the Cream Cheese Frosting

3   cups (340 g) confectioners' sugar

8   ounces (2 sticks/225 g) unsalted butter, softened

2   (8-ounce/226-g) packages cream cheese, softened

1   tablespoon plus 1 teaspoon pure vanilla extract (optional)

½   teaspoon kosher salt

For Décor

Purple sprinkles (optional)

MAKE THE PURPLE VELVET CAKE

1   Preheat the oven to 325°F (165°C). Butter three 8-inch (20-cm) cake pans, line them with parchment paper, and butter the parchment. Dust with flour and knock out the excess.

2   In a small saucepan over very low heat, stir together 2 cups (480 ml) water with the purple yam powder and cook, stirring occasionally, until the mixture is rehydrated, between 5 and 20 minutes depending on the heat. Once the mixture looks and feels like mashed potatoes (or mashed yams) remove it from the heat and whisk in the canola oil.

3   In a large bowl, sift both flours, the baking powder, baking soda, and salt. Set aside.

4   In the bowl of a standing mixer fitted with a paddle attachment, beat the butter and shortening on medium speed until creamy, 3 to 4 minutes. Add the sugar and vanilla and beat on medium speed until the mixture is fluffy, about 3 minutes. Turn the mixer to low. Add the flour mixture in three equal parts, alternating with the purple yam mixture, beginning and ending with the flour mixture. Scrape down the sides of the bowl with a rubber spatula and then mix on low speed for a few more seconds.

5   Mix equal drops of red and blue food dyes in a small bowl to make purple, then scrape it into the cake batter and mix until a pale purple color is achieved.

6   In a clean bowl, whisk the egg whites by hand or in your standing mixer until soft peaks form; do not overbeat. Using a rubber spatula, gently fold the egg whites into the batter.

7   Divide the batter equally among all three pans. Use your spatula to spread the batter evenly. Bake the cakes, rotating the pans halfway through baking, until a toothpick inserted in the center of the cakes comes out clean, 20 to 30 minutes. Transfer the pans to a wire rack and cool for 20 minutes. Invert the cakes onto the rack, remove the pans, and let them cool completely. Remove the parchment.

MAKE THE CREAM CHEESE FROSTING

1   Sift the confectioners' sugar into a large bowl and set aside.

2   In the bowl of a standing mixer fitted with the paddle attachment, beat the butter until it is completely smooth. Add the cream cheese and beat until combined.

3   Add the confectioners' sugar, vanilla, if using, and salt and beat just until smooth; do not overbeat or the frosting will lose structure. Chill the frosting in the refrigerator for about 5 minutes. (The frosting can be made up to 24 hours ahead; cover the bowl tightly, refrigerate, and let the filling soften at room temperature before using.)

ASSEMBLE THE GONZO CAKE

1 Place one cake layer on a serving platter. Trim the top to create a flat surface and evenly spread about 1¼ cups (330 g) of the frosting on top. Add the next layer, trim and frost it, then add the third layer. Trim the top layer. Spread a very thin layer of frosting over the sides and top of the cake (a crumb coat, which helps to keep loose cake crumbs under control when you frost the outside of the cake) and place it in the refrigerator to firm up, about 15 minutes.

2 Remove the cake from the refrigerator. Frost the sides and top with the remaining frosting. Sprinkle the outer edge of the top of the cake with the sprinkles, if you like. Chill the cake in the refrigerator to set the frosting, about 15 minutes. Slice and serve.

HOW TO STORE

This cake can be covered in a cake saver in a cool room for up to 3 days. If you refrigerate it, make sure to cover it tightly and bring it back to room temperature before serving.

SUBSTITUTING SWEET POTATOES FOR YAM POWDER

When you swap out just one ingredient—obscure purple yam powder for standard mashed sweet potatoes—something amazing happens. Essentially, you get a whole new cake: entirely different, but entirely delicious on its own. The main difference is the texture. While the texture of the Purple Velvet cake is akin to a red velvet, this sweet potato version has more in common with an apple cake.

Here's how to do it:

1 Swap the yam powder in the recipe for 2 cups (420 g) roasted, peeled, and mashed sweet potatoes. Ideally, use fresh sweet potatoes, though canned puree without any other ingredients should be okay.

2 Bake the mashed sweet potato cake layers slightly longer than the yam powder layers, 5 to 7 more minutes.

3 Omit the purple food dye. The mashed sweet potato cake is a pretty sherbet-orange color, and the purple dye will just ruin it.

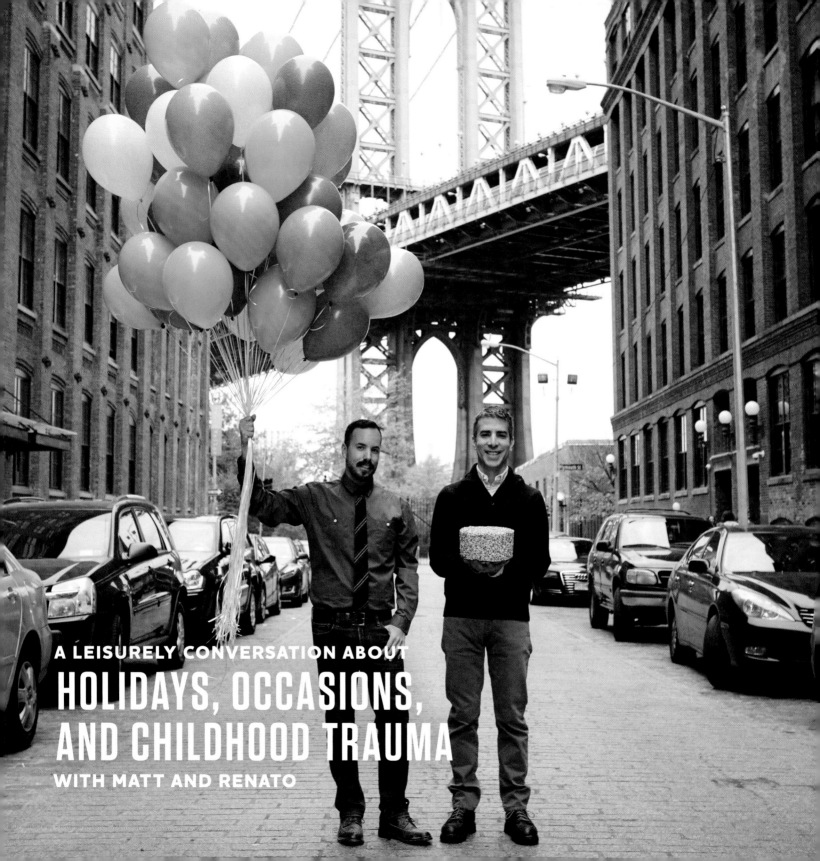

A LEISURELY CONVERSATION ABOUT
HOLIDAYS, OCCASIONS, AND CHILDHOOD TRAUMA
WITH MATT AND RENATO

MATT: So here we are, our fourth book! Can you believe it? I think any discussion about this book inevitably starts with either Secretary's Day or Halloween, in that Secretary's Day was the initial impetus for this book, and we both kind of love Halloween for myriad reasons: scary movies, apple picking, crisp weather, the end of bathing suit season . . . and your obsession with cosplay.

RENATO: My cosplay fascination isn't really cookbook material. I'll be saving that nugget for my bio.

M: Fine. But back to Secretary's Day. It is such a dark holiday. It feels outdated, joyless . . . frozen in time . . . a relic from the Cold War.

R: But it's since been renamed. It is now Administrative Professionals' Day. . . . Actually, that may make it a bit sadder and darker.

M: It is so subservient in nature—the idea of the good-natured, flirty female secretary working arduously for her male boss. If she is good, she gets an unwanted pat on the rump, some flowers, and some chocolate one day a year.

R: Or maybe more, if she looks like Loni Anderson. Wait—that reference dates me. Let me use another example: Joan from *Mad Men*, exhaustedly thwarting the advances of many a fellow office worker.

M: I think that if you dig deep, the entire holiday is built around dominance and power and repression.

R: You're digging too deep. At the end of the day, we are offering up popcorn balls. Good ones at that . . .

M: Let's move on to Halloween, then. You have a memory you'd like to share with our readers, don't you?

R: I do. I'm going to share this story in the hopes that our readers and future generations can learn something from my misfortune. It was 1985. I was an eleven-year-old fey, rotund boy with a penchant for frilly things (if you catch my drift). Halloween was fast approaching and I didn't have a costume. I was desperate, but I fancied myself creative. So after assessing what was available to me, I thought: scarecrow. A costume perfect for the DIY spirit. A costume impossibly easy to pull off. So I wore my older brother's flouncy, blousy shirt, a glittery scarf (the kind Steven Tyler of Aerosmith would tie onto his microphone stand), and an old pair of black panty hose . . . with just my underwear underneath and the long shirt over it. I apparently thought shorts, pants, or any sort of additional covering would not be needed. But the coup de grâce was this punk, spiky, black-and-gold wig.

M: This isn't reading "scarecrow" to me.

R: I caked my face in makeup, slipped on my Reeboks, and left the house. I was so proud. I met up with my friends, I did a little trick-or-treating, and all was okay. I was a bit cold, as it was October and I was technically naked, but I considered it a success. Anyway, because such is my life, we ran into some hooligans. One of these bullies walked right up to me and said, "Who are you supposed to be? Pat Benatar?" Everyone laughed. Even my friends were doubled over. It was one of those life-scarring events.

M: But, in retrospect, you probably did look like Pat Benatar.

R: Love is a battlefield, Matt. But I still love Halloween!

M: Me, too . . . though it has evolved since we were kids. It's become a monstrous holiday. It can be so brutal. People put so much effort into their costumes these days. It's like a mini Fashion Week.

R: If I see one more "sexy [insert noun here]," I will kill. When did that happen? I don't remember anyone trying to look sexy when we were younger. Girls would dress as a mailbox or a pizza and be fine with it! Sexy costumes came in two flavors: nurse and cop. Now everything is sexy. Even for the guys! Ugh.

M: True. But for me, it was always about the candy. The costume was secondary. I lived for my plastic jack-o'-lantern to runneth over with Hershey's Krackel bars and M&M's and Milk Duds. Speaking of which: What the hell happened to Milk Duds? Why aren't they more ubiquitous? Why isn't every kid in America screaming for Milk Duds? Life is so unfair.

R: And what about the Whatchamacallit candy bar? That was my favorite as a kid. I think I ate one or two a day between the ages of six and ten. I was also the size and shape of your standard ottoman.

M: And, if I may (and before this gets away from us), I'd like to reaffirm my love for Christmas as well. After all, Christmas takes up a good portion of this book. No matter how commercialized or overdone it becomes, I still love Christmas, especially in New York. I like Christmas cookies. I like Christmas cakes. I like Christmas trees, and Christmas music, and even Christmas shopping. But if you want a quick preview of the coming apocalypse, I suggest you visit one of those "Christmas-all-year-round" stores in the middle of Florida in July. Where light should envelop, darkness persists. It is an endless, perilous vacuum of cute kitten ornaments and factory-made stockings in a soupy, humid, Tampa suburb. But I digress . . .

R: Um, well . . . Christmas in New York City is what keeps me here year after year. For me, Christmas is about the change of seasons. And linzer cookies. And Pee Wee. Have you ever seen the *Pee-wee's Playhouse* Christmas special?

M: No.

R: Oh, Matt, it is the rare Christmas television special that ages beautifully. It's visionary. It's got Oprah and Cher and Zsa Zsa and Joan Rivers and Grace Jones, and isn't that enough for a lifetime? A lifetime of Christmases?

M: I've never been one for Christmas specials, but holiday music is an altogether different story. I am not even sure I truly like it, but I have to listen to the genre exclusively every December 1 through December 24. In fact, the only reason I can think of for enjoying Barbra Streisand's "Jingle Bells" is that some bizarre form of Stockholm syndrome has taken hold. My parents really overplayed that record. It's the epitome of love/hate for me.

R: And no matter your thoughts on Paul McCartney, his rendition of "Wonderful Christmastime" is the audible equivalent of waterboarding. At the other end of the spectrum, "Hard Candy Christmas" by a certain Miss Dolly Parton always kicks off the Christmas season for me.

M: "Maybe I'll lose some weight . . ." Even Dolly has a page in this book!

R: She's earned it! Dolly is a walking, talking holiday.

M: Can we also discuss some of the less-prominent holidays in this book? I know you love Nutella and that World Nutella Day is an essential part of the calendar, but what about Alaska Day? How did I miss this holiday for so long?

R: Because you have never lived in or near Alaska.

M: But it seems like such an important holiday—I mean, this is the day to celebrate the U.S. purchase of Alaska from Russia for a measly 7.2 million dollars.

R: Less than the price of a three-bedroom condo in NYC.

M: And c'mon, can you think of a more perfect holiday to celebrate the world's most underappreciated dessert, Baked Alaska? Ice cream cake covered in meringue—where have you been all my life? My goal in life is to make Alaska Day more important to the average American.

R: And likewise, what about Eleanor Roosevelt?

M: We should have paid more attention during history class. Thank God for Wikipedia.

R: I have always had a thing for Eleanor. Have you ever heard a recording of her voice? It was the epitome of elocution. She broke the mold on what it means to be the First Lady. Classy, forward thinking, witty . . . I think she would have loved the Peanut Butter and Jelly Crumb Morning Muffins (page 186) we made in her honor for this book.

M: How could she not? Anyway, it's obvious we learned a lot during the writing of this book. We were both surprised and intrigued by the history of so many holidays, both well known and fringe.

R: And that we were influenced by a variety of significant female figures in our lives: our moms, Dolly, Eleanor, Mildred Day . . .

M: Damn right, Mildred Day! Unsung hero to moms everywhere! Creator of the Rice Krispies Treat! My new goal in life is to constantly educate people about Mildred Day. She deserves as much prominence, at least, as Ruth Wakefield [possible creator of the chocolate chip cookie].

R: So this chat ends with Mildred Day, national treasure!

M: "Krispy" perfection.

....

Matt and Renato wish everyone a calendar full of endless happy holidays and sweet occasions. If you see Renato, please do not reference the Pat Benatar/Halloween incident. It still stings.

....

AUGUST

AUG 3 | MARTHA STEWART'S BIRTHDAY
EVERYONE'S FAVORITE BIRTHDAY CAKE 156

AUG 15 | JULIA CHILD'S BIRTHDAY
SALTED CARAMEL SOUFFLÉ 158

AUG 15 | FERRAGOSTO
BRIOCHE ICE CREAM SANDWICHES 161

MONTH FLUCTUATES | BLUEBERRY MONTH
NONNIE'S BLUEBERRY BUCKLE 165

AUG 26 | NATIONAL DOG DAY
CHOCOLATE CHIP HUSH PUPPIES 168

EVERYONE'S FAVORITE BIRTHDAY CAKE

SOUR CREAM CAKE WITH CHOCOLATE CREAM CHEESE FROSTING

YIELD: 1 8-INCH (20-CM) TWO-LAYER CAKE • 10 TO 12 SERVINGS

IN THE FALL OF 2006, when Baked was still in its infancy, we appeared alongside Martha Stewart on her show and made our Sweet and Salty Cake (the recipe is in our first cookbook, *Baked: New Frontiers in Baking*). If you watch the video closely enough, you can pick up hints of my delirium. My smile is big and endless, borderline manic. My eyes lack focus. And, for some unbearable reason, I keep giving the thumbs-up signal to the camera. I was nervous. I had idolized Martha long before appearing on her show (I even tried to get a job working for her upon first moving to New York City), and it was a surreal moment to be baking alongside her. It was like meeting the president (any of them) or Mick Jagger or Carol Burnett. Thankfully, Martha was a trouper. She was as kind as anyone I have met on or off camera. She is a believer in and supporter of the entrepreneurial spirit, and she was DIY before there was a DIY movement. Oh, and she's smart—brutally intelligent—and incredibly kitchen savvy.

I made a version of this cake on Martha's 2011 birthday episode. It is actually a riff on one of our most popular single-layer snack cakes, but it works almost better in multilayer form. At Baked, we rarely make yellow cakes, but this one bakes up golden and elegant and with an adult sensibility, probably attributable to the hint of cinnamon. Our frosting is a bit unusual—the tang of the cream cheese shines through the chocolate—but we wouldn't dress this cake any other way. This is one of our go-to birthday cakes. It is quick and easy to put together, and we insist you make it for someone soon.

●●● BAKED NOTE

In a pinch, you can replace the sour cream in this recipe with 1½ cups (345 g) thick Greek yogurt or crème fraîche with barely noticeable results. Alas, if you don't have any Greek yogurt or crème fraîche, you can replace the sour cream with 1¼ cups (300 ml) buttermilk plus 2 ounces (½ stick/55 g) melted and cooled unsalted butter—the cake will be slightly more tender. If you don't have any of these ingredients, you need to make another trip to the grocery store and stock up.

INGREDIENTS

For the Sour Cream Cake

2½ cups plus 2 tablespoons (330 g) cake flour

1 scant tablespoon baking powder

1½ teaspoons kosher salt

½ teaspoon ground cinnamon

7 ounces (1¾ sticks/200 g) unsalted butter, softened, cut into ½-inch (12-mm) pieces, plus more for the pans

1 cup (200 g) granulated sugar

¾ cup (165 g) firmly packed light brown sugar

4 large eggs

1½ cups (345 g) sour cream

For the Chocolate Cream Cheese Frosting

4 ounces (1 stick/115 g) unsalted butter, softened

1 (8-ounce/226-g) package cream cheese, softened

3 to 3½ cups (340 to 395 g) confectioners' sugar, sifted

¼ teaspoon kosher salt

3 ounces (85 g) dark chocolate, melted and cooled

For Décor

Candles (of course)

MAKE THE SOUR CREAM CAKE

1 Preheat the oven to 350°F (175°C). Butter two 8-inch (20-cm) round cake pans, line them with parchment paper, and butter the parchment. Dust with flour and knock out the excess.

2 In a large bowl, sift together the flour, baking powder, salt, and cinnamon; set aside.

3 In the bowl of a standing mixer fitted with the paddle attachment, beat the butter and both sugars on medium speed until light and fluffy, about 2 minutes. Add the eggs one at a time, and beat until just incorporated, scraping down the sides of the bowl as necessary. Reduce the speed to low; add the flour mixture in three additions, beginning and ending with the flour mixture, alternating with the sour cream, and scraping down the sides of the bowl as necessary.

4 Pour the batter into the prepared pans and bake, rotating the pans halfway through, until a toothpick inserted into the center comes out clean, 35 to 40 minutes. Set the pans on a wire rack to cool for at least 20 minutes before loosening the sides of the cakes from the pans with a small knife and inverting them onto a wire rack. Remove the parchment paper and turn the cakes right side up; let them cool completely.

MAKE THE CHOCOLATE CREAM CHEESE FROSTING

1 Beat the butter in the bowl of a standing mixer fitted with the paddle attachment until smooth. Add the cream cheese and beat until well combined. Add only 3 cups (340 g) confectioners' sugar and the salt; beat until smooth. Add the chocolate and mix until well combined. If the frosting seems too loose, add additional confectioners' sugar, 1 tablespoon at a time, until it becomes thicker. Do not overbeat. The frosting can be made up to 24 hours in advance and stored in an airtight container in the refrigerator; let it soften at room temperature before using.

2 Place one cooled cake layer on a serving platter. If necessary, trim the top to create a flat surface. Spread about ¾ cup (200 g) of frosting on top. Add the top layer and trim if you want (some people prefer a domed cake top). Spread a very thin layer of frosting over the sides and top of the cake (called a crumb coat, this helps to keep loose cake crumbs under control when you frost the outside of the cake), and place it in the refrigerator for 10 minutes to firm up. Spread the sides and top of the cake with the remaining frosting. Refrigerate for another 10 minutes to set before serving.

HOW TO STORE

This cake will keep beautifully in a cake saver in the refrigerator for up to 3 days. Allow to come to room temperature before serving.

SALTED CARAMEL SOUFFLÉ

YIELD: 8 DECADENT SERVINGS

IN JUNE 2007 I rented (with family and friends) a small villa in the South of France just outside the perfectly picturesque town of Paradou. And in a way, I never left. In my mind's eye, I go back there often. Without warning, I am instantly in Paradou again. I am walking to town for warm baguettes and *pain au chocolat*. The bakery is thumbprint size and smells of butter. I am speaking halting (embarrassing) French with the pleasant town butcher. I am drinking magical wines on the magical grounds, with fig trees nearly smack up against a long, rectangular, insanely blue pool. And our entire group is reading the posthumously published autobiography of Julia Child, *My Life in France*, because it is a book about possibilities. For us, our little assembled vacationing group, Julia was not only the master of *sole meunière*; she was also about second chances and midlife career changes. After all, she didn't become Julia Child, chef and personality, until near her fiftieth birthday. Anything is possible.

When we think of Julia Child, rightly or wrongly, we think of soufflés (and Queen of Sheba cake—who can ever not think of the Queen of Sheba cake?). Soufflés are fluffy, and impressive, and decidedly French. Decidedly Julia. Our Salted Caramel Soufflé is a great way to celebrate Julia's birthday, and it is (if we do say so ourselves) a lot of fun to make. True, salted caramel is about as ubiquitous these days as water, but it is put to good use here. The soufflé is neither overly sweet nor overly salty, and the entire effect is one of subtle but sexy flavor; the telltale signs of sugar and smoke linger pleasantly. Happy birthday, Julia.

●●● BAKED NOTE

Two important soufflé tips: First, make sure your eggs are really room temperature. We can't stress this enough. Avoid the temptation to hurry things along and use almost–room temperature eggs. Room-temperature egg whites whip up much more easily and provide more volume. Second, when we say fold, we really mean fold. Don't cheat and stir the egg whites into the caramel mixture—gently fold them. Slow and steady wins the race.

INGREDIENTS

1½ cups (300 g) granulated
   sugar, plus more for the
   soufflé dish
1 tablespoon light corn
   syrup
½ cup (120 ml) heavy cream,
   at room temperature
2 teaspoons fleur de sel
1 cup (240 ml) whole milk
5 large egg yolks, at room
   temperature
3 tablespoons all-purpose
   flour
1 tablespoon cornstarch
6 large egg whites, at room
   temperature
¾ teaspoon cream of tartar
½ teaspoon kosher salt
Unsweetened whipped cream
   (optional)

1 Preheat the oven to 400°F (205°C) and position a rack in the lower third of the oven. Lightly butter the bottom and sides of a 2-quart (2-L) soufflé dish. Dust the soufflé dish with sugar (so that it adheres to the butter) and knock out the excess.

2 In a large saucepan with high sides, combine 1 cup (200 g) sugar, ¼ cup (60 ml) water, and the corn syrup. Stir the mixture gently so you don't splash any of it up the sides of the pan. Turn the heat to medium-high and continue stirring until the sugar dissolves. Increase the heat to high, stop stirring, clip on a candy thermometer (making sure the bulb is immersed in the sugar but not touching the pan), and allow the mixture to boil. Once it begins to turn a rich, dark caramel color and the thermometer reads 345°F (175°C), 5 to 8 minutes (don't worry if it takes longer, the actual time is reliant on so many factors), remove it from the heat; do not overcook. Gently and slowly stream in the heavy cream (it will bubble up, so be careful). Stir in the fleur de sel. Return the mixture to medium-low heat; don't worry if the caramel mixture begins to harden—it will easily melt again as it reheats. Add the milk and stir to combine. Reduce the heat to low. Leave the mixture on the heat while you prep the egg yolks.

3 In a large bowl, whisk together the egg yolks and ¼ cup (50 g) sugar. Sprinkle the mixture with the flour, then the cornstarch, and whisk until completely combined. Pour one-third of the caramel mixture into the egg mixture, whisking the egg mixture constantly. Slowly stream in the rest of the caramel while whisking constantly until combined. Set the bowl aside.

4 In the bowl of a standing mixer fitted with the whisk attachment (or using a whisk and bowl and a ready arm), whisk the egg whites on high speed for 1 minute. Sprinkle the cream of tartar and salt over the whites and continue whisking on high speed until the egg whites form soft peaks. Slowly stream in the remaining ¼ cup (50 g) sugar, and continue beating until stiff (but not dry) peaks form. Using a rubber spatula, gently fold one-quarter of the stiff egg-white mixture into the caramel mixture until almost combined. The caramel mixture will begin to lighten. Fold another quarter of the egg-white mixture into the caramel mixture until nearly combined. Finally, add the remaining egg-white mixture to the caramel mixture and fold gently until completely combined.

5 Transfer the soufflé batter to the prepared dish. For an even rise, run your thumb around the inside edge of the dish to wipe away any stray batter. Place the soufflé in the oven, and immediately reduce the oven temperature to 375°F (190°C). Avoid opening the oven door during the recommended baking time. Bake until the soufflé is puffy and dry to the touch, and the center is just about set but slightly jiggly (that is, slightly jiggly, not crazy ripply), 22 to 30 minutes.

6 Transfer the hot soufflé dish to a serving platter and serve immediately as is or with unsweetened whipped cream, if you like.

BRIOCHE ICE CREAM SANDWICHES

YIELD: 12 ICE CREAM SANDWICHES

FERRAGOSTO, AKA ASSUMPTION DAY, occurs every year on August 15 in Italy. It is a day of feasts, parades, family, and fireworks. More important, Ferragosto is often recognized as the unofficial kickoff to the country's vacation period. This is when Italians close up shop (tourists be forewarned) and head to the coasts. Renato lived in Italy—Sicily, to be precise—on and off during his youth. He ate a lot during this time. After all, it was Italy. It was far, culturally and literally, from the creeping influence of Wonder Bread and Egg McMuffins. Sicily was, for Renato at least, about Ferragosto, Nutella slathered on warm freshly baked bread, and giant cone-shaped *arancini*. It was also about almond granita stuffed in brioche. August in Sicily is hot. Granita is cool. It makes a lot of sense.

We already covered Renato's love of almond granita in our very first cookbook, but we neglected the brioche part. Homemade brioche is usually a little bit of a headache (see sidebar, page 164). It is also about the smell of warm butter wafting through your house, but it is, well, a bear. Then, we stumbled upon a Michael Ruhlman recipe, a recipe for brioche that he wrote for his eleven-year-old daughter. If she could make her own brioche on a regular basis, so could we. Unlike most recipes, his called for only one bowl and just a few steps. He removed several extraneous efforts (the kind that made making brioche slightly a drag). We only adapted it slightly. We prefer using instant yeast (we hate those little packets). And we reduced the butter a tiny bit, but otherwise the spirit of the simple, easy-enough-for-an-eleven-year-old-to-make brioche is still intact. And, it is dreamy. The smell it produces during the bake is reason alone to make this recipe before guests arrive.

People love our brioche ice cream sandwiches. They are different yet achingly familiar to the American palate—soft bread cradling cool, firm ice cream—and we recommend you dress them up on occasion. Toast the bread. Roll the sandwiches in nuts. Drizzle them with chocolate.

●●● **BAKED NOTE**

This recipe makes 12 individual brioche buns. That may seem like a lot, but we go through them fast: Sometimes we eat one or two immediately from the oven (how can you not?), turn a handful into ice cream sandwiches, and save the rest for bread pudding. You can also bake this brioche as a loaf, by using a 9-by-5-inch (23-by-12-cm) loaf pan instead of a 12-cup muffin tin.

INGREDIENTS

For the Brioche

1¾ teaspoons instant yeast

2¾ cups (385 g) bread flour

¼ cup (60 ml) whole milk, at room temperature

3 tablespoons granulated sugar

¼ teaspoon kosher salt

4 large eggs, at room temperature

10 ounces (2½ sticks/285 g) unsalted butter, softened, cut into 2-tablespoon-size pieces, plus more for the pan

For the Assembly

1 recipe Brown Sugar Praline Ice Cream (see page 59), or 2 to 3 pints (946 ml to 1.4 L) of your favorite ice cream or gelato

MAKE THE BRIOCHE

1 In the bowl of a standing mixer fitted with the paddle attachment, stir together the yeast with ½ cup (70 grams) of the bread flour. Add the milk, and mix on low speed until combined. Turn off the mixer, cover the mixing bowl with plastic wrap, and set aside for 45 to 60 minutes so the mixture can ferment.

2 In a medium bowl, whisk together the sugar and salt with the remaining bread flour.

3 Replace the paddle attachment with the dough hook. Add the flour mixture and eggs to the bowl. Mix on low the speed for 1 minute, then increase the speed to medium-high. Mix until a dough forms and begins to pull cleanly from the sides and bottom of the bowl, 8 to 10 minutes. At this point, the dough will have a nice sheen and look very elastic.

4 With the mixer running on medium-high, slowly add the butter, one chunk at a time, waiting for each addition to incorporate before adding the next piece. After all the butter has been added, keep mixing until the dough is smooth and uniform. This whole process should take anywhere from 7 to 10 minutes. Remove the dough hook, use your hands to scrape any dough on the hook back into the bowl, cover the bowl lightly with plastic, and place it in a draft-free environment until the dough doubles in volume, between 1 hour and 1 hour 30 minutes. While the dough is rising, butter a standard 12-cup muffin tin.

5 Use a dough scraper to scrape the light, silky dough onto a lightly floured surface. Knead the dough by hand for about a minute, folding it in half and then over itself. Divide the dough into 12 equal portions (use a scale if you have one), about 2½ ounces (70 g) each. Form each piece into a ball by rolling it on the counter between your thumb and fingers; don't incorporate too much flour, as the dough should retain a little bit of stickiness. Place each ball in a greased muffin cup. The dough might pop over the top of the tin by about ½ inch (12 mm) or so. Cover the muffin pan lightly with plastic wrap and refrigerate it for at least 8 hours (or overnight).

6 Prior to baking, remove the dough from the refrigerator and let it sit at room temperature for at least 90 minutes, but no more than 2 hours. At this point, the dough may have risen a full inch (2.5 cm) over the top of the tin. During the last 30 minutes of the rise, preheat the oven to 375°F (190°C).

7 Bake the brioches until the crust is golden and the bread is cooked all the way through, 12 to 18 minutes; the internal temperature should hover near 195°F (90°C) on an instant-read thermometer. If the crusts brown too quickly before the center of the bread is ready, cover the tops of the bread with foil until finished baking.

8 Allow the bread to cool for a few minutes and pop the individual brioches out of the pan.

ASSEMBLE THE ICE CREAM SANDWICHES

1 Slice each brioche in half (slightly warm is divine, though room temperature is fine), separating the "muffin top" from the bottom. Place one generous scoop, about ¾ cup (180 ml), of ice cream on the flat surface of the bottom of the muffin and sandwich it with the top. Serve immediately. We have also been known to toast the brioche before filling it; this is a must-try at least once in your life.

HOW TO STORE

If you want to make the sandwiches ahead to serve later, it is better to freeze the components individually rather than in sandwich form. Wrap the completely cooled brioches in foil and freeze until ready to use. Bring the brioches back to room temperature before filling with ice cream.

THE TRUTH ABOUT BRIOCHE

You can mess this recipe up and still get a decent-quality bread, but there are a few things you should know about brioche before starting:

- During the 8-to-10-minute mixing period, you really want the dough to come together in one elastic mass. It should be flying off the sides and bottom of the bowl in one big lump.

- The butter does not always behave. Often, when throwing chunk after chunk of butter into the dough as it mixes, a piece of butter will start climbing the mixing bowl. Go ahead and stop the bowl, push it back down into the dough, and resume mixing.

- You don't want to overproof the dough during the rising period. It should double in volume, not triple. Check on it every 30 minutes or so just to be sure.

- Now there is no way around this: Brioche is hell on your mixer. My mixer has handled it fine, over and over again, but the dough does make it strain and it does, on occasion, make the mixer jump. This is just par for the course. My KitchenAid has survived thus far. And I am fairly certain it has many more lives left.

- Last, we don't egg-wash our brioche, but we know a lot of people are obsessed with the final egg wash. If you want to use an egg wash, whisk 1 large egg with 1 teaspoon of water until well beaten. Brush the top of each brioche with a little bit of the egg wash.

NONNIE'S BLUEBERRY BUCKLE

YIELD: 1 TUBE CAKE • 12 GENEROUS SERVINGS

WE LOVE BLUEBERRIES, and we are pleased someone (in this case the North American Blueberry Council) thought well enough of them to give them not just an entire month, but two. Accordingly, America celebrates the month in July and Canada celebrates it in August. Though we classified this recipe as one for August, if you plan correctly and live in North America, you can *officially* embrace all of your blueberry dreams for most of the summer.

Blueberry buckle is really just blueberry cake dressed up with a fancy, alliterative naming device. We are okay with that. We will still eat buckets of blueberry buckle or cake or ring (so-called because of the shape) or whatever you want to call this dessert as long as the blueberries are fresh and the days are summery. This is one of those Nonnie (aka Grandma) desserts. It is the kind of recipe you might see in a church cookbook, and the kind of dessert you might taste at a local farmers' market. Needless to say, at the prodding of a great Baked friend, we made this delicious blueberry buckle, and we loved it. We fell hard. The texture is mostly cakey, a little loafy, chock-full of blueberries (four cups!), and topped with a lovely contrasting crumb. It is as if this buckle were crafted especially for lazy mornings and dark coffee.

●●● BAKED NOTE
This is one of those cakes that tastes better 12 to 24 hours after baking; however, we have never received a complaint from someone eating it warm from the oven.

INGREDIENTS

For the Blueberry Cake

1½ cups (170 g) all-purpose
    flour
1½ cups (170 g) cake flour
2   teaspoons baking powder
¾   teaspoon kosher salt
¾   teaspoon ground ginger
¼   teaspoon baking soda
1   cup plus 2 tablespoons
    (225 g) granulated sugar
¼   cup plus 2 tablespoons
    (90 ml) canola oil
2   ounces (½ stick/55 g)
    unsalted butter, softened
1   large egg
1   large egg yolk
2   teaspoons pure vanilla
    extract
Zest of 1 lemon (about
    1 tablespoon)
¼   cup (60 ml) heavy cream
½   cup (115 g) sour cream
4   cups (14 ounces/395 g)
    fresh blueberries

For the Cinnamon Topping

¾   cup (165 g) firmly packed
    dark brown sugar
⅓   cup (40 g) all-purpose
    flour
⅓   cup (40 g) cake flour
¾   teaspoon ground cinnamon
3   ounces (¾ stick/85 g)
    unsalted butter, melted
    and cooled slightly

MAKE THE BLUEBERRY CAKE

1 Preheat the oven to 375°F (190°C). Generously spray the inside of a 10-cup (2.4-L) tube pan with a removable bottom with nonstick cooking spray; alternatively, butter it thoroughly, dust it with flour, and knock out the excess flour. (You can make this cake in a tube pan without a removable bottom or a 12-cup Bundt pan; just make sure it is extra well greased.) If you want to ensure super-simple removal, you can cut out a ring of parchment paper to fit into the bottom of the pan.

2 In a large bowl, whisk together both flours, the baking powder, salt, ginger, and baking soda. Set aside.

3 In the bowl of a standing mixer fitted with the paddle attachment, beat the sugar, oil, and butter on medium speed until light and fluffy, 3 to 4 minutes. Add the egg and egg yolk and beat until incorporated. Scrape down the sides and bottom of the bowl, add the vanilla and lemon zest, and beat again for 10 seconds.

4 Measure out the cream into a glass measuring cup. Add the sour cream and whisk until combined. Add the flour mixture to the sugar mixture in the standing mixer in three parts, alternating with the cream mixture, beginning and ending with the flour mixture; beat at medium speed after each addition until incorporated, 10 to 15 seconds.

5 Using a rubber spatula, fold the blueberries into the batter, which will be very thick, and transfer the batter to the prepared pan. Smooth the top with an offset spatula and prepare the topping.

MAKE THE CINNAMON TOPPING

1 In a large bowl, whisk together the brown sugar, both flours, and cinnamon (do not worry if large pieces of the sugar remain). Drizzle the butter over the mixture and use your very clean hands to pick up the mixture, squeeze it in your fist, and let the mixture fall back into the bowl, repeating until the topping comes together.

2 Pinch off chunks of the topping and drop them over the top of the buckle batter. Use all of the topping and cover the batter completely.

3 Bake the cake until a toothpick inserted in the center of the cake comes out with a few moist crumbs, 50 to 60 minutes. Set the pan on a wire rack to cool for at least 20 minutes. Loosen the cake from the sides of the pan with a paring knife, then push the bottom of the pan up to release the cake. Use the knife to loosen and remove the cake from the bottom of the pan, then cool completely, topping side up, on a cooling rack.

HOW TO STORE

The cake can be stored, tightly covered, at room temperature for up to 3 days.

CHOCOLATE CHIP HUSH PUPPIES

YIELD: 24 TO 30 HUSH PUPPIES

ONE OF RENATO'S GREAT JOYS IN LIFE is his Chihuahua, Tina. I wish I could tell you that Renato and Tina are swimming around in all manner of imaginable gay man/small dog stereotypes. It would be much more fun. But, alas, Renato does not dress Tina up in Wonder Woman outfits. He does not push her around in a carriage, or truck her around town in a baby sling or murse (aka man purse). Sadly, the story of Renato and Tina is much less camp than that. It is the age-old tale of man's best friend, of loyalty and devotion. Quite simply, it is the story of always having a best friend to greet you at the door at the end of a long workday. The fact that Tina is adorable and tiny just means she is more suited to urban dwellings and nothing more. And because of Tina, Renato celebrates National Dog Day every day.

Sweet Chocolate Chip Hush Puppies seemed like the perfect snack for National Dog Day, if only because so few other desserts have the word *puppy* in their name. Forgive us this terrible pun, because these hush puppies are so damn good. They are hot, crispy little nostalgic bites best served in the deep dog days (another terrible pun) of summer. The exterior is crackly, tasty cornmeal, and the interior gives way to a soft, dreamy texture with a few chocolate chips thrown in for good measure.

●●● **BAKED NOTE**

Three important things: (1) Don't scoop your puppies too large (i.e., larger than the recipe suggests) or the outside will burn before the interior is cooked, (2) hot fritters right out of the pan are best, and they deteriorate quickly after being fried, and (3) if you prefer not to fry, see the last step of the directions for an alternative.

INGREDIENTS

¾ cup (150 g) granulated
    sugar
1   tablespoon ground
    cinnamon
1½ cups (115 g) pastry flour
1½ cups (210 g) fine- to
    medium-grain cornmeal
1   cup (220 g) firmly packed
    light brown sugar
2   teaspoons baking powder
¾ teaspoon kosher salt
¼ teaspoon baking soda
3   ounces (85 g) chocolate
    chips (about ½ cup)
1   large egg
1   large egg yolk
1   cup (230 g) sour cream
2   tablespoons unsalted
    butter, melted and cooled
1   tablespoon pure maple
    syrup, plus more for serving
    (optional)
2   teaspoons pure vanilla
    extract
Vegetable oil for frying

1   In a small shallow bowl, stir together the granulated sugar and cinnamon. Set aside.

2   In a large bowl, whisk the flour, cornmeal, brown sugar, baking powder, salt, and baking soda together, using your hands to rub most of the chunks of brown sugar into the flour mixture. Stir in the chocolate chips.

3   In another large bowl, whisk together the egg, egg yolk, sour cream, butter, maple syrup, and vanilla.

4   Make a well in the dry ingredients and pour the wet ingredients into the well. Using very clean hands, bring the ingredients together by pulling the dry ingredients from the sides into the wet ingredients in the middle and kneading gently until just combined; do not overmix.

5   Pour 1 to 1½ inches (2.5 to 4 cm) of oil into a deep skillet or large pot (if you need to fill the pan more than halfway, choose a larger pan). Slowly heat the oil over medium-high heat until it registers 350°F (175°C) on a deep-fry thermometer. Line a plate with a double layer of paper towels and set it near your work area.

6   Using a small ice-cream scoop with a release mechanism, scoop no more than 1 tablespoon of dough and release it into the hot oil (alternatively, you can use a spoon). Add a few more to the oil, but do not crowd the pot. Cook until the fritters have browned on one side, about 2 minutes. Using a slotted spoon or tongs, turn them over and continue to cook until browned, another minute; do not overcook. Use a slotted spoon to transfer the fritters to the prepared plate. Continue with the rest of the dough. Allow the fritters to dry for about 5 minutes. Working quickly, roll the hot fritters in the cinnamon-sugar mixture until coated. Serve immediately, with a side of maple syrup for dipping, if you like—they are dangerously good that way. (Alternatively, if you prefer not to fry, spoon the batter into greased muffin tins, filling each three-quarters full, sprinkle the tops with cinnamon-sugar, and bake at 350°F/175°C for 13 to 15 minutes.)

HOW TO STORE

Hot fritters are best right out of the pan, as they deteriorate in quality quickly after being fried; 2 or 3 hours is pushing it, but not unheard of.

SEPTEMBER

●●●

1ST SUN AFTER LABOR DAY | NATIONAL GRANDPARENTS' DAY

FROZEN SWISS CHOCOLATE PIE 172

DATE FLUCTUATES | ROSH HASHANAH

ORANGE PANCAKES WITH HONEY BUTTER 175

DATE FLUCTUATES | FIRST DAY OF SCHOOL

MINI CHOCOLATE BROWNIE CUPCAKES 178

SEP 24 | MILDRED DAY'S BIRTHDAY

CHOCOLATE RICE CRISPY "CAKE" WITH HOMEMADE MARSHMALLOW "ICING" 181

FROZEN SWISS CHOCOLATE PIE

YIELD: 1 9-INCH (23-CM) PIE • 10 TO 12 SERVINGS

I AM REMARKABLY FORTUNATE. Not only did all four of my grandparents survive until my late thirties (here's hoping for good genes), they thrived; they embraced life into their golden years and well beyond. They traveled, gambled, swam, hiked, cooked, baked, and read mountains of books. They were, across the board, very active, and they were very much a part of my life. I don't ever remember specifically celebrating Grandparents' Day; I was vaguely aware of the holiday, but it seemed superfluous. Every moment I spent with either set of grandparents felt holiday-ish— every moment was celebratory. Grandma Boreali always made ricotta cavatelli and a cheesecake very nearly the size of Omaha. Grandma Lewis always made cocktails (usually screwdrivers) and heirloom shortbread. Every day I spent with my grandparents was National Grandparents' Day.

I have a thick volume of recipes, copied from aging, handwritten notecards, from each grandmother. So I couldn't choose just one recipe to represent National Grandparents' Day; I wanted to include them all. I was stuck. Thankfully, Jessie Sheehan (great friend and avid recipe developer) freed me with this amazing Frozen Swiss Chocolate Pie recipe. It is directly from her husband's mom (aka Nonnie, aka Grandma) and emblematic of all the things a family-heritage recipe should be: simple, delicious, and accessible (meaning every ingredient can be found at the corner store). The pie is dreamy, with the texture and taste of a rich Fudgsicle, and it's practically made for early September's temperate weather. And remember: Visit your grandparents frequently. Grandparents' Day deserves to occur at least four or five times per year.

●●● **BAKED NOTE**

If you want to go over the top—and, really, we should all go over the top once in a while—serve this pie with hot fudge (see page 250) and more whipped cream. This recipe includes uncooked egg whites, so please exercise caution.

INGREDIENTS

For the Walnut Crust

2 cups (200 g) walnuts, toasted (see page 19)

½ cup (100 g) granulated sugar

3 ounces (¾ stick/85 g) unsalted butter, melted and cooled

For the Frozen Swiss Chocolate Filling

12 ounces (340 g) good-quality dark chocolate (60 to 72% cacao), coarsely chopped

1½ teaspoons instant espresso powder

1 (8-ounce/226-g) package cream cheese, softened

½ cup (100 g) sugar

1 teaspoon pure vanilla extract

2 cups plus 3 tablespoons (525 ml) heavy cream

2 large egg whites

¼ cup (60 ml) whiskey

¼ cup (25 g) walnut pieces, toasted (see page 19) and coarsely chopped

MAKE THE WALNUT CRUST

1 Lightly spray a 9-inch (23-cm; preferably deep dish) pie plate with nonstick cooking spray.

2 In a food processor, process the walnuts until they are finely chopped (do not pulverize); you should have about 1½ cups (200 g). Place them in a bowl, add the sugar, and stir until combined. Pour the melted butter over the walnut mixture, mix well, transfer to the prepared pie plate, and press it into the bottom and up the sides; use the back of a large metal measuring cup to get an even crust. If you are having trouble getting it to adhere to the sides, first refrigerate the crust for 5 to 7 minutes. Refrigerate the crust while you make the filling.

MAKE THE FROZEN SWISS CHOCOLATE FILLING

1 Place the chocolate in a large heatproof bowl and set it over a saucepan of simmering water (double-boiler method, see page 19). Heat the chocolate, stirring occasionally, until it is 80 percent melted. Sprinkle the espresso powder over the chocolate and stir until it is incorporated and the chocolate is just fully melted. Remove the top of the double boiler from the heat and continue to stir the chocolate mixture for another minute to release excess heat. Set aside to cool to room temperature.

2 In the bowl of a standing mixer fitted with the paddle attachment, beat the cream cheese, ¼ cup (50 g) of the sugar, the vanilla, and 3 tablespoons of the cream on medium speed until the mixture is combined, 1 to 2 minutes. Add the cooled chocolate mixture and beat again until just combined. Scrape down the sides and bottom of the bowl and beat again for 10 seconds.

3 Place the egg whites and the remaining ¼ cup (50 g) sugar in a clean, heatproof medium bowl and set it over the saucepan of simmering water you used for the chocolate. Gently whisk the whites and sugar until warm to the touch; remove the pan from the heat. Using a handheld whisk or the whisk attachment on the standing mixer, whisk the mixture just until stiff peaks form. Using a rubber spatula, fold the egg whites into the chocolate mixture and set aside.

4 In the bowl of the standing mixer fitted with the whisk attachment, whisk the remaining 2 cups (480 ml) cream until soft peaks form. Turn the mixer to low and drizzle in the whiskey, then increase the mixer speed to medium and continue beating until stiff peaks form. Using a rubber spatula, fold the whipped cream into the filling until just combined, then pour the filling into the crust. Smooth the top with an offset spatula and sprinkle with the walnuts. Cover gently with foil and place the pie in the freezer until frozen, about 4 hours.

5 Before serving, place the pie in the refrigerator for 2 hours or at room temperature for 20 minutes. Dip a large knife in hot water, dry it off, and use the hot knife to slice and serve.

HOW TO STORE

Leftover pie, covered with foil (tented with toothpicks), can be frozen for up to 1 week.

ORANGE PANCAKES WITH HONEY BUTTER

YIELD: 10 TO 12 (6-INCH / 15-CM) PANCAKES

THIS BOOK IS FULL OF VARIOUS New Year celebrations for good reason. We believe in the cleansing power of beginning anew, of closing chapters and starting new ones. That we have co-opted two New Year celebrations that were not part of our backgrounds, but occasionally part of our upbringings—Chinese New Year and Rosh Hashanah (aka Jewish New Year)—only speaks to our (mild) obsession with starting over.

As (almost) lifelong New Yorkers, we both have absorbed many customs from our Jewish pals. But perhaps their biggest influence is their gusto for celebration and food. In other words, our Jewish friends know how to throw a party. Our Italian Catholic upbringings were similarly imbued with bounteous tables of gorgeous food, but the party aspect was dialed down a bit overall. The Jewish celebrations we have attended define merriment and break records for highest decibel levels.

While we have tried to replicate a few typical Jewish delicacies in the past (the pumpkin kugel was nixed from our previous book with good reason), we thought we would nod toward the Jewish New Year with a foodstuff we are intimate with: pancakes. The batter for these pancakes is really thick. Really stout. It creates a serious, puffy, and crispy orange-scented pancake. While we know the impulse will be to soak them in syrup (and we wouldn't stop you), we encourage you to let the orange flavor shine by eating them sans syrup. Instead, layer them with a schmear of our simple honey butter, and you will begin to feel transformed. The New Year awaits.

●●● **BAKED NOTE**

We are not scientists, but we have formulated a pancake hypothesis while making (and eating) many, many pancakes. Pancakes are generally best when eaten within minutes of being cooked. Though we provide instructions for keeping them warm while making them in batches, this is much too formal for us. We prefer to cook and serve as we go.

INGREDIENTS

For the Honey Butter

8   ounces (225 g) unsalted high-fat/European-style (cultured) unsalted butter, softened, cut into cubes
3   tablespoons clover honey

For the Orange Pancakes

2   cups (255 g) all-purpose flour
1   teaspoon baking powder
1   teaspoon baking soda
¾   teaspoon kosher salt
1   cup (240 ml) freshly squeezed orange juice
1   cup (230 g) plain full-fat Greek yogurt, strained
½   cup (120 ml) well-shaken buttermilk
4   ounces (1 stick/115 g) plus 2 tablespoons unsalted butter, melted and cooled
2   large eggs
2   tablespoons (25 g) granulated sugar
Zest of 2 oranges (about 3 tablespoons)

MAKE THE HONEY BUTTER

1   In the bowl of a standing mixer fitted with the paddle attachment, beat the butter and honey on medium speed until smooth and creamy, about 4 minutes. Scrape the honey butter into a ramekin to use immediately with the pancakes. Leftover honey butter should be covered and refrigerated for up to 1 week.

MAKE THE ORANGE PANCAKES

1   Preheat the oven to 200°F (90°C), if you plan to make all of the pancakes before serving them.
2   In a large bowl, whisk together the flour, baking powder, baking soda, and salt.
3   In a separate bowl, whisk together the orange juice, yogurt, buttermilk, 4 ounces (115 g) of the butter, the eggs, sugar, and orange zest.
4   Make a well in the dry ingredients, pour the wet ingredients into the well, and stir together until just combined.
5   Heat a large skillet over medium heat. Brush the pan with some of the remaining 2 tablespoons of melted butter. Add ⅓ cup (75 ml) batter to the pan per pancake, cooking until bubbles form on the tops and the pancakes are browned on the bottom. Flip and continue cooking them until they are completely browned on both sides, another minute or so. Continue buttering the pan and making pancakes until all the batter is used.
6   Serve immediately as the pancakes are made, or keep them in the oven on a heatproof plate just until you've cooked them all (don't leave them in the oven longer). Serve with copious amounts of honey butter.

MINI CHOCOLATE BROWNIE CUPCAKES

YIELD: 48 MINI CUPCAKES

MY MOM, VERY VOCALLY and very enthusiastically, always celebrated the first day of my brother's and my return to school. In fact, she counted the days on the calendar, giddy but guilty, a color creeping into her cheeks as each giant X brought us one day closer to the beginning of the school year. For her, as for millions of other moms (and dads) around the country, the date signified a return to sanity, a brief but needed tranquility. The endless suburban shuttle—of kids to malls, of kids to other kids' houses, of kids to beaches (we lived in Florida)—would cease temporarily. Mom would finally be able to finish a chapter in her book uninterrupted.

Our Mini Chocolate Brownie Cupcakes are tailor-made for any fall celebration, but they seem especially well suited for a back-to-school event. Nutritionally minded parents (and sugar high–minded teachers alike) will appreciate the mini "pop-the-whole-thing-in-your-mouth" portions. And they transport from kitchen to classroom with ease, having no frosting to fret over. But most important, they are a scrumptious commingling of walnuts and chocolate that manage to flawlessly walk the line between rich, fudgy brownie and adorable cupcake. It is impossible to eat just one.

●●● BAKED NOTE

We are well aware that nut allergies are prevalent these days. Feel free to substitute even more chocolate chips for the walnuts in this recipe if you are baking for a nut-free crowd (or if you happen to be a chocolate addict).

INGREDIENTS

1 tablespoon unsalted butter

1½ cups (150 g) walnuts

8 ounces (225 g) good-quality dark chocolate (60 to 72% cacao), coarsely chopped, or mini dark chocolate chips

¼ cup plus 1 tablespoon (25 g) unsweetened dark cocoa powder

1½ teaspoons instant espresso powder

1 cup (240 ml) very hot water

2 cups (255 g) all-purpose flour

¾ teaspoon kosher salt

1 cup (220 g) firmly packed dark brown sugar

¾ cup (150 g) granulated sugar

¾ cup (180 ml) canola oil

2 teaspoons pure vanilla extract

1 large egg

2 large egg yolks

1 teaspoon baking soda

1 Preheat the oven to 350°F (175°C). Line two mini cupcake pans with liners. (Alternatively, use one pan and bake in batches.)

2 Place the butter in a medium bowl and set aside.

3 Spread the nuts on a rimmed baking sheet and toast until fragrant, tossing and flipping the nuts halfway through, approximately 10 minutes. Transfer the hot nuts to the bowl with the butter. Wait approximately 1 minute, then turn to coat the nuts in the butter as it melts. Let the nuts cool completely, then chop them into fine pieces. Return to the bowl. Add the chocolate and toss with the walnuts until combined.

4 In a small bowl, whisk together the unsweetened cocoa powder, espresso powder, and ½ cup (120 ml) of the very hot water. Set aside.

5 In a medium bowl, whisk together the flour and salt. Set aside.

6 In the bowl of a standing mixer fitted with the paddle attachment, beat both sugars, the canola oil, and vanilla on medium-low speed until combined. Add the egg and egg yolks and continue beating until the mixture is uniform and completely combined. Scrape down the sides and bottom of the bowl and add the flour mixture in three parts, alternating with the cocoa-powder mixture, beginning and ending with the flour mixture. Scrape down the sides and bottom of the bowl, then mix on low speed for a few more seconds.

7 Stir the baking soda into the remaining ½ cup (120 ml) hot water to dissolve. Pour the mixture into the batter and mix on low speed until incorporated. Spoon about 1 tablespoon of the batter into each of the prepared cups, then spoon about 1 tablespoon of the walnut-chocolate mixture directly over the batter. Bake, rotating the pan halfway through the baking time, until a toothpick inserted into the side of the cupcake (not the melty chocolate topping part) comes out with a few moist crumbs, 19 to 22 minutes. Do not overbake.

8 Allow the cupcakes to cool for 15 minutes in the pan on a wire rack, then turn them out onto a wire rack to cool completely. Serve at room temperature.

HOW TO STORE

The cupcakes can be stored in an airtight container at room temperature for up to 3 days.

CHOCOLATE RICE CRISPY "CAKE" WITH HOMEMADE MARSHMALLOW "ICING"

YIELD: 1 9-BY-5-INCH (23-BY-12-CM) LOAF CAKE

CHANCES ARE you are already familiar with Mildred Day's artistry. Her invention, Rice Krispies Treats (perhaps co-invented with Malitta Jensen), is ubiquitous, the lifeblood of untold children's birthday parties and a billion after-school snacks. Mildred concocted the celebrated treat (formerly known as "marshmallow squares") sometime between 1929 and 1938 (yup, the exact date is a little elusive depending on the source). A few months later, Kellogg's sent Mildred out to Kansas City to re-create the treats for a mega-successful Camp Fire Girls fund-raiser (she carried her own mixer and specially made sheet trays on the train).* A dessert monster was born. Kellogg's printed the recipe on the back of their Rice Krispies cereal box. The Rice Krispies Treat became an instant American icon, alongside the chocolate chip cookie and classic brownie, and virtually overnight, the puffed-rice cereal became more famous as an ingredient than as . . . well . . . cereal.

While we are big fans of Mildred's original recipe, we enjoy continually riffing (the Peanut Butter Crispy Bar from our first book, *Baked: New Frontiers in Baking*, is a perennial best seller), hence our tribute here to Mildred Day's birthday: the Chocolate Rice Crispy Treat Cake. The "cake" base is an über-chocolaty cocoa-crisp concoction, straightforward and delicious (and, by the way, perfectly substantial on its own, sans "icing"). And the "icing" portion is an even layer of our simple and lovely homemade marshmallow. It's kind of kitschy, but immensely delicious. My three-year-old nephew tore the marshmallow top from the cocoa-crisp base and ate each part separately, like an Oreo. I asked him which part was his favorite. He said both.

●●● **BAKED NOTE**
The "icing" in this recipe is our traditional marshmallow recipe—it yields enough to ice the "cake," be the binder for the "cake," and yield some extra for snacking. If you want to make only marshmallows, follow the Homemade Marshmallow "Icing" directions below, except pour the product into only one greased 9-by-13-inch (23-by-33-cm) pan (no need for parchment) and sprinkle confectioners' sugar over the whole thing. (This recipe will make approximately 48 marshmallows.)

* Tom Longden, "Mildred Day," *Des Moines Register.*

INGREDIENTS

For the Homemade Marshmallow "Icing"

Vegetable shortening, for greasing the pans
12   sheets gelatin
Ice cubes
1   cup (240 ml) light corn syrup
2   cups (400 g) granulated sugar
2   teaspoons pure vanilla extract
⅛   teaspoon kosher salt
½   cup (50 g) sifted confectioners' sugar, plus more for dusting

For the Chocolate Rice Crispy "Cake"

3   tablespoons unsalted butter
7½   ounces (210 g) home-made marshmallows (recipe above)
4   ounces (115 g) dark chocolate, coarsely chopped
6½   ounces (185 g) cocoa-flavored crisp rice cereal (about 4½ cups)

MAKE THE HOMEMADE MARSHMALLOW "ICING"

1   Grease the sides and bottoms of two 9-by-5-inch (23-by-12 cm) loaf pans with vegetable shortening. In one pan, line the bottom with parchment so that it comes up on the long sides and overhangs slightly. Grease the parchment. Set aside.

2   Place the gelatin sheets in a medium or large heatproof bowl, fill the bowl with very cold water, and set it aside; add a few ice cubes to keep the water cold.

3   Fill a medium saucepan halfway with water and bring it to a simmer over medium-low heat.

4   Place ½ cup (120 ml) of the corn syrup in the bowl of a standing mixer fitted with the whisk attachment. Set aside.

5   In a medium saucepan, gently stir together the granulated sugar, the remaining ½ cup (120 ml) corn syrup, and ½ cup (120 ml) water. Be careful not to splash the ingredients onto the sides of the pan. Put the saucepan over medium-high heat and clip a candy thermometer to the side of the saucepan, making sure the bulb is submerged but not touching the bottom of the pan.

6   When the temperature of the sugar mixture reaches 210°F (100°C), drain the water from the bowl of gelatin and quickly wring out the gelatin sheets. Place the gelatin back in the heatproof bowl and place the bowl over the saucepan of simmering water; stir the gelatin sheets with a heatproof spatula until the gelatin is completely melted. Turn the mixer on low speed and slowly pour the melted gelatin into the corn syrup. Keep the mixer on low.

7   Bring the sugar mixture to the soft-ball stage on the candy thermometer (234°F to 240°F / 112°C to 116°C), then remove it from the heat. Turn the standing mixer up to medium speed and beat for 1 minute. Then, still on medium speed, slowly pour the sugar mixture into the gelatin mixture. When all of the sugar mixture has been added, turn the mixer to medium-high and beat for about 5 minutes. The marshmallow mixture will begin to turn white and fluffy. Add the vanilla and salt and turn the mixer up to its highest setting for another minute.

8   Working very quickly, scoop approximately one-third of the marshmallow mixture into the parchment-lined loaf pan, and place the remaining marshmallow mixture into the other pre-pared pan. Using a lightly oiled offset spatula, spread out the mixtures evenly. Sprinkle a little bit of confectioners' sugar over the pan filled with the larger amount of marshmallow. Do not sprinkle confectioners' sugar over the pan filled with the lesser amount. Cover both pans loosely with plastic wrap (the wrap should not touch the surface of the marshmallow) and let sit at room temperature for about 4 hours or overnight.

9   Place ½ cup (50 g) confectioners' sugar in a small bowl. Lightly dust a flat surface with confectioners' sugar.

10 Using a knife, loosen the marshmallow from the edges of the pan containing the larger amount of marshmallow. Pull the giant marshmallow out of the pan and onto the dusted surface. Using a lightly oiled chef's knife, cut the marshmallow into 9 or 10 slices, then cut each slice into 1- to 1½-inch (2.5- to 4-cm) squares (feel free to cut them into larger or smaller sizes at will). Roll each marshmallow in confectioners' sugar. Weigh out and set aside 7½ ounces (210 g) of marshmallows. The remaining cut marshmallows will last for up to 1 week in an airtight container, and they make a great s'mores. Reserve the pan with the smaller amount of marshmallow.

MAKE THE CHOCOLATE RICE CRISPY "CAKE"

1 Remove the plastic wrap from the pan with the smaller amount of marshmallow.

2 In a medium saucepan over medium-low heat, melt the butter. Add the reserved 7½ ounces (210 g) marshmallows and half of the dark chocolate. Keep stirring the mixture until it is completely melted, then remove it from the heat. Add the cereal, stir for a few seconds, then add the remaining chocolate. Once it is completely incorporated, scoop out the mixture and place it on top of the marshmallow that is still in the parchment-lined pan and press the mixture into an even layer. Let the mixture set at room temperature for about 30 minutes.

3 To unmold, loosen the sides of the pan with an offset spatula and pull up on the parchment. Invert the cake onto a serving platter and remove the parchment. Slice and serve.

HOW TO STORE

Leftovers will keep, tightly covered, at room temperature for up to 5 days.

OCTOBER

● ● ●

OCT 11 | ELEANOR ROOSEVELT'S BIRTHDAY
PEANUT BUTTER AND JELLY CRUMB MORNING MUFFINS 186

2ND MON IN OCT | COLUMBUS DAY
PUMPKIN SWIRL CHEESECAKE CHOCOLATE BROWNIES 189

OCT 18 | ALASKA DAY
INDIVIDUAL BAKED ALASKAS WITH VANILLA AND COFFEE ICE CREAM 193

OCT 31 | HALLOWEEN
MILK CHOCOLATE MALTED BROWNIES WITH CHOCOLATE GANACHE 195

OCT 31 | HALLOWEEN
CHOCOLATE POP TARTS WITH PEANUT BUTTER AND JAM FILLING 199

PEANUT BUTTER AND JELLY CRUMB MORNING MUFFINS

YIELD: 12 MUFFINS

IF WE HAD TO PLAY FAVORITES with First Ladies (as of yet, no one has ever asked us to do so, but still . . .), we would probably choose Eleanor Roosevelt. In politics, she was a trailblazer. She was, arguably, the first First Lady to use her position of power to develop her own persona and agenda within the White House. She was a First Lady with an impressive lists of, well, firsts: She was the first presidential spouse to hold press conferences; to pen a regularly (and often opinionated) syndicated newspaper column, "My Day"; and to speak at the national convention. Her advocacy for civil rights was dogged (and controversial for the time), and her attention to the poor was unprecedented. That her personal life was equally intriguing just makes Eleanor all the more appealing.

The Roosevelts had "hearty, typically American food" preferences, so we made a delectable and worthy Peanut Butter and Jelly Crumb Morning Muffin to celebrate Eleanor's birthday.* After all, peanut butter and jelly practically screams "typical American food." And, supposedly, the Roosevelts loved breakfast (whatever that means). These morning muffins are peanut buttery without being oily, and the jelly provides just the right amount of bright, fruity contrast. Of course, we topped the whole thing with a heaping peanut crumb, because what isn't made better by a heaping peanut crumb? We would be pleased as punch to wake up to these on our birthday. Or Eleanor's.

●●● **BAKED NOTE**

We opt not to use liners for most muffins for purely superficial, visual reasons. We like our muffins bare. Feel free to use them, however, to aid in removing the muffins from the pan once baked. Also, while we both grew up with grape jelly—and therefore interpret most "peanut butter and jelly" combos as peanut butter and *grape* jelly combos—feel free to swap the grape jelly in the recipe with your favorite flavor of jelly or jam.

* Poppy Cannon and Patricia Brooks, *The Presidents' Cookbook: Practical Recipes from George Washington to the Present.* New York: Funk & Wagnalls, 1968.

INGREDIENTS

For the Crumb

½ cup (75 g) lightly salted peanuts, toasted (see page 19)
1 cup (130 g) all-purpose flour
⅓ cup (75 g) firmly packed dark brown sugar
½ teaspoon kosher salt
3 ounces (¾ stick/85 g) unsalted butter, melted and warm

For the Peanut Butter and Jelly Muffins

1¾ cups (225 g) all-purpose flour
½ cup (100 g) granulated sugar
½ cup (110 g) firmly packed dark brown sugar
2 teaspoons baking powder
1 teaspoon ground cinnamon
½ teaspoon baking soda
½ teaspoon kosher salt
½ cup (120 ml) whole milk
½ cup (115 g) sour cream (not low-fat)
½ cup (130 g) creamy peanut butter (natural is fine here)
⅓ cup (75 ml) canola oil
1 large egg
1 teaspoon pure vanilla extract
⅓ to ½ cup (105 to 160 g) grape jelly

MAKE THE CRUMB

1 Place the peanuts in the bowl of a small food processor and pulse until finely chopped (a few coarser crumbs won't hurt), or finely chop them by hand.

2 Transfer the chopped peanuts to a large bowl. Whisk in the flour, brown sugar, and salt. Drizzle the butter over the mixture and use a rubber spatula (or your very clean fingers) to fold and cut the ingredients together until the mixture is crumb-like. Set aside.

MAKE THE PEANUT BUTTER AND JELLY MUFFINS

1 Preheat the oven to 400°F (205°C). Lightly spray each cup of a standard 12-cup muffin pan with a little bit of nonstick cooking spray and use a paper towel to spread the oil evenly along the bottom and up the sides of each cup.

2 In a large bowl, whisk together the flour, both sugars, the baking powder, cinnamon, baking soda, and salt, breaking up any lumps of brown sugar if necessary.

3 In another large bowl, whisk together the milk, sour cream, peanut butter, oil, egg, and vanilla.

4 Make a well in the middle of the dry ingredients. Pour the wet ingredients into the well, and fold until just combined.

5 Drop about 2 tablespoons of batter into each cup of the prepared muffin pan. Use the back of a clean, lightly oiled spoon to flatten the batter out. Place 1 rounded teaspoon of grape jelly onto the muffin batter in each cup, trying to keep it in the center of the cup, if possible. Top the jelly with another 2 tablespoons of muffin batter to cover the jelly completely, using the back of a spoon to gently spread the batter into an even layer. The muffin cups should be not quite full. (You might end up with excess batter. Do not try to force it into the cups; simply make extra muffins.) Cover the surface of each muffin cup with a small handful of crumbs, pressing the mixture ever so gently so that it adheres to the top.

6 Bake, rotating halfway through the baking time, until the crumb topping turns a golden brown, 14 to 18 minutes. Check them; if a toothpick inserted into a muffin near the edge (avoiding the jelly center) should come out clean (disregarding any topping or jelly that might stick), bake them for a minute more—these muffins might sink in the middle if not baked all the way.

7 Let the muffins cool almost completely in the pan on a cooling rack. Since the crumb topping is messy, I found the easiest way to remove the muffins is to angle the muffin pan over the sink and tilt the pan until the muffins almost fall out. Grab each muffin and set it on the cooling rack until completely cool.

HOW TO STORE

Serve the muffins within 24 hours. These muffins freeze well: Just wrap them in a few layers of plastic wrap to fend off frost.

PUMPKIN SWIRL CHEESECAKE CHOCOLATE BROWNIES

YIELD: 24 BROWNIES

THERE ARE NOT, to the best of our knowledge, strictly regimented and traditional menus for Columbus Day. It is not Thanksgiving. Though one could skew toward Italian delicacies in a nod to Christopher's heritage, one could also skew iconic American (hamburgers, fried chicken, apple pie) in homage to Columbus arriving *in the Americas.* We chose an entirely different route. We went with pumpkin cheesecake brownies, because Christopher Columbus Day is in October (to celebrate the anniversary of his arrival in America in 1492), and as bakery owners, the only thing we associate with October is pumpkin.

Here is the thing about these brownies: We like them too much. We don't mention this to be glib; we say this because they are a problem. It is the rare dessert that disrupts and overturns our years-honed self-control. Give us one bite of pumpkin cheesecake chocolate chunk brownie, and we will eat the whole tray. At first glance, that shouldn't happen: We like pumpkin, and we like chocolate (that is obvious), but not always together. However, the tang of the cream cheese brings everything into alignment. The brownies are super moist, the kind of moist that will leave your fingers tacky with chocolate. They are pumpkiny and fudgy in all the right ways. It's a great dessert to welcome fall and celebrate Christopher.

●●● BAKED NOTE
Be sure to make the recipe in the order specified. The pumpkin cheesecake swirl should be made first, as the brownie batter will stiffen if it sits too long, and it will be difficult to pull a swirl through. It is not the easiest batter to swirl, but a few hefty repetitions of pulling the knife through the batter will do it. Also, try these cold: This is the rare brownie that we like directly from the refrigerator.

INGREDIENTS

For the Pumpkin Cheesecake Swirl

- 1 (8-ounce/226-g) package cream cheese, softened
- ¼ cup plus 2 tablespoons (75 g) granulated sugar
- ¾ cup (170 g) solid pack pumpkin or pumpkin puree (not pumpkin pie filling)
- 1 large egg yolk
- 2 tablespoons all-purpose flour
- 1 teaspoon ground cinnamon
- ¼ teaspoon ground nutmeg
- ¼ teaspoon ground allspice
- ¼ teaspoon ground ginger

For the Brownie Layer

- ¾ cup plus 2 tablespoons (105 g) all-purpose flour
- 1 tablespoon unsweetened cocoa powder
- ½ teaspoon kosher salt
- 8 ounces (225 g) dark chocolate (60 to 72% cacao), coarsely chopped
- 6 ounces (1½ sticks/170 g) unsalted butter, cut into 1-inch (2.5-cm) cubes, plus more for the pan
- ¾ cup (150 g) granulated sugar
- ¼ cup plus 2 tablespoons (85 g) firmly packed light brown sugar
- 3 large eggs, at room temperature
- 1 teaspoon pure vanilla extract

MAKE THE PUMPKIN CHEESECAKE SWIRL

1 In a medium bowl, whisk the cream cheese and sugar until smooth and creamy (it should almost look like frosting). Add the pumpkin, egg yolk, flour, cinnamon, nutmeg, allspice, and ginger and whisk again until well blended. Cover and refrigerate while you make the brownie layer.

MAKE THE BROWNIE LAYER

1 Preheat the oven to 350°F (175°C) and position a rack in the center. Butter the sides and bottom of a glass or light-colored metal 9-by-13-inch (23-by-33-cm) pan. Line the bottom with a sheet of parchment paper with a 1-inch (2.5-cm) overhang on the long sides of the pan, and butter the parchment.

2 In a medium bowl, whisk together the flour, cocoa, and salt.

3 Place the chocolate and butter in a large heatproof bowl and set it over a saucepan of simmering water (double-boiler method, see page 19), stirring occasionally, until the chocolate and butter are completely melted, smooth, and combined. Turn off the heat, but keep the bowl over the water and add both sugars. Whisk until completely combined, then remove the bowl from the pan. The mixture should be at room temperature. Add 2 eggs to the chocolate mixture and gently whisk until just combined. Add the remaining egg and whisk until combined. Add the vanilla and whisk until combined. Do not overbeat the batter at this stage or your brownies will be cakey.

4 Sprinkle the flour mixture over the chocolate mixture. Using a spatula, fold them gently together until just a bit of the flour mixture is visible.

5 Pour two-thirds of the batter into the prepared pan and smooth the top. Pour the pumpkin cheesecake mixture over the brownies and smooth into an even layer with the back of an offset spatula. Drop the remaining one-third of the brownie batter by heaping tablespoons here and there over the pumpkin layer. Use a knife to gently pull through the batters to create a swirl. (The brownie batter is thick, so you might need to pull several times before you start to create the swirl.)

6 Bake, rotating the pan halfway through the baking time, until a toothpick inserted into the center of the brownies comes out with a few moist crumbs sticking to it, 30 to 40 minutes. Let the brownies cool almost completely.

7 You can eat the brownies slightly warm or at room temperature, when they have a more pumpkin-y flavor. Or cover and refrigerate them for about 3 hours and enjoy them slightly chilled (this is our favorite). Either way, when you're ready, release the brownies from the side of the pan with a small paring knife. Pull straight up on the parchment to remove them from the pan, place them on a cutting board, cut, and serve.

HOW TO STORE

The brownies will keep, tightly covered, in the refrigerator for up to 5 days.

INDIVIDUAL BAKED ALASKAS WITH VANILLA AND COFFEE ICE CREAM

YIELD: 12 INDIVIDUAL BAKED ALASKAS

AS WITH MANY DESSERTS that originated long ago, the history of baked Alaska is convoluted. There seems to be solid evidence, however, that a gentleman named Charles Ranhofer popularized and named the dessert in 1876 at Delmonico's in New York City to commemorate the United States' acquisition of the Alaska Territory on October 18, 1867 (now known as Alaska Day). And though we are not Alaskans (but it is on our list to visit), if we were in charge of such things, we would institute a rule whereby every restaurant in America must replace one boring dessert item on their menu with some variation of baked Alaska. Baked Alaska is often visually exquisite (true showmen light the whole thing on fire tableside), and, more important, it is also insanely delicious. If you aren't acquainted with this fine dessert, it is, at the very basic level, an ice cream cake encased in a torched meringue. As someone who used to live for Fudgie the Whale (a beloved Carvel ice cream cake with a cult following), I find that baked Alaska is the answer to many of life's questions.

Our baked Alaska is special. We "individualized" the dessert, because we can't think of anything more fun than receiving your very own swirly, torched-meringue-coffee-ice-cream-chocolate-cake at a dinner party. They are easy to make (though, yes, the process of freezing the components takes some time), and they keep well in the freezer if you want to prepare them a day or two ahead of time. And last, we should probably tell you that during the testing phase of our baked Alaskas, we almost never had leftovers, and we always wore stretchy pants.

●●● BAKED NOTE

Use your favorite chocolate cupcake recipe for the baked Alaska bases. We tested this recipe several times using batches of our Red Wine Chocolate Cupcakes (unglazed, of course; page 117), and they were perfect—great crumb for the ice cream.

MAKE THE BAKED ALASKA BASES

1 Pull one or two very large pieces of plastic wrap across the top of a 12-cup muffin tin. The plastic wrap should cover the entire tin, plus there should be overhang (6 to 8 inches/15 to 20 cm) on either

INGREDIENTS

For the Baked Alaska Bases

1 pint (473 ml) coffee ice cream, slightly softened
12 unglazed, unfrosted chocolate cupcakes (see Baked Note)
1 pint (473 ml) vanilla ice cream

For the Baked Alaska Meringue

7 large egg whites
1¾ cups (350 g) granulated sugar
½ teaspoon cream of tartar
2 teaspoons pure vanilla extract

side. Press the plastic wrap into the bottoms and sides of the cups. Don't worry if it doesn't adhere to the sides of the tin; you just want to make sure it conforms to the general shape of the cups.

2 Equally divide the coffee ice cream among the prepared muffin cups. Use your fingers to press it into a compact, even layer. Cover the pan loosely with more plastic wrap and freeze for 1 hour.

3 Slice the cupcakes horizontally through the exact middle. Remove the pan from the freezer, and fold back the plastic wrap on top. Take the bottom piece of each cupcake (right side up is fine) and place it directly over the coffee ice cream, smushing the cake a little to create an even layer. Cover again and freeze for 20 minutes. Meanwhile, remove the vanilla ice cream from the freezer to soften.

4 Remove the pan from the freezer, and fold back the plastic wrap on top. Equally divide the softened vanilla ice cream among the 12 frozen cupcake layers. Use your fingers to press it into a compact, even layer. Immediately cover each with the top piece of cupcake (dome facing up) and press gently to adhere to the ice cream. Cover again loosely and freeze for at least 5 hours or overnight.

5 Invert the cupcake pan, pulling gently on the plastic wrap to help release the Alaskas. Remove all of the plastic wrap and divide the Alaskas onto two separate, parchment-lined baking sheets or 9-by-13-inch (23-by-33 cm) pans (this will make it easier to brown the meringue on just 6 at a time, which is ideal) and freeze for another 30 minutes.

MAKE THE BAKED ALASKA MERINGUE

1 After the Alaskas have been frozen for 30 minutes, whisk the egg whites and sugar together in a nonreactive metal bowl (ideally from your standing mixer) until combined. Set the bowl over a saucepan of simmering water. Cook, whisking constantly, until the sugar is completely dissolved and the mixture registers 140°F (60°C) on an instant-read thermometer, 6 to 8 minutes.

2 In the bowl of a standing mixer fitted with the whisk attachment, beat the mixture on high speed until stiff peaks form, adding the cream of tartar when the mixture begins to thicken, after about 3 minutes. When it holds stiff peaks, after about 6 minutes, add the vanilla and beat to incorporate.

3 Working quickly, remove 6 of the baked Alaska bases from the freezer. Cover each base in a thick coating of meringue—from top to bottom—taking care that no part of the base is showing, swirling and spiking the meringue as you like. Return to the freezer and repeat with the remaining bases. Freeze for 2 hours or up to 24 hours.

FINISH THE BAKED ALASKAS

1 Position a rack in the middle of the oven. Preheat the oven to 500°F (260°C).

2 Bake just 6 meringue-covered bases at a time (do not bake one tray on the top shelf and one below), until the meringue starts to brown, 1 to 3 minutes. Keep the remaining bases in the freezer until the oven is free, then bake them at once. Alternatively, you can brown the meringue with a kitchen torch; just a few passes of the flame should do the trick. Plate individually and serve immediately.

MILK CHOCOLATE MALTED BROWNIES WITH CHOCOLATE GANACHE

YIELD: 36 TO 48 MINI BROWNIES

APOLOGIES ARE IN ORDER. We gilded the lily. It was inevitable. We took a sublime brownie—a brownie that is impeccable and delicious in its own right—cut it into bite-size squares, and drenched it in chocolate. For those of you keeping score at home, the base of this brownie is actually a variation of our classic brownie layered with milk chocolate and malt powder (it contrasts beautifully with the dark chocolate shell). Then, we committed the ultimate sacrilege. We went a little cutesy in décor. We blame Halloween. A Baked chocolate-glazed brownie is pure heaven, but a Baked chocolate-glazed brownie with a hand-piped pumpkin on top is heaven on a roller coaster.

●●● **BAKED NOTE**

There is no wrong way to decorate these brownies. While we provide instructions for replicating our favorite Halloween icons, we know that decorating time is a luxury we don't always have. Don't worry—these brownies are just as tasty, and just as attractive, topped with a few tablespoons of chocolate, orange, or white sprinkles or nonpareils as soon as you finish pouring the ganache. (The sprinkles and nonpareils will stick to the chocolate better while it is still "wet.")

INGREDIENTS

For the Brownies

1¼ cups (160 g) all-purpose flour

½ cup (70 g) malted milk powder

1 tablespoon unsweetened cocoa powder

½ teaspoon kosher salt

6 ounces (170 g) milk chocolate (40 to 60% cacao), coarsely chopped

4 ounces (115 g) dark chocolate (60 to 72% cacao), coarsely chopped

6 ounces (1½ sticks/170 g) unsalted butter, cut into 1-inch (2.5-cm) cubes, plus more for the pan

1 cup (200 g) granulated sugar

½ cup (110 g) firmly packed light brown sugar

5 large eggs, at room temperature

2 teaspoons pure vanilla extract

For the Chocolate Ganache

6 ounces (170 g) dark chocolate (60 to 72% cacao), coarsely chopped

½ cup (120 ml) heavy cream

For the Royal Icing

3 to 4 cups (340 to 450 g) confectioners' sugar, sifted

2 large egg whites

1 teaspoon fresh lemon juice

Blue, yellow, red, and black food dyes or gels (optional)

MAKE THE BROWNIES

1 Preheat the oven to 350°F (175°C) and position a rack in the center. Butter the sides and bottom of a glass or light-colored metal 9-by-13-inch (23-by-33-cm) pan. Line the bottom with a sheet of parchment paper so that it overhangs about 1 inch (2.5 cm) on the long sides of the pan, and butter the parchment.

2 In a medium bowl, whisk together the flour, malted milk powder, cocoa, and salt.

3 Place both chocolates and the butter in a large heatproof bowl and set it over a saucepan of simmering water (double-boiler method, see page 19), stirring occasionally, until the chocolate and butter are completely melted, smooth, and combined. Turn off the heat, but keep the bowl over the water and add both sugars. Whisk until completely combined, then remove the bowl from the pan. The mixture should be at room temperature.

4 Add 3 eggs to the chocolate mixture and whisk until combined. Add the remaining 2 eggs and whisk until combined. Add the vanilla and whisk until combined. Do not overbeat the batter at this stage or your brownies will be cakey.

5 Sprinkle the flour mixture over the chocolate mixture. Using a spatula, fold the flour mixture into the chocolate until just a bit of the flour mixture is visible.

6 Pour the batter into the prepared pan and smooth the top. Bake, rotating the pan halfway through the baking time, until a toothpick inserted into the center of the brownies comes out with a few moist crumbs sticking to it, about 30 minutes. Remove from the oven, place the pan on a cooling rack, and let the brownies cool completely.

MAKE THE CHOCOLATE GANACHE

1 Place the chopped chocolate in a medium heatproof bowl. Place the cream in a saucepan over medium heat and heat just until bubbles form around the edge of the pan. Pour the hot cream over the chopped chocolate and let sit for 1 minute. Whisk until smooth. Pour the warm chocolate ganache over the cooled brownies in the pan and use an offset spatula to spread it into an even layer. Allow the ganache to sit for about 10 minutes, then refrigerate for another 15 minutes to set completely.

2 Using a small paring knife, release the brownies from the sides of the pan and pull straight up on the parchment to remove them from the pan, then place the brownies onto a cutting board and remove the parchment. Place the brownies in the freezer for 30 minutes (this will make them easier to cut). Run a chef's knife under hot water, wipe dry, and cut the brownies into 36 to 48 bite-size pieces (or smaller—these brownies are rich).

MAKE THE ROYAL ICING

1 In a medium bowl, whisk together 3 cups (340 g) confectioners' sugar, the egg whites, and lemon juice until the mixture is completely smooth. The mixture should have the texture of a thick glaze. If it is too thin, add more powdered sugar, a few tablespoons at a time, until it is thick enough to hold its shape when piped. Divide the icing into four bowls. Royal icing will begin to harden when exposed to air. If you are not using a particular color, make sure to cover the bowl tightly with plastic wrap or place the icing in a pastry bag and cover the tip.

2 Leave one bowl white for skulls and ghosts. In another bowl, create a black icing (about 8 drops of black gel or 2 drops each of blue, yellow, and red dye) for outlines and eyes. In the other two bowls, we recommend mixing orange for pumpkins and green for embellishments (green eyes are spooky). Put each color in its own pastry bag fitted with the smallest tip. (Pastry bags provide more control, but, if needed, you can fill four zip-tight plastic bags and cut a small corner from the bottom of each.) In essence, you want to pipe and fill all of your base layers first, then go back and add your final embellishments. (It is more difficult to decorate each brownie from start to finish.)

3 For skulls and ghosts: Pipe on the shapes of skulls or ghosts in white and allow them to harden for a few minutes (see photo 1). Then fill them in completely (see photo 2). Gently pipe final embellishments (eyes, mouths, etc.) directly on top of the white icing with any other color you like (see photos 3 and 4).

4 For pumpkins: Pipe on the shape of the pumpkins (not the stem) in orange and allow to harden for a few minutes (see photo 1), then fill them in completely. Gently pipe on the stem in green.

5 Allow the icing to harden completely before serving.

HOW TO STORE

The brownies will keep, tightly covered with plastic wrap, at room temperature for up to 4 days.

CHOCOLATE POP TARTS WITH PEANUT BUTTER AND JAM FILLING

YIELD: 10 POP TARTS

IN THEORY, WE COULD PROBABLY DEVOTE an entire recipe book to Halloween (many people already have). True, it has been co-opted and marketed and overdone—whole swaths of the country blanketed in orange and black faux-fright doodads—but it is still high on our list of favorite holidays. If you block out the noise, Halloween is nearly perfect. It is the bliss of pumpkin desserts, dark chocolate treats, fall sweaters, and horror-movie marathons. That the Halloween-themed *It's the Great Pumpkin, Charlie Brown* is also the best Charlie Brown TV special (by a landslide) is simply the cherry on top of a great holiday.

If you aren't gorging yourself on Halloween-themed candy—we have a weakness for the Reese's Peanut Butter Cup in the shape of a pumpkin—we encourage you to make these tasty Chocolate Pop Tarts with Peanut Butter and Jam Filling. We think they are an amazing and surprising Halloween dinner-party dessert (guaranteed to get at least one squeal of delight), but they also work well as high-end after-school snacks. They riff on the original nostalgic treat, but they are better—and not just because they are homemade. The chocolate dough is sweet, almost the texture of soft sugar cookies, and thoroughly toothsome, and they are filled with a burst of peanut butter tempered with a bit of jam. It's just the sort of thing you need while watching Jamie Lee Curtis outrun Michael Myers in John Carpenter's 1978 classic, *Halloween*.

●●● BAKED NOTE

As we are well-known peanut butter fanatics, we wouldn't dream of making these without the peanut-butter portion of the filling; however, if you or any loved ones have peanut allergies, you should know that we also love these with just the jam filling (double it up if you are cutting the peanut butter). And other nut-butter and jam combos work well here too; almond butter and blueberry jam are kind of insanely good together in this chocolate pop tart.

INGREDIENTS

For the Chocolate Pop Tart Dough

1 cup (130 g) all-purpose flour

1 cup (130 g) cake flour

2 tablespoons unsweetened dark cocoa powder

2 tablespoons granulated sugar

1½ teaspoons kosher salt

1 large egg

1 tablespoon whole milk

1 tablespoon heavy cream

1 tablespoon pure vanilla extract

8 ounces (2 sticks/225 g) frozen unsalted butter, cut into ½-inch (12-mm) cubes

For the Peanut Butter and Jam Filling

¾ cup (195 g) creamy peanut butter

4 ounces (115 g) dark chocolate, coarsely chopped

½ cup (120 ml) heavy cream

½ teaspoon pure vanilla extract

1½ to 2 cups (480 to 640 g) strawberry jam or preserves

MAKE THE CHOCOLATE POP TART DOUGH

1 In the bowl of a standing mixer fitted with the paddle attachment, stir together the all-purpose flour, cake flour, cocoa powder, sugar, and salt.

2 In a glass measuring cup, whisk together the egg, milk, cream, and vanilla until combined. Set aside.

3 Remove the mixing bowl from the standing mixer and scatter the frozen butter over the dry mixture. Using a pastry cutter, cut the butter into the dry mix until the mixture is pebbly and the butter chunks are lentil size.

4 Place the mixing bowl back on the mixer, add the wet ingredients, and beat on the lowest or second-lowest speed until the mixture comes together and a dough starts to form. Turn the dough out onto a very lightly floured surface and bring it fully together with your hands, kneading ever so gently. Do not overwork this dough. Form into a disk. Wrap in plastic wrap and refrigerate for at least 30 minutes or overnight.

MAKE THE PEANUT BUTTER AND JAM FILLING

1 Place the peanut butter and chocolate in a medium heatproof bowl.

2 In a small saucepan, heat the cream over medium heat until it just begins to bubble around the edges of the pan. Remove from the heat and immediately pour it over the peanut butter and chocolate. Let stand for 1 minute. Starting in the center of the bowl and working your way out to the edges, whisk the mixture by hand until it is completely smooth. Whisk in the vanilla until just combined. Set aside to cool to room temperature. The mixture will thicken as it sets.

ASSEMBLE THE POP TARTS

1 Line two baking sheets with parchment paper.

2 Remove the dough from the refrigerator and divide it in half. Rewrap half of the dough and return that portion to the refrigerator. Place the other half on a flour-dusted work surface and dust a rolling pin with flour as well. Roll out the dough (it will be sticky) into a rectangle approximately 10 by 13 inches (25 by 33 cm), about ⅛ to ¼ inch (3 to 6 mm) thick. (If the dough becomes too sticky, return it to the refrigerator to chill.) Cut the dough into 3-by-4-inch (7.5-by-10-cm) rectangles. If you have scraps, you should be able to reroll them at least once and cut more rectangles. Place the rectangles on one of the prepared pans and refrigerate them. Roll out and cut up the second half of the dough, place the rectangles on the second prepared pan, and refrigerate for at least 45 minutes. You should end up with approximately 20 rectangles in total, the same amount on each sheet and an even number altogether.

INGREDIENTS (CONT.)

For the Cocoa Frosting

2 to 2½ cups (225 to 280 g) confectioners' sugar

¼ cup plus 1 tablespoon (25 g) unsweetened dark cocoa powder

¼ cup plus 2 tablespoons (90 ml) whole milk

2 teaspoons pure vanilla extract

2 ounces (½ stick/55 g) unsalted butter, softened, cut into cubes

For Décor

White, yellow, and orange sprinkles (optional)

3 Place the peanut butter filling in a large zip-tight plastic bag. If it does not feel thick enough to pipe just yet, pop the filling in the refrigerator for 5 to 10 minutes to help it set quickly. Snip a small corner off the bag to create a do-it-yourself pastry bag and set aside. Do the same with another plastic bag and the jam.

4 Remove the first pan of chilled dough. Pipe the peanut butter filling in a Z shape over the top of the rectangles, making sure to leave a ½-inch (12-mm) space along the perimeter. Pipe the jam in an inverse Z shape over the peanut butter filling, again making sure to leave a ½-inch (12-mm) space along the perimeter. Using a pastry brush, brush water along the exposed ½-inch (12-mm) perimeter of the dough.

5 Remove the second pan of dough from the refrigerator. Carefully place each of these chilled rectangles directly on top of the filling on the first pan of rectangles, lining up the edges of the rectangles. Seal the pop tarts by pressing the dough together along all four edges. Dip the tines of a fork in flour and use the tines to crimp the sealed border of the dough. Using the same fork, prick the surface of each pop tart three or four times to create vents. Place the pan back in the refrigerator for 20 to 30 minutes.

6 Preheat the oven to 350°F (175°C).

7 Bake the pop tarts, rotating the pan halfway through the baking time, until the tops of the tarts appear dry to the touch, 12 to 18 minutes. Transfer the pan to a wire rack to cool completely.

MAKE THE COCOA FROSTING

1 In the bowl of a standing mixer fitted with the paddle attachment, mix 2 cups of the confectioners' sugar with the cocoa powder until uniform in color. Add ¼ cup of the milk and the vanilla and keep mixing until the frosting starts to come together; the texture should be thick and almost sandy. Add the cubed butter all at once and beat on medium-high speed until the frosting looks spreadable. If the frosting is too thin, add a little more sugar; if it is too thick, add a little more milk.

2 Use an offset spatula to frost each cooled pop tart. Top with a pinch of white, yellow, and orange sprinkles, if you like. Allow to set for 15 minutes, then serve immediately.

HOW TO STORE

The pop tarts taste best when eaten within 24 hours.

NOVEMBER

●●●

NOV 1-2 | DAY OF THE DEAD
CHOCOLATE CINNAMON CHIPOTLE SUGAR COOKIES 204

DATE FLUCTUATES | ELECTION DAY
ELECTION PALMIERS 208

4TH THU IN NOV | THANKSGIVING
BROWN BUTTER APPLE CRANBERRY GALETTE 212

4TH THU IN NOV | THANKSGIVING
SWEET POTATO TART WITH GINGERSNAP CRUST AND HEAVENLY MERINGUE 217

FRI FOLLOWING THANKSGIVING | BLACK FRIDAY
CHOCOLATE ESPRESSO TAPIOCA PUDDING WITH KALHÚA WHIPPED CREAM 220

CHOCOLATE CINNAMON CHIPOTLE SUGAR COOKIES

YIELD: ABOUT 12 LARGE COOKIES

WITHOUT AN OUNCE OF HESITATION, I can honestly state that experiencing Día de Muertos (Day of the Dead, a day to remember family and loved ones who have died) in Oaxaca, Mexico, in 2005 is one of my life's highlights. It was an intense, beautiful, Technicolor experience. It was the purest form of celebration, lacking sarcasm, crass marketing, and all the other things that make celebrations decidedly impure. It was—forgive my childlike exuberance here—epic. Being a tourist, I scooped up many items featuring variations of La Calavera Catrina (the Dapper Skull or Elegant Skull) and other masks. After several moves, only my set of hand-formed mugs etched in skull markings survived. Obviously, this is a sign: I am meant to return soon.

Our Chocolate Cinnamon Chipotle Sugar Cookies are as tasty as they are striking. They are crunchy and spicy, pleasantly smoky without a lot of residual heat. But, perhaps, nearly too attractive to eat. Much credit to Susanna Caliendo for decorating these cookies for the book; they are pure artistry. Our cookies (meaning mine and Renato's) do not look as perfect as the ones in the photo. We tell you this to encourage you to attempt to make them nonetheless. Even if your cookies look more akin to Scooby-Doo (sadly, this is about as far as my skill set has evolved), they are still quite enjoyable to make. Or, you can just bake the cookies and eat them plain. We would never tell.

●●● **BAKED NOTE**
We recommend breaking this recipe up over the course of two days. On Day One, make and bake the cookie dough, then make and apply the filler icing to the cooled cookies. Allow the cookies to sit out overnight; the filler icing needs to dry over an eight-hour period. Then, on Day Two, add the decorative flourishes with the royal icing.

INGREDIENTS

For the Chocolate Cinnamon Chipotle Cookies

2 cups (255 g) all-purpose flour
½ teaspoon kosher salt
½ teaspoon ground cinnamon
¼ teaspoon baking powder
¼ teaspoon chipotle chile powder, or ancho chile powder
6 ounces (1½ sticks/170 g) unsalted butter, cool but not cold
2 tablespoons cold (unflavored, non-hydrogenated) vegetable shortening
⅔ cup (130 g) granulated sugar
1 large egg
1 teaspoon pure vanilla extract
2 ounces (55 g) dark chocolate (60 to 72% cacao), melted and cooled

For the Filler Icing

3½ to 4 cups (395 to 450 g) confectioners' sugar
½ teaspoon cream of tartar
3 large egg whites, plus more if needed
1 teaspoon fresh lemon juice

For the Royal Icing

3 cups (340 g) confectioners' sugar
2 large egg whites
1 to 2 teaspoons fresh lemon juice
Various food gels

MAKE THE CHOCOLATE CINNAMON CHIPOTLE COOKIES

1 In a medium bowl, whisk together the flour, salt, cinnamon, baking powder, and chipotle. Set aside.

2 In the bowl of a standing mixer fitted with the paddle attachment, beat the butter and shortening together on medium speed until just combined. Add the sugar and cream together until the mixture is light and fluffy, about 3 minutes. Scrape down the bowl, add the egg and vanilla, and beat until just combined. Add the melted and cooled chocolate and beat until uniform in color. Scrape down the sides and bottom of the bowl, add half of the flour mixture, and beat for 15 seconds. Again, scrape down the bowl, then add the remaining flour mixture and beat until just incorporated. Loosely shape the dough into two disks (it will be sticky, so work quickly and feel free to flour your hands first), wrap them tightly in plastic wrap, and refrigerate for at least 2 hours.

3 Preheat the oven to 325°F (165°C). Line two baking sheets with parchment paper.

4 Unwrap one disk of dough, leaving the other in the refrigerator while you are working, and place it on a lightly flour-dusted work surface. Dust your hands and rolling pin with a little flour. Roll the dough ¼ inch (6 mm) thick, flipping and lightly flouring the dough a few times, as needed, while you work. Using your favorite Day of the Dead cookie cutter (we use the easy-to-find skull), cut shapes in the dough, then transfer them to the prepared baking sheets, leaving about 1 inch (2.5 cm) of space around each cookie. Dough scraps can be rerolled and recut, if desired. Continue the process with the remaining dough. Place the cut dough on the baking sheets in the freezer for about 15 minutes.

5 Bake the cookies, rotating the baking sheets halfway through the baking time, until the tops of the cookies look set and are just beginning to appear dry, 10 to 12 minutes. Place the baking sheets on a cooling rack for 5 minutes. Using a spatula, transfer the cookies to the rack to cool completely.

MAKE THE FILLER ICING

1 In the bowl of a standing mixer fitted with the paddle attachment, combine 3½ cups (395 g) confectioners' sugar and the cream of tartar; turn the mixer to the lowest speed to mix them together and remove any possible lumps. Increase the speed to medium-low, add the egg whites and lemon juice, and mix until the icing is completely smooth. It should have the texture of a thick, shiny glaze, but be just thin enough to pour. If the mixture is too thick, add additional egg whites to thin it. If the mixture is too thin, add the additional sugar a tablespoon at a time. Scrape the icing into a piping bag fitted with a large round tip (#3). First, outline each of the cookies with the icing and wait 15 minutes for the outlines to harden.

2 After 15 minutes, return to the first cookie and flood the icing within the outline. If you feel confident and steady, you can flood each cookie just by using a pastry bag filled with the icing; I recommend using less icing in the flooding process than you imagine you will need, as it should spread to the outline and fill it in. If you are not quite confident using just the pastry bag, or if you want to be extra careful, squeeze a few dollops of the icing over the top of the cookie and use a dry

paintbrush or the back of a spoon to gently spread it to the outline. (We don't recommend pastry brushes; craft-store paintbrushes with synthetic bristles work best.) Let the frosting dry completely before adding the décor (royal icing), at least 8 hours or overnight.

MAKE THE ROYAL ICING

1 In the bowl of a standing mixer fitted with the paddle attachment, combine the confectioners' sugar with the egg whites and 1 teaspoon lemon juice and beat on low to medium-low speed until the icing is completely smooth, 3 to 5 minutes. When the paddle is lifted from the icing, a peak in the icing should be created, which should fall over just a bit; it's slightly thicker than the filler icing. To reach the right consistency, add ½ teaspoon more egg white and/or lemon juice at a time to thin the icing, or 1 teaspoon more confectioners' sugar at a time to thicken the icing.

2 Divide this icing into five or six small prep bowls. Add pea-size amounts of food gel to all of the bowls save one, and mix, adding more gel as needed to achieve the colors you desire. Keep the last bowl plain (white). Place each color in a pastry bag fitted with a small tip (#1). (Alternatively, though we don't wholly recommend this method, as you will get cleaner lines using pastry bags and tips, you can place the icing in zip-tight plastic bags, cut off just a tiny bottom corner of the bag—as small as possible—and use the bag to pipe.)

3 Apply the royal icing to the outlined, filled, and completely dry cookies. Use the accompanying photo as a guide for traditional Day of the Dead décor or (obviously) decorate as you want. If you need to or want to overlap decorating colors, just make sure the bottom color is dry before applying the top color over it. Let the décor harden completely before serving, at least an hour or up to overnight.

HOW TO STORE

The cookies can be kept in an airtight container in a cool and dry environment for 3 to 5 days; do not wrap in plastic wrap.

ELECTION PALMIERS

SPICY MINI ELEPHANT EARS

YIELD: 20 TO 24 MINI PALMIERS

SIMPLY STATED, we are proudly American. If this were a different type of book, we would fall rapidly into a long, earnest dialogue about the power of democracy. We would cite famous historical (mostly long-dead) people regarding the moral obligation of "pulling the lever" for a representative of your choosing. But this is a different book. This is a celebratory book. And that Tuesday in November is one giant celebration, especially every four years, during the presidential election. At least for members of one party. Election Day has evolved into a media event on a par with the Oscars and the Super Bowl. It is a time to gather with friends and food in front of the television and root for a "team," holding your collective breath for the results.

Election Day (or Night) parties are not especially known for their food. If anything, they are usually themed red, white, and blue. We've eaten a lot of blueberries and blue cheese while waiting to see who captured Ohio's electoral votes. Our choice for Election Day treats are a rather obvious play on the elephant (Republican)/donkey (Democratic) symbols of the parties. We are definitely not Republicans, but our elephant ears are quite delicious nonetheless. A good palmier is an easy palmier, and this recipe is no exception. You will likely have most of the ingredients in your cabinet already, and though they look complicated, they are easier to put together than the average cake. They are crunchy and spicy in all the right places. Most important, they look quite impressive, as though you labored for hours. And until we come up with a satisfying donkey dessert (still thinking), everyone will eat a lot of palmiers at our Election Night parties.

●●● **BAKED NOTE**

The beauty of this recipe is the ease with which it comes together in the food processor; however, it can just as easily be made by cutting the very cold butter into the very cold flour with a pastry cutter and a little elbow grease. As with the food processor method, cut the butter quickly, just until it is in chunks that are slightly bigger than peas.

INGREDIENTS

- 1½ cups (170 g) all-purpose flour
- ¾ teaspoon kosher salt
- 7 ounces (1 ¾ sticks/200 g) unsalted butter, cut into ½-inch (12-mm) cubes
- ¾ teaspoon fresh lemon juice
- 1 large egg
- ½ cup (125 g) raw sugar
- 1 tablespoon ground cinnamon
- 1½ teaspoons cayenne pepper (optional, but worth it)

1 In a medium bowl, whisk together the flour and ½ teaspoon of the salt and place in the freezer. Place the butter in a separate bowl in the freezer. Finally, in a small prep bowl or measuring cup, stir together 2 tablespoons water with the lemon juice and place in the freezer. Allow all the items to chill in the freezer for 12 to 15 minutes.

2 Remove all items from the freezer. Place the flour mixture in a food processor and pulse for 1 or 2 short bursts. Add about half of the cold butter chunks and pulse about 3 to 4 times in short bursts. Do not overprocess; the butter pieces should be slightly bigger than pea size. Add the remaining butter and pulse a few more times; the butter should still be quite visible and pronounced in the mixture. Drizzle in a few drops of the lemon juice mixture and pulse 2 or 3 times until crumbly. Test the dough by pinching a bit in your fingers; it should just hold together. If the dough does not hold together, continue to add drops of the lemon juice mixture and pulse as needed. (Note: you may not use all of the mixture, or you may need to add additional drops of tap water; this is usually dependent on flour brand.) Again, be careful not to overprocess; the dough should not form a ball.

3 Transfer the chilled dough to a lightly floured work surface and knead until it just comes together. Use your hands to shape it into a rough 6-by-9-inch (15-by-23-cm) rectangle about ½ inch (12 mm) thick, with a short side closest to you. Make the first letter fold: Fold the bottom third of the dough on top of the middle third, then fold over the top third to cover, just like folding a letter. Rotate the rectangle so the short side is facing you, and letter-fold the dough again. Rotate again and use your hands to gently shape the dough into another rough 6-by-9-inch (15-by-23-cm) rectangle. Perform the final letter fold. If, at any time, the dough starts feeling soft or the butter starts to warm, refrigerate until cool again. Once all three letter folds are finished, cover the dough loosely in plastic wrap, and refrigerate it for 30 minutes.

4 Remove the chilled dough from the refrigerator and place it on a lightly floured surface. Using a rolling pin this time, roll the dough into an 8-by-15-inch (20-by-38-cm) rectangle, with the short side closest to you. Make the first letter fold: Fold the bottom third of dough on top of the middle third, then fold over the top third to cover. Rotate the rectangle so the short side is facing you and letter-fold the dough again. Rotate again, gently roll the dough back into a rough 8-by-15-inch (20-by-38-cm) rectangle, and perform a final letter fold. Cover the dough loosely in plastic wrap and refrigerate for 30 more minutes.

5 In a small bowl, whisk the egg with a fork. Set aside.

6 Place a rectangle of parchment (about the size of a half sheet pan, 18 by 13 inches/46 by 33 cm) on your workspace. Whisk together the sugar, cinnamon, cayenne (if using), and remaining ¼ teaspoon salt. Dust the parchment with one-third of the sugar mixture. Place the dough on top of the parchment and sprinkle the dough with another third of the sugar mixture. Roll the dough into a 12-by-15-inch (30.5-by-38-cm) rectangle about ⅛ to ¼ inch (3 to 6 mm) thick, sprinkling a tablespoon or two more of the sugar mixture over the dough if it becomes too sticky to work with.

Refrigerate the dough for 5 to 10 minutes to firm up. Roll up both of the long sides of the dough toward the center so that they meet in the exact middle. Brush the egg wash where the two sides of the dough meet; this will act as the glue to keep the rolls stuck together. Wrap in parchment paper and refrigerate for 20 minutes.

7 Preheat the oven to 425°F (220°C). Line two baking sheets with parchment. Add a teaspoon or two of water to the parchment and use your hands to spread it around; you want the parchment to be slightly damp.

8 Remove the dough from the refrigerator and cut crosswise into ½-inch (12-mm) slices; place the slices on the prepared baking sheets about 1 inch (2.5 cm) apart. Sprinkle the remaining sugar over the slices.

9 Bake for 5 minutes, then remove from the oven and flip the cookies over with a spatula. Bake the other side of the cookies until they have spread slightly and are puffy and golden brown, about 5 more minutes. Allow to cool slightly, then serve warm or at room temperature.

HOW TO STORE

Palmiers taste best when eaten within 12 hours.

BROWN BUTTER APPLE CRANBERRY GALETTE

YIELD: 1 10-BY-14-INCH (25-BY-36-CM) GALETTE • ABOUT 10 SERVINGS

TRY AS WE MIGHT, our respective Thanksgiving tables never look like the ones depicted in fancy food magazines. For starters, we don't own large Versailles-length tables, thousands of chairs, and acres of space. We each live in typical (space-challenged) Brooklyn apartments. More important, we don't have as much stuff as these magazine families. We don't have (i.e., we can't fit into our humble abodes) the place-card holders, the runners, the centerpieces, the endless china, the so-specific serving ware, and the various napkins. Who are these people who own an infinite supply of color-coordinated linens? Our Thanksgiving tables are simpler affairs. They have to be, and that is okay with us.

Our Brown Butter Apple Cranberry Galette happens to look stunning on a simple Thanksgiving table. In fact, it is so beautiful, it could be a centerpiece unto itself. Galettes, often described as rustic or hand-formed pies, might look intimidating, but they are actually easy to make. We filled ours, of course, with a bounty of typical Thanksgiving-inspired fare, a pleasing mix of apples and cranberries. And, like all good pies, the crust is also a star, super buttery and flaky. Our galette will definitely stand on its own on a Thanksgiving table, or you could just as easily serve it alongside the more typical pumpkin and pecan pies.

●●● BAKED NOTE

Why do we use bread crumbs in this dessert? The bread crumbs help absorb some of the excess juice in the fruit filling, which results in an overall crisper galette. Also, if you don't have access to fresh cranberries (not in season or otherwise available), dried cranberries will work wonderfully, though the texture will be slightly chewier. Frozen cranberries are perfect as well, though be sure to thaw them first, and discard any liquid they may exude before tossing them with the apples. Finally, we rarely strain our brown butter; we like the mottled appearance it can give baked goods, and we think the slightly browned bits are the best part.

INGREDIENTS

For the Galette Dough

4   ounces (1 stick/115 g) cold unsalted butter, cut into ½-inch (12-mm) cubes
¼   cup (50 g) very cold vegetable shortening, cut into ½-inch (12-mm) cubes
Ice cubes
1½ cups (170 g) all-purpose flour, plus more for rolling out the dough
¾   cup (90 g) cake flour
2   tablespoons granulated sugar
1   teaspoon kosher salt

For the Spiced Apple Filling

3   Granny Smith apples
½   cup (55 g) fresh cranberries, or dried (65 g), or frozen (60 g), thawed and drained (see Baked Note)
¼   cup plus 2 tablespoons (85 g) firmly packed dark brown sugar
¼   teaspoon ground cinnamon
¼   teaspoon kosher salt
2   ounces (½ stick/55 g) unsalted butter

For the Assembly

3   tablespoons very fine bread crumbs or panko
1   tablespoon sanding sugar
Vanilla ice cream (optional)

MAKE THE GALETTE DOUGH

1 Place the butter and shortening in a small bowl and freeze for at least 15 minutes and up to 30.

2 Add ¼ cup (60 ml) water to a measuring cup. Add a few ice cubes to the water to keep it cold, and place in the freezer for 15 minutes.

3 Place both flours, the sugar, and salt in a food processor and pulse until combined. Add the cold butter and shortening chunks. Pulse until the mixture is coarse and pebbly, with a few small chunks of butter and shortening still visible, 5 to 7 quick pulses. Remove the ice water from the freezer. Add 1 tablespoon ice water to the dough at a time, pulsing in between, until the mixture just starts to come together; it will likely take 3 to 4 tablespoons. Keep pulsing until a mass forms or until a pinch of dough in your fingers holds together. Turn the dough out onto a very lightly floured work surface and bring it together by kneading gently but briefly. Form the dough into a disk, wrap it tightly in plastic wrap, and refrigerate it for at least 1 hour or overnight.

MAKE THE SPICED APPLE FILLING

1 Peel and core the apples. Slice them into very thin (about ⅛-inch/3-mm) slices. Place the apples in a large bowl and toss together with the cranberries. Sprinkle the brown sugar, cinnamon, and salt over the fruit and toss again until the fruit is well coated and the mixture is combined.

2 Place the butter in a small saucepan over medium-high heat and cook, swirling the pan occasionally, until the foam subsides and the butter turns a light nut brown, 3 to 4 minutes; watch carefully so it does not burn. Remove from the heat and set aside to cool, about 5 minutes (pick up the pan and swirl it constantly to cool the butter more quickly). Remove 2 tablespoons of the butter to a small glass or mini prep bowl, then pour the remaining melted butter over the fruit mixture and toss with your hands to combine.

ASSEMBLE THE GALETTE

1 Place a 12-by-16-inch (30.5-by-40.5-cm) piece of parchment paper on a work surface and sprinkle it with a tiny bit of flour. Sprinkle the chilled dough with a little flour and place it on the parchment. Using a rolling pin, roll the dough out into a rough rectangle ⅛ to ¼ inch (3 to 6 mm) thick that covers or almost covers the parchment, sprinkling the dough with flour if necessary. Lift the parchment with the dough and place it inside a half sheet pan. Refrigerate the dough in the pan for about 15 minutes.

2 Preheat the oven to 400°F (205°C).

3 Remove the dough from the refrigerator and sprinkle the bread crumbs in the center of the dough, leaving a 2-inch (5-cm) empty border from the edge. Use your hands to lift the apples out of the bowl, shake them gently to remove excess liquid, and arrange decoratively (we like slightly overlapping concentric circles or a spiral pattern) over the bread crumbs, again keeping a 2-inch (5-cm) border all the way around. Next, use your hands to remove the cranberries from the bowl,

leaving excess liquid behind (if using dried cranberries, give a slight squeeze to remove excess liquid), and arrange them in a circle in the center of the galette over the apples. Feel free to sprinkle the apples with a few tablespoons of the juice, but no more; discard any remaining liquid. Use the parchment paper to help turn the plain border of dough over the apples, using your fingers to pinch together any tears (much of the apple filling will be left exposed). Using a pastry brush, brush the reserved brown butter onto the dough and exposed apples. Sprinkle the dough and apples with the sanding sugar.

4 Bake for 35 to 45 minutes, until the crust is browned; try lifting the corner of the galette with a metal spatula—the bottom should be browned as well. (If the top of the galette crust or the fruit begins to brown too much before the galette is baked through, tent the top with foil for the remaining baking time.) Remove from the oven and let cool for 15 minutes.

5 Serve warm or at room temperature with vanilla ice cream, if you like.

HOW TO STORE

The best way to store leftover galette is to allow it to cool completely, then wrap tightly and refrigerate. Rewarm in a 350°F (175°C) oven for about 10 minutes, until warmed throughout. Galette, like pie, will get soggy starting on the third day.

SWEET POTATO TART WITH GINGERSNAP CRUST AND HEAVENLY MERINGUE

YIELD: 1 9-INCH (23-CM) TART • ABOUT 10 TO 12 SERVINGS

FROM A FOOD PERSPECTIVE, Thanksgiving is a holiday that needs little, if any, reinvention. A few riffs are fine, but ultimately the core basics are stronger when simpler: roast turkey, thick gravy, starchy sides, and autumnal desserts. A kind but misinformed soul once brought a pizza to my Thanksgiving table. It was like she had set a bomb down in the middle of the festivities. Sad to say, she was never invited back. Pizza is not appropriate. Sweet potato tart is.

Happily, Renato's approach to this tart is gentle and affirming and 100 percent Thanksgiving. He is not rocking the boat; he is just giving it a new coat of paint. Our sweet potato tart is really all about the sweet potato; the filling is all warm spicing without a lot of sugar. We cover the top in a thick and glossy and dramatic marshmallowy meringue (everything is better in a thick and glossy meringue), and the whole thing is cradled in a sprightly gingersnap crust. This is the kind of unexpected/expected dessert you crave after a dose of tryptophan by way of turkey. It is also the kind of thing you crave the day after Thanksgiving with your morning coffee.

●●● **BAKED NOTE**

Canned candied yams will not work here; they will make the filling way too sweet. Roasting sweet potatoes is best and often provided the best flavor in our tests. But if you are crunched for time, microwave them until tender, about 5 minutes, then wrap them in foil until they've cooled slightly.

INGREDIENTS

For the Sweet Potato Puree

3   medium to large sweet
    potatoes

For the Gingersnap Crust

8   ounces (225 g) ginger-
    snap cookies (about 30
    cookies)
2   tablespoons firmly
    packed light brown sugar
⅛   teaspoon kosher salt
2   ounces (½ stick/55 g)
    unsalted butter, melted

For the Sweet Potato Filling

⅓   cup (75 ml) evaporated
    milk
3   large eggs, at room
    temperature
1   tablespoon maple syrup
2   cups (480 ml) sweet
    potato puree (recipe
    opposite)
1   cup (220 g) firmly packed
    light brown sugar
½   teaspoon ground cinnamon
⅛   teaspoon ground ginger
¼   teaspoon ground nutmeg
1   tablespoon unsalted
    butter, melted

For the Meringue

3   large egg whites, at room
    temperature
¾   cup (150 g) granulated
    sugar
¼   teaspoon cream of tartar
½   teaspoon pure vanilla
    extract

For the Assembly

Ground cinnamon (optional)

MAKE THE SWEET POTATO PUREE

1   Position a rack in the middle of the oven. Preheat the oven to 400°F (205°C). Line a sheet tray with foil.

2   Wash the sweet potatoes vigorously with a scrubber. Pat dry and prick the potatoes multiple times with a fork. Place them on the prepared sheet tray. Roast the potatoes until fork tender, rotating the pan halfway through the baking time, about 1 hour. Remove the sheet tray from the oven, place on a cooling rack, and allow the potatoes to cool. Peel and cut them into 1-inch (2.5-cm) chunks, discarding the peels. Puree the sweet potato chunks in a food processor until completely smooth. Add 1 tablespoon water at a time and pulse to reach a typical pumpkin puree–like consistency (thinner than mashed potatoes); this is usually between 1 and 2 tablespoons water. Measure out 2 cups (480 ml) of the puree for the pie and save the rest for another use. (Sweet potato puree lasts 5 to 7 days in the fridge, and 30 days in a freezer bag in the freezer.)

MAKE THE GINGERSNAP CRUST

1   Preheat the oven to 350°F (175°C). Position a rack in the middle of the oven.

2   In a food processor, pulse the cookies until pulverized into a very fine crumb. You should have a scant 2 cups (230 g). Add the brown sugar and salt, and pulse until incorporated, about 10 seconds. Pour in the melted butter and pulse until the butter is fully incorporated and the mixture has the consistency of wet sand.

3   Transfer the mixture to a 9-inch (23-cm) tart pan with removable bottom (or a 9-inch/23-cm springform pan for a smooth-sided finish). Press the crumbs into the bottom and up the sides, using the back of a large spoon or the bottom of a large measuring cup to pack the crumbs into an even layer. Freeze the pan just to set, 8 to 10 minutes. Place the tart pan on a sheet tray and bake until the crust is fragrant and appears set, 6 to 8 minutes. Remove from the oven and cool completely on a wire rack.

MAKE THE SWEET POTATO FILLING

1   Turn the oven temperature to 375°F (190°C).

2   Measure the evaporated milk into a glass measuring cup. Whisk in the eggs and maple syrup.

3   In the bowl of a standing mixer fitted with the paddle attachment, add the sweet potato puree and mix on the lowest setting to loosen. Add the evaporated milk mixture and beat on medium speed until incorporated, about 1 minute. In a small bowl, stir the brown sugar, cinnamon, ginger, and nutmeg together until combined, then add to the sweet potato mixture and mix on medium speed until just combined. Add the melted butter and mix again.

4   Pour the mixture into the cooled tart shell. Place the tart on a sheet pan (for easier cleanup in case of seepage), and bake until a toothpick inserted into the middle of the tart comes out clean, 20 to 25 minutes. Cool completely.

MAKE THE MERINGUE

1 In a nonreactive metal bowl (ideally the one from your standing mixer), whisk the egg whites and sugar together until combined.

2 Set the bowl over a saucepan of simmering water. Cook, whisking constantly, until the sugar is completely dissolved and the mixture registers 140°F (60°C) on an instant-read thermometer, 6 to 8 minutes. Remove the bowl from the pan.

3 In the bowl of a standing mixer fitted with the whisk attachment, beat the mixture on high speed until stiff peaks form, adding the cream of tartar when the meringue begins to thicken, or after 3 minutes. When the mixture holds stiff peaks, after about 6 minutes, add the vanilla and beat to incorporate.

ASSEMBLE THE TART

1 Scoop out the meringue and generously pile it over the top of the tart, swirling and peaking to create your desired look. (You may have some meringue left over.) Use a kitchen torch to gently brown the meringue. (Do not use a broiler.)

2 To serve, gently push up on the bottom of the tart pan to release it and transfer it to a plate or stand. Dust with a light coating of cinnamon before slicing, if you like.

HOW TO STORE

The tart tastes best if eaten within 24 hours but can be kept, covered, in the refrigerator for up to 2 days.

CHOCOLATE ESPRESSO TAPIOCA PUDDING WITH KAHLÚA WHIPPED CREAM

YIELD: 8 SERVINGS

BLACK FRIDAY HAS EVOLVED into a treacherous beast, an event unto itself. Theoretically, it is often the kickoff to the holiday shopping season (the day that tips retailers from "in the red" to "in the black," i.e., the day they become profitable), and stores play into this mythology with hourly sales, deep but limited discounts, and special festivities (live music, free coffee and doughnuts, etc.). We are not Black Friday people. It's not in our blood. The crowds, the jostling, the predawn hours are too much—much too much—especially coming off the maddening pie-making marathon that swallows our bakery whole the three days prior to Thanksgiving. No, for us, Black Friday is about rest and reruns. It is *I Love Lucy* and leftovers.

While we ourselves do not participate in Black Friday, we have several friends and family members who attack the day with gusto. They load out at 2 A.M. with a thermos of coffee and a thorough military-style plan of attack. For them, we present this dessert. It's very wink-wink (note the heaps of espresso added to get the early-morning blood circulating), but lovingly made nonetheless. Regardless of whether or not you enjoy Black Friday, we promise you will enjoy this pudding. It is a rich chocolate pudding all studded up with a pearl tapioca surprise. It's the kind of dessert that makes you wish you cooked with tapioca more often (completely unscientific evidence suggests Americans have a skewed view of tapioca overall), the kind of dessert that will make you question why pudding hasn't made a resurgence in popularity along the lines of cupcakes and Bundts.

●●● **BAKED NOTE**

Do not fear small pearl tapioca. It is easy to work with and ten times more pleasingly textured than the instant variety. For some reason, instant tapioca cooks up into a gelatinous blob (we are of the not-so-humble opinion). Besides, as long as you stay the course and stir the small pearl tapioca constantly (not unlike polenta or risotto) in a heavy-bottomed pot, you will find great success and satisfaction with going the slow and steady route.

INGREDIENTS

For the Espresso Tapioca

- ⅓ cup (60 g) small pearl tapioca (not instant), such as Bob's Red Mill
- 1 cup (240 ml) heavy cream
- 2 large eggs, separated
- ½ teaspoon kosher salt
- ½ cup (100 g) granulated sugar
- 2 cups (480 ml) whole milk
- 2 tablespoons instant espresso powder
- 1 tablespoon unsweetened dark cocoa powder, such as Valrhona
- 2 ounces (55 g) high-quality dark chocolate, chopped
- 1 teaspoon pure vanilla extract

For the Kahlúa Whipped Cream

- 1¼ cups (300 ml) heavy cream
- 2 tablespoons superfine sugar
- 1 to 2 tablespoons Kahlúa

MAKE THE ESPRESSO TAPIOCA

1. Place the tapioca in a medium heavy-bottomed saucepan. Cover it with ¾ cup (180 ml) of the cream and let it soak for 30 minutes.

2. About 25 minutes into the soak, place the egg whites and salt in the bowl of a standing mixer fitted with the whisk attachment (or, if you are feeling strong, a whisk, a bowl, and a ready arm), and whisk on high speed for 1 to 2 minutes, until right before soft peaks form. Sprinkle the top of the mixture with the sugar and continue beating until soft peaks form. Set aside.

3. Add the remaining ¼ cup (60 ml) cream, the milk, and the egg yolks to the tapioca mixture. Whisk gently until just combined. Place the pan over medium heat and, stirring constantly (be very careful—tapioca scorches easily), bring the mixture to a boil. Immediately reduce the heat to low and simmer, continuing to stir constantly, until the tapioca is swollen and translucent, and the entire mixture thickens, 10 to 15 more minutes. Remove it from the heat. Add the espresso powder, cocoa, and chocolate and stir until the chocolate is melted and the mixture is combined.

4. Using a rubber spatula, gently fold one-fourth of the tapioca mixture into the egg whites until almost combined, then transfer the mixture back to the medium saucepan containing the rest of the tapioca. Place the pan over medium-low heat and cook for a few more minutes, until the mixture is completely combined. Allow it to cool briefly, then stir in the vanilla. Transfer the mixture to 8 individual ramekins or coffee mugs. Cover with plastic wrap and place in the refrigerator for at least 4 hours, until the mixture is no longer jiggly.

MAKE THE KAHLÚA WHIPPED CREAM

1. Pour the cream into a chilled metal bowl and beat vigorously with a chilled whisk for about 1 minute, until soft peaks form. Sprinkle the sugar and Kahlúa to taste over the cream and continue whisking vigorously until stiff peaks form. Spoon dollops on top of the chilled puddings and serve immediately.

HOW TO STORE

Individual puddings (without whipped cream) will keep in the refrigerator, covered in plastic wrap, for up to 3 days.

DECEMBER

HOLIDAY BAKING INTERLUDE
TWELVE DAYS OF COOKIES 224-240

DEC 17 | NATIONAL MAPLE SYRUP DAY
BROWN SUGAR OATMEAL WHOOPIE PIES WITH MAPLE MARSHMALLOW FILLING 242

DATE FLUCTUATES | WINTER SOLSTICE
WINTERMINT CAKE 244

DEC 24 | CHRISTMAS EVE
PINK PEPPERMINT STICK ICE CREAM WITH HOMEMADE HOT FUDGE 249

DEC 25 | CHRISTMAS
TRICOLOR CAKE 252

DEC 25 | CHRISTMAS
ORANGE PINEAPPLE WALNUT FRUITCAKE 257

DEC 26 | BOXING DAY
SALTED CARAMEL CHOCOLATE CUPCAKE SHAKES 260

HOLIDAY BAKING INTERLUDE
TWELVE DAYS OF COOKIES

WE MAY BE SLIGHTLY JADED NEW YORKERS, but we still get the "warm fuzzies" each and every December. Biting cold and gray skies be damned, it is hard not to fall a lot in love with our adopted city during the run up to the big holidays. The skyline is ablaze with a million multicolored holiday bulbs. The air is (finally) refreshingly scented (or at least we romanticize it so) with chimney smoke, cinnamon, and peppermint. It's a month of motion, friends, feasts, hot toddies (many, many hot toddies), Rockefeller Center, Frank Capra movies, and Dickens's novels. And cookies . . . hundreds upon hundreds of cookies.

Each December we undertake a cookie marathon. It's a visceral reflex born of family tradition. Our moms were Christmas cookie enthusiasts, more often than not engaging neighbors, family, friends, and friends of friends to join in a few days of hard-core cookie baking near the middle of December. I was usually tasked with cookie shaping. My dad was the dutiful kitchen cleaner. Mom's friends boxed and bowed. It was a beautiful flurry of flour, sugar, butter, and cocoa powder.

We continue this custom because we have to. It is part of our DNA. We bake, eat, gift, and swap untold amounts of cookies starting the first week of December, gradually increasing the pace and production as we race toward the twenty-fifth. It's the Olympics of cookiedom.

Our Twelve Days of Cookies Baking Interlude is pure homage, the recipes within carefully curated by our kitchen staff and us. Each of these cookies has a story. Some are archival, clipped or carefully handwritten, and passed down through generations. Some are slightly new inventions, quirkier takes on what a Christmas cookie should be. All are quite simple. All are delicious. We encourage you to tackle all twelve cookies. And, if you happen to make all twelve recipes back to back, we salute you. (See photo on page 241 for a key to all twelve cookies.)

S COOKIES

YIELD: 50 TO 60 COOKIES

THIS IS A COOKIE RENATO KNOWS WELL. S cookies are biscotti-like in nature, crisp and brittle, but toothsome. They are meant to be dunked in something: perfect for midday tea or coffee (dip away) or midnight snack (with wine). You will notice the baking powder is not whisked together with the other dry ingredients. This is extremely rare. When Renato asked his mother for an explanation (for every Italian household has an S cookie, and Renato's house was no different; his mom was taught by her cousin Sadie), her answer was simple: She always had. Perhaps we should have tested it the other way. But, then it wouldn't be Renato's mother's cousin's true recipe, and that would be a shame.

INGREDIENTS

- 6 cups (770 g) all-purpose flour
- ¼ teaspoon kosher salt
- ⅓ cup (75 ml) whole milk
- 1½ cups (300 g) granulated sugar
- 3 large eggs, at room temperature
- ¾ cup (180 ml) vegetable oil
- 1 teaspoon vanilla bean paste
- 2 tablespoons baking powder
- 2 to 3 tablespoons vegetable shortening

1 In a medium bowl, whisk together the flour and salt. Set aside.

2 In a small saucepan over low heat, heat the milk and sugar. Stir gently until the sugar is mostly dissolved and the mixture is warm to the touch. Remove the pan from the heat and set it aside to cool.

3 In the bowl of a standing mixer fitted with the paddle attachment, beat the eggs at medium-low speed for a few seconds. Keep the mixer on low and stream in the sugar mixture, followed by the oil and vanilla bean paste. Keep mixing until the liquid is completely incorporated. Stop the mixer and add the baking powder. Mix on low speed to incorporate. Scrape down the sides and bottom of the bowl and add the flour mixture in four parts, mixing after each addition until just incorporated.

4 Very lightly grease a kneading surface with the vegetable shortening. Rub the shortening into your hands and knead the crumbly dough until it is shiny and uniform, about 1 minute. Wrap the dough in plastic wrap and let it rest at room temperature for about 30 minutes.

5 Preheat the oven to 350°F (175°C). Line two baking sheets with parchment paper.

6 Cut off a handful of dough, rewrapping the remaining dough so it doesn't dry out.

7 Using your hands, roll the dough into one 15-inch- (38-cm-) long rope, then cut the rope into three 5-inch (12-cm) segments. Form each into a tight, compact S shape on the baking sheets. Space the cookies about 1 inch (2.5 cm) apart. (If the dough starts to tear while you are bending it, add a pea-size amount of the vegetable shortening to the dough and reknead.) Using a small, very sharp knife, make a small slash (no more than ¼ inch/6 mm in length and depth) on the top of both ends of the S (in the same direction as the S; see page 241).

8 Bake, rotating the sheets halfway through the baking time, until the cookies are puffed up and the edges are golden brown, 15 to 18 minutes. Transfer the sheets to wire racks to cool for about 5 minutes, than transfer the cookies directly to wire racks to cool completely.

HOW TO STORE

The cookies can be kept, tightly covered, at room temperature for about 1 week.

PEANUT BUTTER BLOSSOMS

YIELD: 36 TO 48 COOKIES

I CHOSE THIS COOKIE because I had to. It was a complete nostalgia play. It was one of the few cookies my mom made every December, and it surely precipitated my love for all things peanut butter and chocolate.

The recipe is virtually unchanged from Mom's, via Hershey's (not sure where she dug up the recipe, maybe a Hershey's cookbook or the back of the Hershey's Kisses package). We only made a tweak here and there, as we are wont to do. It is one of my favorite cookies, regardless of the holiday, and I can't stop making them.

INGREDIENTS

36 to 48 Hershey's Kisses
1½ cups (170 g) all-purpose flour
1 teaspoon baking soda
½ teaspoon kosher salt
¼ cup (50 g) vegetable shortening, cool but not cold
2 ounces (½ stick/55 g) unsalted butter, cool but not cold
¾ cup (195 g) creamy natural peanut butter
⅓ cup (65 g) granulated sugar
⅓ cup (75 g) firmly packed dark brown sugar
1 large egg
2 tablespoons whole milk
1 teaspoon pure vanilla extract
⅓ cup (80 g) demerara sugar

1 Remove the wrappers from all 48 Hershey's Kisses and place in a bowl. Set aside.

2 In a small bowl, whisk together the flour, baking soda, and salt.

3 In the bowl of a standing mixer fitted with the paddle attachment, beat the shortening and butter on medium-high speed until smooth and combined. Add the peanut butter and beat again on medium speed until combined, about 1 minute. Scrape down the sides and bottom of the bowl, and add the granulated and brown sugars. Continue beating until fluffy, about 2 minutes. Add the egg, milk, and vanilla, and beat until completely blended, 1 to 2 minutes. Scrape down the sides and bottom of the bowl and add half of the flour mixture. Beat on medium speed for about 30 seconds, stop the mixer, and add the remaining flour mixture. Continue beating until completely blended, about 1 more minute.

4 If the dough feels a little wet, cover the bowl with plastic wrap and refrigerate to firm it up, about 30 minutes or up to 1 hour. Otherwise, move directly on to the next step.

5 Preheat the oven to 375°F (190°C). Line two baking sheets with parchment paper. Place the demerara sugar in a small shallow bowl.

6 Scoop and roll the dough into balls about 1 inch (2.5 cm) in diameter. Roll them in the demerara sugar to coat and place them on the prepared baking sheets about 1½ inches (4 cm) apart. Bake, rotating the sheets halfway through the baking time, until the cookies appear set and are dry to the touch, 8 to 10 minutes.

7 Remove the sheets from the oven, and place them on cooling racks. Immediately gently press a Hershey's Kiss into the center of each cookie, making sure it's good and snug so it doesn't fall out when cooled. The cookie will crack around the edges. Cool completely and serve.

HOW TO STORE

The cookies can be kept, tightly covered, at room temperature for up to 3 days.

GINGERSNAPS WITH LEMON SUGAR

YIELD: ABOUT 36 COOKIES

MOLLY MARZALEK-KELLY, the head baker at Baked, is a gingersnap magician. Her recipe for Gingersnaps with Lemon Sugar is pivotal. She says that if your gingersnap love is waning, this recipe will surely pull you back from gingersnap purgatory. It is a glorious and simple cookie. It is chewy on the inside, crunchy on the outside, and, as befits a cookie such as this, covered in a splendid lemon-scented sugar. It is also worth mentioning that it is a mixer-free recipe. All you need is your hands, a bowl or two, and a few minutes.

INGREDIENTS

For the Lemon Sugar

½ cup (100 g) granulated sugar
Zest of 1 lemon (about 1 tablespoon)

For the Gingersnaps

1¼ cups (250 g) granulated sugar
¾ cup plus 1 tablespoon (195 ml) canola oil
1 large egg
1 large egg yolk
¼ cup plus 1 tablespoon (75 ml) molasses
2⅔ cups (340 g) all-purpose flour
1 tablespoon ground ginger
2 teaspoons baking soda
1½ teaspoons ground cinnamon
½ teaspoon ground allspice
½ teaspoon kosher salt

MAKE THE LEMON SUGAR

1 Place the sugar in a small shallow bowl. Sprinkle the zest over the sugar. Use your fingers to rub the lemon zest and sugar together.

MAKE THE GINGERSNAPS

1 Preheat the oven to 325°F (165°C). Line two baking sheets with parchment paper.

2 In a large bowl, whisk together the sugar and canola oil until combined. Add the egg and egg yolk and whisk to combine. Add the molasses and whisk to combine.

3 In another large bowl, whisk together the flour, ginger, baking soda, cinnamon, allspice, and salt.

4 Add the dry ingredients to the wet ingredients. Using your (very clean) hands, combine the dry and wet ingredients together in the bowl, kneading as necessary.

5 Scoop and roll the dough into balls about 1 inch (2.5 cm) in diameter. Roll them in the lemon sugar to coat and place them on the prepared baking sheets about 1½ inches (4 cm) apart. For soft cookies, bake 12 to 15 minutes; for a cookie that is crunchy on the outside yet soft on the inside, bake 15 to 20 minutes. Remove the sheets from the oven and place them on cooling racks. Serve warm or transfer the cookies directly to the racks to cool completely.

HOW TO STORE

The cookies can be kept, tightly covered, at room temperature for up to 3 days.

EXCEEDINGLY CHOCOLATY CRINKLES

YIELD: 24 TO 30 COOKIES

THIS IS YET ANOTHER TYPE OF COOKIE I remember seeing regularly around the household come winter. Mom was of the "if it's not chocolate, it's not worth eating" philosophy, so this cookie is, in essence, dedicated to her. Cobbled together Frankenstein-style from a few of our family "crinkle" recipes, it is the most chocolaty cookie I could create that is not just a slab of chocolate. Slightly firm on the outside. Melt-in-your mouth goodness on the inside.

INGREDIENTS

- 1¼ cups (160 g) all-purpose flour
- 2 tablespoons unsweetened cocoa powder
- ½ teaspoon baking powder
- ¼ teaspoon kosher salt
- 6 ounces (170 g) dark chocolate (60 to 72% cacao), coarsely chopped
- 2 ounces (½ stick/55 g) unsalted butter, cut into tablespoons
- 1 teaspoon instant espresso powder
- 2 large eggs, at room temperature
- ¼ cup (50 g) granulated sugar
- ½ cup (110 g) firmly packed dark brown sugar
- 2 teaspoons pure vanilla extract
- ¾ cup (85 g) confectioners' sugar, sifted
- 2 tablespoons fleur de sel (optional)

1 In a medium bowl, sift together the flour, cocoa powder, baking powder, and salt. Set aside.

2 Place the chocolate and butter in a large heatproof bowl set over a pan of simmering water (double-boiler method, see page 19), and stir occasionally until they are almost completely melted and combined. Stir in the espresso powder. Remove from the heat and continue stirring until the last remaining chunks of chocolate and butter are melted. Let cool to room temperature.

3 In the bowl of a standing mixer fitted with the paddle attachment, beat the eggs, granulated sugar, and brown sugar together on medium speed until smooth and the color of a very light cappuccino, 3 to 4 minutes. Add the vanilla and beat again until incorporated. Scrape the chocolate mixture into the bowl and beat until combined. Scrape down the sides and bottom of the bowl, and add the flour mixture all at once. On the lowest speed possible, beat the mixture until just incorporated; do not overmix. Cover the bowl tightly and refrigerate the dough for at least 2 and up to 24 hours.

4 Preheat the oven to 350°F (175°C). Line two baking sheets with parchment paper. Place the confectioners' sugar in a small wide bowl.

5 Remove the dough from the refrigerator. Scoop and form the dough into balls about 1 inch (2.5 cm) in diameter. Roll them in the confectioners' sugar to coat and place on the prepared baking sheets about 1½ inches (4 cm) apart. If the cookies do not pick up enough confectioners' sugar at first pass (which is important for visual flair), go back and give the cookies a second roll.

6 Bake, rotating the sheets halfway through the baking time, until the cookies start to firm up along the edges, 9 to 12 minutes. If anything, pull these cookies a minute before you think they are done; they still taste fantastic slightly underbaked (with a gooey brownie-like texture inside). While they are still hot from the oven, sprinkle the tops of them with a little fleur de sel, if you like. Let the cookies cool on the baking sheets for 5 minutes. Serve warm or transfer the cookies to a wire rack and let them cool completely.

HOW TO STORE

The cookies can be kept, tightly covered, at room temperature for up to 2 days.

WHIPPED SHORTBREAD

YIELD: 48 SMALL COOKIES

ONE OF BAKED'S FINEST CAKE DECORATORS, Veronika Mautunin, submitted this recipe for our Twelve Days of Cookies because she is enamored of shortbread. And it happens to be a family tradition. We have to agree with Veronika, these are great cookies. They are melt-in-your-mouth tender and crumbly. While we both grew up with more traditional shortbread, the "whipped" aspect of these, which creates that pleasingly smooth texture, is entirely addictive. Surely they will disappear at light speed at any cookie swap.

This recipe has endless variations. Our testers loved playing with all of them. They started subbing all variety of things for the pecan topping, like candied ginger, Skor bars, and flavored salts. And a few testers thought the shortbread was beautiful with just a little lemon zest in the batter. We encourage you to experiment—it is your holiday cookie table.

INGREDIENTS

3   cups (385 g) all-purpose flour
1   cup (115 g) confectioners' sugar, sifted
1   cup (120 g) cornstarch
1   teaspoon kosher salt
1   pound (4 sticks/455 g) unsalted butter, softened
1   cup (100 g) pecans, coarsely chopped

1   Preheat the oven to 325°F (165°C). Line two baking sheets with parchment paper.
2   In a large bowl, whisk together the flour, confectioners' sugar, cornstarch, and salt. Set aside.
3   In the bowl of a standing mixer fitted with the paddle attachment, beat the butter on high speed until it is lump-free and smooth.
4   Turn the mixer to low, and slowly stream in the dry ingredients until combined. Scrape down the sides and bottom of the bowl. Mix again for 10 seconds.
5   Using a small ice-cream scoop with a release mechanism (or spoons), scoop out the cookie dough by heaping tablespoons onto the prepared sheets about ½ inch (12 mm) apart. Once all the cookies have been scooped, press down on each one with the tines of a fork in a crosshatch pattern. Press a few pecan pieces into the top of each cookie. Bake until the bottoms of the cookies start to turn a light brown, 10 to 15 minutes. Transfer the sheets to cooling racks for about 5 minutes, then transfer the cookies to the racks to cool completely.

HOW TO STORE
These cookies will keep, tightly covered, at room temperature for about a week.

PEPPERMINT CHOCOLATE CHIP MERINGUES

YIELD: ABOUT 40 COOKIES

IT WOULDN'T BE CHRISTMAS without heaps of peppermint. This recipe is a favorite of Katie Page, resident Baked decorator. It is her family recipe—a mom recipe—that she tweaked over time to balance out the right amount of peppermint with the right amount of chocolate. The result is a blissful bite-size (or two), airy meringue. It looks great—a pale pinkish/reddish kiss—it basically screams Santa Claus and tastes even better.

INGREDIENTS

4   large egg whites, at room
     temperature
¼   teaspoon cream of tartar
1   cup (200 g) granulated
     sugar
¼   teaspoon peppermint
     extract
Red food dye or gel
4   ounces (115 g) mini
     chocolate chips, or
     regular chocolate chips,
     roughly chopped (about
     ¾ cup)

1 Preheat the oven to 250°F (120°C). Line two baking sheets with parchment paper.

2 In the bowl of a standing mixer fitted with the whisk attachment, beat the egg whites on medium speed for 1 minute. Sprinkle the egg whites with cream of tartar and beat on medium-high speed until soft peaks form.

3 Turn the mixer to medium speed and add the sugar, 2 tablespoons at a time. After all of the sugar has been added, increase the mixer speed to high and beat just until stiff peaks form; the whites should still be shiny, not dry.

4 Remove the bowl from the mixer and use a rubber spatula to fold in the peppermint extract, food dye (a few drops at a time until the desired color is reached), and chocolate chips until combined.

5 Drop the mixture by heaping teaspoons onto the prepared baking sheets 1 inch (2.5 cm) apart. (Alternatively, you can pipe the meringues into a Hershey's Kiss–like shape using a pastry bag fitted with the largest round tip so that the chocolate chips can pass through.) Bake just until the meringues color and are not wet at all, 55 to 60 minutes, then turn off the oven, crack the oven door, and allow the meringues to cool completely in the oven.

HOW TO STORE

The meringues will keep, tightly covered, at room temperature for up to 4 days.

PEANUT BUTTER BUTTERSCOTCH COOKIES

YIELD: ABOUT 24 COOKIES

THOUGH I AM A PEANUT BUTTER FANATIC, I was never completely sold on the old-school peanut butter cookie recipe, the kind with the crosshatch pattern on top. I always thought they were too one-note, and impossible to eat without a gallon of whole milk at the ready. On the rare occasion my mom made these cookies, she would stud them with M&M's to liven them up with some chocolate. As previously noted, Mom rarely baked anything without chocolate. I liked her version, but they usually just made me crave a chocolate chip cookie with M&M's instead.

I decided to give these cookies another go-round with butterscotch chips instead. It was a mini revelation. They are the kind of peanut butter cookies you would have dreamt about when you were a kid: sweet (make no mistake, they are sweet) and peanut buttery—and super tasty. I don't crosshatch them, but I do sprinkle them with sea salt for a little balance. It's like a peanut butter cookie with a little holiday cheer added throughout.

INGREDIENTS

- 1 cup plus 2 tablespoons (145 g) all-purpose flour
- ¾ teaspoon baking soda
- ½ teaspoon baking powder
- ½ teaspoon kosher salt
- 5 ounces (1¼ sticks/140 g) unsalted butter, softened
- 5 ounces (140 g) smooth peanut butter, at room temperature
- ½ cup (100 g) granulated sugar
- ½ cup (110 g) firmly packed dark brown sugar
- 1 large egg
- 1 teaspoon pure vanilla extract
- 4 ounces (115 g) butterscotch chips
- 1 tablespoon sea salt (optional)

1. Preheat the oven to 350°F (175°C). Line two baking sheets with parchment paper.
2. In a medium bowl, whisk together the flour, baking soda, baking powder, and kosher salt. Set aside.
3. In the bowl of a standing mixer fitted with the paddle attachment, beat the butter on medium speed until smooth and lump-free. Add the peanut butter and beat until combined.
4. Add both sugars and continue beating on medium-high speed until light and fluffy, 3 to 4 minutes. Scrape down the sides of the bowl, add the egg and vanilla, and beat again until completely incorporated. Scrape down the sides and bottom of the bowl, add the flour mixture all at once, and beat until just incorporated, about 30 seconds. Use a wooden spoon or rubber spatula to stir in the butterscotch chips.
5. Scoop and roll the dough into balls about 1 inch (2.5 cm) in diameter. Place them on the prepared baking sheets about 1½ inches (4 cm) apart. Bake the cookies for 5 minutes, then sprinkle the tops with the sea salt, if you like. Continue baking until the cookies just start to brown on the edges, another 5 to 6 minutes. Remove from the oven and place the sheets on cooling racks for 5 minutes. Transfer the cookies from the sheets to wire racks and allow to cool completely.

HOW TO STORE

The cookies can be served immediately or stored in an airtight container at room temperature for up to 3 days.

LEBKUCHEN

YIELD: 24 COOKIES

THIS FABLED COOKIE COMES TO US DIRECTLY from Germany, via Renato's very German boyfriend, Sven Wiedmann. Like America's chocolate chip cookie, *Lebkuchen* differ from region to region, household to household, but the general idea is the same: a spiced cookie base that is more cakey than crispy, with a sweet (usually a chocolate, sugar, or candied nut) topping.

These *Lebkuchen* bear all the hallmarks of classic (er, classy) European tastes. The cookie is not too sweet—it has a fairly low sugar-to-flour ratio (though there is some honey)—and it is filled with some mighty fine chunks of candied orange. The crowning feature is the chocolate glaze. It is the pièce de résistance that brings it all together, the cherry on top of the sundae.

INGREDIENTS

For the Lebkuchengewürz (Gingerbread Spices)

1 tablespoon plus 1 teaspoon ground cinnamon
½ teaspoon ground cloves
¼ teaspoon ground allspice
⅛ teaspoon ground nutmeg
¼ teaspoon ground coriander
¼ teaspoon ground cardamom
¼ teaspoon ground ginger

For the Lebkuchen

8 ounces (225 g) honey (about ⅔ cup)
3 ounces (¾ stick/85 g) unsalted butter
¼ cup (55 g) firmly packed dark brown sugar
1 large egg yolk
1 tablespoon unsweetened dark cocoa powder
2 teaspoons Lebkuchengewürz (see above)

MAKE THE LEBKUCHENGEWÜRZ

1 In a bowl, whisk together all of the ingredients. Set aside.

MAKE THE LEBKUCHEN

1 Preheat the oven to 350°F (175°C). Line two baking sheets with parchment paper.
2 In a medium saucepan, stir together the honey, butter, and brown sugar, and cook over medium heat until the butter is melted and the brown sugar is dissolved. Remove the pan from the heat and set aside. Let cool.
3 In the bowl of a standing mixer fitted with the whisk attachment, add the cooled honey mixture and mix briefly. Add the egg yolk, cocoa powder, Lebkuchengewürz, and lemon zest, and mix at medium speed until fully combined.
4 In a small prep bowl, stir together the rum and baking soda. Add to the batter and whisk to combine, about another 15 seconds.
5 Replace the whisk attachment with the dough-hook attachment.
6 Sift the flour into a large bowl. Stir in the almonds and candied orange peel. Add the flour mixture all at once to the mixer bowl, and stir on the lowest speed until just combined. Turn onto a well-floured surface.
7 Use your hands to knead the dough until it is pliable, then form it into a small disk; the dough will be very tacky. Roll the dough into a round ½ inch (12 mm) thick, flipping it and sprinkling more flour as needed so it doesn't stick. Use a 3-inch (7.5-cm) round (or thereabouts) cookie cutter to press out your cookies; place them on the prepared baking sheets about 1 inch (2.5 cm) apart.

INGREDIENTS (CONT.)

Zest of 1 lemon
  (about 1 tablespoon)
2   tablespoons rum
1   teaspoon baking soda
2¼ cups (285 g) all-purpose
    flour
4   ounces (115 g) almonds,
    finely ground
¾   cup (140 g) finely chopped
    candied orange peel

For the Chocolate Glaze

1   cup (115 g) confectioners'
    sugar
3   tablespoons unsweetened
    cocoa powder
3 to 4 tablespoons (45 to
    60 ml) whole milk
1   teaspoon pure vanilla
    extract

8   Bake until the cookies appear set and are just dry to the touch, about 12 minutes. Use a spatula to transfer the cookies to wire racks to cool completely.

MAKE THE CHOCOLATE GLAZE

1   Line the two baking sheets with new parchment paper.

2   Sift the confectioners' sugar and cocoa into a small bowl. Add 3 tablespoons milk and the vanilla and whisk until smooth. If the glaze is too stiff, add additional milk a teaspoon at a time to loosen.

3   Working quickly, dip each cooled cookie face down into the glaze. Turn the cookies over and place them on the parchment. Allow to set completely, about 15 minutes.

HOW TO STORE

The cookies can be served immediately or stored in an airtight container at room temperature for up to 3 days.

MAE'S CRESCENT COOKIES

YIELD: 24 COOKIES

JORDAN, BAKED'S OMNIPRESENT MANAGER, is Jewish, but he loves Christmas. In fact, some of his best childhood memories are of making (and eating) other people's Christmas cookies. Specifically Mae's Crescent Cookies. Mae, a dear friend and neighbor of Jordan's mother, spent entire December afternoons in her kitchen cranking out holiday cookies, often enlisting the help of Jordan's mother for the monumental task. While Jordan enjoyed all of the goodies produced in Mae's kitchen, the crescent cookie was his standout favorite, and not just because he and his sister used to have confectioners' sugar fights while making them. Mae's Crescent Cookies, a very old-school recipe indeed, are rich and buttery and sugar-cookie-like in texture but with a ton more butter and a sprinkling of nuts. Jordan remembers devouring the cookies still warm from the oven. This is the kind of cookie Jordan associates with friends and family and, well, Christmas.

INGREDIENTS

½ cup (55 g) confectioners' sugar, sifted

8 ounces (2 sticks/225 g) unsalted butter, cool but not cold

2 cups (255 g) all-purpose flour

½ cup (50 g) walnuts, coarsely chopped

⅓ cup (65 g) granulated sugar

1 teaspoon pure vanilla extract

1 Preheat the oven to 300°F (150°C). Line two baking sheets with parchment paper.

2 Place the sifted confectioners' sugar in a wide bowl. Set aside.

3 In the bowl of a standing mixer fitted with the paddle attachment, beat the butter on high speed until smooth and creamy, 2 to 3 minutes. Add the flour, walnuts, granulated sugar, and vanilla, and beat on medium speed until completely combined.

4 Scoop and roll heaping tablespoons of dough between your hands just until they form a short, stubby log, then form them into crescents or half-moon shapes by pinching the ends slightly. Toss the crescents in the confectioners' sugar to coat (reserving any remaining) and place them on the prepared baking sheets about 1 inch (2.5 cm) apart.

5 Bake until the cookies just start to color, 25 to 30 minutes. Cool them on the baking sheets for 5 minutes, then toss them one more time in the confectioners' sugar to coat, and serve warm.

HOW TO STORE

Crescent cookies taste best within 24 hours, but you can store them, tightly covered, at room temperature for up to 2 days.

CAMPFIRE COOKIES

YIELD: ABOUT 36 COOKIES

HEAD BAKER MOLLY MARZALEK-KELLY made a double contribution to the Twelve Days of Cookies (thankfully), and one is the amazing Campfire Cookie. It is a Baked customer favorite. While at first glance, it might not scream "holiday" (the cookie is neither peppermint focused, nor red, nor a riff on a Christmas classic), it is a worthy (if not downright necessary) addition to the Santa cookie extravaganza. The inspiration for it is a bit of a lark. Molly was so moved by the painterly summer nostalgia in the 2012 movie *Moonrise Kingdom* that she felt the urge to encapsulate the famous s'more into a perfect Christmas cookie. The combination of marshmallows, chocolate, and graham crackers will ace any cookie swap, and brighten any gray December afternoon.

INGREDIENTS

- 1¾ ounces (50 g) homemade marshmallows (see page 182) or mini store-bought or plain marshmallows
- ¼ cup (25 g) sifted confectioners' sugar (only if using homemade marshmallows)
- 3 ounces (85 g) graham crackers (about 6 crackers)
- 1¾ cups (225 g) all-purpose flour
- 1 teaspoon ground cinnamon
- ½ teaspoon baking soda
- ½ teaspoon kosher salt
- 4 ounces (1 stick/115 g) unsalted butter, cool but not cold
- ½ cup (110 g) firmly packed light brown sugar
- ½ cup (100 g) granulated sugar
- 1 large egg
- 2 tablespoons honey
- 1 teaspoon pure vanilla extract
- 6 ounces (170 g) chocolate chips (about 1 cup)

1. If you are using homemade marshmallows, cut them into small cubes about the size of sugar cubes. Place the confectioners' sugar in a medium bowl and roll or dip the marshmallows in the confectioners' sugar to coat the newly exposed sticky sides and keep the marshmallows from clumping together. (If you are using store-bought mini marshmallows, you do not need the confectioners' sugar.)

2. Place the graham crackers in a zip-tight plastic bag. Roll a rolling pin back and forth over the graham crackers until they are crushed into coarse crumbs.

3. In a large bowl, whisk together the graham cracker crumbs, flour, cinnamon, baking soda, and salt. Set aside.

4. In the bowl of a standing mixer fitted with the paddle attachment, beat the butter and sugars together until smooth and creamy, about 3 minutes. Add the egg, honey, and vanilla, and beat until well incorporated. Scrape down the sides and bottom of the bowl and beat again for another 15 seconds. Add the flour mixture all at once and beat just until the dough comes together. Add the chocolate chips and marshmallows, and mix again for 15 seconds. Cover the bowl tightly and refrigerate the dough for at least 4 hours or overnight (in fact, up to a week is fine).

5. Preheat the oven to 325°F (165°C). Line two baking sheets with parchment paper.

6. Using a small ice-cream scoop with a release mechanism or a spoon, scoop 2-tablespoon balls of dough and place them on the prepared baking sheets about 1 inch (2.5 cm) apart. Bake, rotating the pans halfway through the baking time, until the edges of the cookies are set and they begin to darken, 14 to 20 minutes. Set the sheets on wire racks for 10 minutes to cool. Using a spatula, transfer the cookies to the wire racks to cool completely.

HOW TO STORE

The cookies can be stored in an airtight container at room temperature for up to 3 days.

TRADITIONAL LINZER COOKIES

YIELD: 24 COOKIES

A HOLIDAY DESSERT PLATTER without a linzer cookie is a travesty. It's like Easter without a bunny, Halloween without a jack-o'-lantern, Valentine's Day without chocolate. In short, linzer cookies are necessary come December. Not only are they quite beautiful—the jam windowpane feature is all shimmery elegance—but the taste is always pleasing. Simple. Addictive.

Renato's version of the linzer conforms closely to the traditional cookie with very slight modifications. A little unsweetened cocoa powder is added, and he recommends a less ordinary jam: Blueberry rhubarb adds an unexpected and bright flair.

INGREDIENTS

1   cup (150 g) blanched almonds, toasted (see page 19)
½   cup (100 g) granulated sugar
2   cups (255 g) all-purpose flour
1   tablespoon unsweetened cocoa powder
½   teaspoon baking powder
½   teaspoon kosher salt
8   ounces (2 sticks/225 g) unsalted butter, softened
1   large egg
1   large egg yolk
1   teaspoon almond extract
8   ounces (225 g) jam (we recommend blueberry rhubarb)
2   tablespoons confectioners' sugar

1   Put the almonds and ¼ cup (50 g) of the sugar in the bowl of a food processor and pulse until the almonds are finely ground.

2   In a large bowl, whisk together the flour, unsweetened cocoa powder, baking powder, and salt. Set aside.

3   In the bowl of a standing mixer fitted with the paddle attachment, beat the butter and remaining ¼ cup (50 g) sugar until light and fluffy. Add the egg, egg yolk, and almond extract and beat until incorporated. Scrape down the sides and bottom of the bowl and add the flour mixture in three parts, alternating with the almond mixture, beginning and ending with the flour mixture. Scrape down the sides and bottom of the bowl one more time and then mix again.

4   Turn the dough out (it will be tacky) onto a lightly floured surface and bring it together with your hands. Form the dough into two disks and wrap them tightly in plastic wrap. Refrigerate for at least 3 hours or overnight.

5   Preheat the oven to 350°F (175°C). Line two baking sheets with parchment paper.

6   Unwrap one dough disk and place it on a lightly floured surface. Roll the dough into a round ⅛ inch (3 mm) thick, flipping and lightly sprinkling it with flour as needed so it doesn't stick. Using a 2½-inch (6-cm) round cookie cutter, cut the dough and transfer the pieces to the prepared baking sheets, leaving about 1 inch (2.5 cm) of space around each cookie. Extra dough scraps can be refrigerated and rerolled, if desired. Continue the process with the remaining dough disk, and distribute the pieces equally between the two trays. Freeze the trays of cookies for 5 minutes.

7 If you like, you can bake the windowpane cutout scraps as well. Line one more baking sheet with parchment (if you don't have another baking sheet, you can place them on a large platter or plate lined with parchment until the sheet is free). Remove one sheet of dough from the freezer. Make the windowpane cutout: Working quickly, using a small cookie cutter (round, or heart- or star-shaped, about 1 inch/2.5 cm in diameter), cut out shapes directly in the middle of each round of cookie dough. Place the cutout shape scraps on the last sheet or platter, if desired. Set aside. Remove the other sheet from the freezer, but leave the cookies intact. (In total, only half of your cookies should have cutouts.)

8 Bake the cookies, rotating the sheets halfway through the baking time, until they are set, 8 to 10 minutes. Place the baking sheets on wire racks to cool for 5 minutes. Then, using a spatula, transfer the cookies to the wire racks to cool completely. (If you reserved your cutout shape scraps on a platter, transfer them to one of the empty baking sheets and bake until set, 6 to 8 minutes. Again, place the baking sheet on a wire rack to cool for 5 minutes, then transfer the cookies to the wire rack to cool.)

9 Flip the cookies that are wholly intact (with no cutout) and spread an even layer of jam, about 1 teaspoon, over the cookie bottom. Dust the cookies with the cutout with a little confectioners' sugar, then place them directly over the jam-covered cookies. Dust the cutout shapes with confectioners' sugar as well, to eat alongside the assembled linzers. Allow the cookies to set for about 10 minutes before serving.

HOW TO STORE

The cookies can be stored in an airtight container at room temperature for up to 4 days.

DATE SQUARES

YIELD: ABOUT 24 BARS

EVEN IF YOU DON'T CONSIDER YOURSELF A DATE PERSON, you would be remiss not to give these a whirl. Even Katie Page, the talented Baked decorator who introduced us to these, was a slow convert. Katie's mom regularly made these delicious date squares, but Katie was cautiously curious about the main ingredient—until after the first amazing bite. Like all good grandma-style date squares, the center of these are gooey and sweet, and the crumbs are like a delicious oatmeal cookie sandwich.

INGREDIENTS

For the Date Filling

1   pound (455 g) dried pitted dates, chopped into very small pieces
1   cup (220 g) firmly packed light brown sugar

For the Crumb Mixture

1½ cups (170 g) all-purpose flour
½   teaspoon kosher salt
½   teaspoon baking soda
1½ cups (120 g) quick-cooking oats
4   ounces (1 stick/115 g) unsalted butter, cool but not cold, cut into cubes, plus more for the pan
1   cup (220 g) firmly packed light brown sugar

MAKE THE DATE FILLING

1   In a medium saucepan, stir together the dates, brown sugar, and 1 cup (240 ml) water. Over medium-high heat, bring the mixture to a low boil, then reduce the heat to low. Simmer until the dates are soft and have absorbed most of the water, 7 to 10 minutes. Set aside to cool.

MAKE THE CRUMB MIXTURE

1   In a large bowl, sift together the flour, salt, and baking soda. Stir in the oats.

2   In the bowl of a standing mixer fitted with the paddle attachment, beat the butter and sugar on medium speed until light and fluffy, 2 to 4 minutes. Add the flour mixture all at once and mix on low speed until crumbly.

ASSEMBLE THE BARS

1   Preheat the oven to 350°F (175°C) and position a rack in the center. Butter the sides and bottom of a glass or light-colored metal 9-by-13-inch (23-by-33-cm) pan. Line the bottom with a sheet of parchment paper so that it overhangs about 1 inch (2.5 cm) on the long sides of the pan, and butter the parchment.

2   Press half of the crumb mixture into the bottom of the prepared pan. Spread the date mixture in an even layer over the crumb mixture. Finally, sprinkle the remaining half of the crumb mixture over the date layer to cover. Using the palm of your hand (lightly greased if you like), very gently press the crumb mixture into the dates so it will adhere.

3   Bake, rotating the pan halfway through the baking time, until the crumb turns golden brown, about 30 minutes. Remove the pan from the oven, place on a cooling rack, and let cool completely. Use a paring knife to release the sides of the bars from the pan, pull up on the parchment to remove them, then cut and serve.

HOW TO STORE

The squares can be stored in an airtight container in the refrigerator for up to 5 days.

LEBKUCHEN
(PAGE 234)

**TRADITIONAL
LINZER COOKIES**
(PAGE 238)

**PEANUT BUTTER
BLOSSOMS**
(PAGE 228)

DATE SQUARES
(PAGE 240)

S COOKIES
(PAGE 227)

WHIPPED SHORTBREAD
(PAGE 231)

**EXCEEDINGLY CHOCOLATY
CRINKLES** (PAGE 230)

**PEANUT BUTTER
BUTTERSCOTCH
COOKIES** (PAGE 233)

CAMPFIRE COOKIES
(PAGE 237)

MAE'S CRESCENT COOKIES
(PAGE 236)

**PEPPERMINT CHOCOLATE
CHIP MERINGUES**
(PAGE 232)

**GINGERSNAPS WITH
LEMON SUGAR**
(PAGE 229)

BROWN SUGAR OATMEAL WHOOPIE PIES WITH MAPLE MARSHMALLOW FILLING

YIELD: 15 TO 17 SMALL WHOOPIE PIES

WE GREW UP (like many, many American kids coming of age in the late '70s and early '80s) eating boatloads of pancakes and waffles doused in a Frankenstein-like food substance we just assumed was maple syrup. In fact, what we ate at home, at Denny's, at Bob's Big Boy, and at the many roadside diners clinging to I-95 was not even a relative of maple syrup. It was (breathe deep) mostly a confluence of high fructose corn syrup, cellulose gum, caramel color, and artificial flavor. It's a tiny miracle we're still here.

Needless to say, real maple syrup was a revelation. It was an explosion of flavors. Real maple syrup—produced from the sap of red maple, sugar maple, and black maple trees—strikes chords of almond, coffee, chestnut, and whiskey (at least in my brain), and some studies suggest it might be a natural antioxidant. Real maple syrup is reason alone to hug a tree. So if you feel like celebrating National Maple Syrup Day, we suggest you make our Brown Sugar Oatmeal Whoopie Pies with Maple Marshmallow Filling. They are moist little maple cakes sandwiching a frothy, marshmallowy, mapley filling. Adults like them, kids love them, and maple fanatics crave them.

●●● **BAKED NOTE**

To boost the maple experience and to reduce ingredient costs (pure maple syrup is pricey, but worth it), we use a few drops of pure natural maple extract. Again, look for an all-natural version. Do not use an imitation maple flavor/extract.

MAKE THE BROWN SUGAR OATMEAL WHOOPIE PIES

1 In a food processor, pulse the oats into coarse crumbs, leaving some large pieces for texture (ideally a mixture of oat powder and broken-up oat pieces).

2 In a large bowl, whisk together the oat crumbs, flour, baking powder, baking soda, salt, and cinnamon. Set aside.

3 In another large bowl, whisk together the brown sugar and oil. Add the eggs, yogurt, sour cream, maple syrup, and maple extract and whisk until smooth.

INGREDIENTS

**For the Brown Sugar
Oatmeal Whoopie Pies**

½ cup (80 g) rolled oats
3¼ cups (415 g) all-purpose
flour
1½ teaspoons baking powder
1 teaspoon baking soda
½ teaspoon kosher salt
½ teaspoon ground cinnamon
2 cups (440 g) firmly
packed dark brown sugar
¾ cup (180 ml) canola oil
2 large eggs
½ cup (115 g) plain whole
milk yogurt
½ cup (115 g) sour cream
1 tablespoon pure maple
syrup
1½ teaspoons pure maple
extract (not imitation)

**For the Maple
Marshmallow Filling**

1½ teaspoons powdered
gelatin
2 tablespoons cold water
3 large egg whites
¾ cup (150 g) granulated
sugar
2 to 3 teaspoons pure maple
extract

4 Using a rubber spatula, gently fold the dry ingredients into the wet ingredients. Make sure to scrape down the sides and bottom of the bowl as you fold. Cover and chill the dough in the refrigerator for at least 20 minutes.

5 Preheat the oven to 350°F (175°C). Line two baking sheets with parchment.

6 Use a small ice-scream scoop with a release mechanism to drop heaping tablespoons of the dough about 1 to 2 inches (2.5 to 5 cm) apart on the prepared baking sheets (alternatively, use a larger ice-cream scoop to yield approximately 8 to 10 larger whoopies). Bake until the cookies are just starting to crack on top and feel dry to the touch, and a toothpick inserted into the center of the cookie comes out clean, 12 to 15 minutes. Let the cookies cool completely.

MAKE THE MAPLE MARSHMALLOW FILLING

1 In a small glass measuring cup, sprinkle the gelatin over the cold water. Let soften (5 to 10 minutes).

2 Place the egg whites in the bowl of a standing mixer fitted with the whisk attachment and beat on medium-high speed until soft peaks form.

3 In a small saucepan, gently stir together the sugar and ¼ cup (60 ml) water. Set the saucepan over medium-high heat and clip a candy thermometer to the side of the saucepan. When the sugar mixture reaches 235°F (113°C), remove from the heat. Very gently stir in the softened gelatin. Turn the mixer with the egg whites on low speed and slowly pour the sugar-gelatin mixture in a slow, steady stream into the egg whites. Increase the mixer speed to high and continue to whip until stiff peaks form, about 10 minutes. Add the maple extract to taste and mix for another 30 seconds, or until completely incorporated.

4 Place the marshmallow filling in a pastry bag with a large round tip. (Alternatively, you can use a small ice-cream scoop with a release mechanism.)

ASSEMBLE THE WHOOPIE PIES

1 Turn half of the cooled cookies upside down (flat side facing up).

2 Pipe the marshmallow filling from the center of the flat side of each cookie until the filling almost reaches the edge of the cookie. (Alternatively, use the ice-cream scoop to place the filling.) Place another cookie, flat side down, on top. Press down slightly so that the filling spreads to the edges of the cookie. Continue filling the whoopie pies until all cookies are used. (It is possible you will have leftover filling, depending on how full you like your whoopies.) If you like, use a kitchen torch to gently toast the exposed sides of the marshmallow frosting. Allow the whoopies to firm up before serving, about 15 minutes.

HOW TO STORE

The whoopie pies will keep on a parchment-lined baking sheet covered with plastic wrap in the refrigerator for 3 days. Bring them back to room temperature before serving.

WINTERMINT CAKE

YIELD: 1 8-INCH (20-CM) THREE-LAYER CAKE • 10 TO 12 SERVINGS

I LIKE WINTER IN THE CITY. MOSTLY. Winter in New York is a low and pleasant hum, while summer is a loud—and often fragrant—roar. I still get a goofy delight watching the ice-skaters glide by in Central Park in the middle of January, dusk fast approaching. I still find some joy in the careful, treacherous bundling and layering, a fashion exercise unto itself. True, the days are shorter and the nights are longer, but the cold weather was practically invented for baking. I prefer to bake breads and cakes and cookies in the naturally chilled December air of an improperly insulated New York City apartment, as opposed to the artificial breeze offered by a barely passable window air-conditioning unit in the soup of July.

At Baked, our tribute to winter is the stately Wintermint Cake. It is a staff and customer favorite. It is the feature of our winter menu, which usually makes its debut on or around the solstice, and it is anticipated. The dark chocolate cake sponge is one of our classic recipes; we suggest using part black cocoa powder if you can find it (see page 19). It is rich and moist (but not too moist), and it stands up beautifully to the light peppermint buttercream and mint ganache. It is winter exemplified, a cake tailor-made for snowy backdrops and January birthdays.

●●● **BAKED NOTE**

We decorate this cake using an ombré technique, but obviously, you can cover the whole thing in just our elegant, off-white peppermint buttercream—it still looks beautiful. Also, this cake is pepperminty, but not overly so; we prefer subtler peppermint flavor. If you want to up the peppermint experience, we suggest adding a tiny bit more extract (about ¼ teaspoon) to both the ganache and the buttercream.

INGREDIENTS

For the Classic Chocolate Cake

- ½ cup (40 g) unsweetened dark cocoa powder (such as Valrhona) plus ¼ cup (20 g) unsweetened black cocoa powder; or just ¾ cup (60 g) unsweetened dark cocoa powder
- 1¼ cups (300 ml) hot water
- ⅔ cup (150 g) sour cream
- 2⅔ cups (340 g) all-purpose flour
- 2 teaspoons baking powder
- 1 teaspoon baking soda
- ½ teaspoon kosher salt
- 6 ounces (1½ sticks/170 g) unsalted butter, softened, plus more for the pans
- ½ cup (100 g) unflavored vegetable shortening
- 1 ½ cups (300 g) granulated sugar
- 1 cup (220 g) firmly packed dark brown sugar
- 3 large eggs, at room temperature
- 1 tablespoon pure vanilla extract

For the Peppermint Buttercream

- 1½ cups (300 g) granulated sugar
- ⅓ cup (40 g) all-purpose flour
- 1½ cups (360 ml) whole milk
- ⅓ cup (75 ml) heavy cream
- 12 ounces (3 sticks/340 g) unsalted butter, soft but cool, cut into ½-inch (12-mm) cubes
- 1 teaspoon pure vanilla extract

MAKE THE CLASSIC CHOCOLATE CAKE

1 Preheat the oven to 325°F (165°C).

2 Butter three 8-inch (20-cm) round cake pans, line them with parchment, and butter the parchment. Dust with flour and knock out and discard excess flour.

3 In a small bowl, mix the cocoa powder, hot water, and sour cream together and set aside to cool.

4 In a large bowl, sift the flour, baking powder, baking soda, and salt and set aside.

5 In the bowl of a standing mixer fitted with the paddle attachment, beat the butter and shortening together on medium speed until light and smooth, about 5 minutes; the mixture will appear to string or ribbon throughout the bowl. Add both sugars and beat until light and fluffy, about 5 more minutes. Add the eggs one at a time, beating after each until incorporated, then add the vanilla and beat together. Scrape down the sides of the bowl and mix again for 30 seconds. Add the flour mixture in three parts, alternating with the cocoa mixture, beginning and ending with the flour mixture, beating to incorporate after each addition. Scrape down the bowl and beat for a few more seconds.

6 Divide the batter among the three prepared pans (about 1¼ pounds/565 g of batter per pan). Use your spatula to spread the batter evenly. Bake, rotating the pans halfway through, until a toothpick inserted in the center of the cakes comes out clean, 35 to 40 minutes. Transfer the cakes to a wire rack and let cool for 20 minutes. Invert the cakes onto the rack and let them cool completely. Remove the parchment.

MAKE THE PEPPERMINT BUTTERCREAM

1 In a medium heavy-bottomed saucepan, whisk the sugar and flour together. Add the milk and cream and cook over medium heat, whisking constantly but gently, until the mixture comes to a boil and has thickened, 8 to 12 minutes.

2 Transfer the mixture to the bowl of a standing mixer fitted with the paddle attachment. Beat on high speed until cool, at least 7 to 9 minutes of mixing; you can speed up the process by pressing bags of frozen berries or corn against the sides and bottom of the mixing bowl. Reduce the speed to low and add the butter a few cubes at a time, beating well after each addition. Once all of the butter is thoroughly incorporated, increase the speed to medium-high and beat until the frosting is light and fluffy, 1 to 2 minutes. Add the vanilla and peppermint extracts and continue mixing until combined. If the frosting is too soft, put the bowl in the refrigerator to chill slightly, then beat again until it is the proper consistency; if the frosting is too firm, set the bowl over a pot of simmering water and beat with a wooden spoon until it is the proper consistency.

MAKE THE PEPPERMINT CHOCOLATE GANACHE

1 Place the chocolate in a medium heatproof bowl and set aside.

2 In a small saucepan over medium heat, bring the cream just to a boil. Remove from the heat and pour it over the chocolate. Let the cream sit for 2 to 4 minutes, then, starting in the center of the

INGREDIENTS (CONT.)

1 teaspoon pure peppermint extract (not mint or spearmint extract)

For the Peppermint Chocolate Ganache

6 ounces (170 g) dark chocolate (60 to 72% cacao), coarsely chopped

½ cup (120 ml) heavy cream

1 tablespoon crème de menthe (optional)

½ teaspoon pure peppermint extract

For the Assembly

Food dye or gel

bowl and working your way out to the edges, slowly stir the chocolate-and-cream mixture in a circle until the chocolate is completely melted and the mixture is smooth. Whisk for another few minutes to release the excess heat from the mixture. Stir in the crème de menthe, if using, and the peppermint extract. Let the ganache come to room temperature, whisking occasionally, about 15 minutes.

ASSEMBLE THE CAKE

1 Place one cake layer on a serving platter (or, better yet, a cake turntable). Trim the cake layer to create a flat top surface. Use an offset spatula to spread about ¼ cup (60 ml) of the mint chocolate ganache on the top (not sides) of the layer. Put the cake in the refrigerator to set the ganache for a few minutes. Remove from the refrigerator and spread approximately 1¼ cups (160 g) of the peppermint buttercream on top of the ganache. Top with the next cake layer, trim, add ganache, chill, and then add buttercream as with the first layer. Then add the third layer and trim the top. Spread a very thin layer of peppermint buttercream (known as crumb coating) over the sides and top of the cake and put it in the refrigerator to firm up for about 15 minutes. (See photo 1.)

2 To frost the cake ombré-style, distribute the remaining frosting into three separate bowls, putting about ¼ cup (30 g) more frosting in one bowl than in the other two. Add a few drops of food dye to each bowl and mix to create three different shades of pink: dark, medium, and light; the one with slightly more frosting should be the light pink. Obviously, if pink is not your color, you can use any color on the spectrum.

3 Starting with the bottom of the cake, apply a band of the dark pink frosting up one-third of the cake and all the way around. (See photo 2.) Wipe the spatula. Apply an equal band of medium pink frosting above the dark pink frosting and wipe the spatula. Then apply an equal band of light pink frosting above the medium pink band, bringing it all the way up to the top edge of the cake. (See photo 3.) Wipe the spatula. Immediately, use an offset spatula to smooth the bands (you can spin

the cake turntable against the edge of the offset spatula to make this step easier; see photo 4); while continuing to smooth the color bands, bring some of the light pink frosting up and just slightly over the top of the cake.

4   Using the same offset spatula, wiping it as necessary, start from the bottom and dimple the cake in even rows up the sides of the cake (if you are using a cake turntable, rotate the cake and just lift and press with the curved end of the spatula). (See photo 5.)

5   Finally, once all of the dimples have been applied to the sides of the cake, spread the remaining light pink frosting over the top of the cake (you might need to add a smidge more light pink icing to your spatula as you work) and continue the dimpling process in toward the center. (See photo 6.)

6   To frost the cake more conventionally (not ombré-style), follow the instructions in step 1 to apply the crumb coat. Frost the sides and top of the cake with the remaining buttercream, and refrigerate for about 15 minutes to firm up the entire cake.

HOW TO STORE

This cake will keep beautifully in a cake saver at room temperature for up to 3 days, as long as the weather is cool and humidity-free. Otherwise, place it in a cake saver and refrigerate it for up to 3 days; let the chilled cake sit at room temperature for at least 2 hours before serving.

PINK PEPPERMINT STICK ICE CREAM WITH HOMEMADE HOT FUDGE

YIELD: ABOUT 1½ QUARTS (1.4 L) OF ICE CREAM AND 1¼ CUPS (300 ML) OF HOT FUDGE • ABOUT 6 SERVINGS

CHRISTMAS IN FLORIDA IS NOT CHRISTMAS. Christmas in Florida is one giant miscalculation. A mutation. It is a disturbing blend of overly scented coconut suntan lotion, humidity, and housecoats (there is a proclivity for housecoats in Florida). It is the sacrilege of Christmas lights on a palm tree. It is not okay. We have the authority to say this because we spent a fair number of Christmases in Florida (not by choice). We opened presents in our shorts. We much prefer Christmases in New York. These are the Christmases of movies. These are the Christmases of roaring fires, hot chocolate, warm cookies, gentle snows, Bing Crosby, mittens, wool blankets, and scarves.

The insanity wrought by the scourge of spending Christmas in Florida produced one everlasting (and worthwhile) habit. We are perfectly okay with ice cream for Christmas. In fact, we are fine with ice cream any time of the year, but there is something sublime about our Pink Peppermint Stick Ice Cream at Christmas. It is suitable for warm, sandy, Florida beach–type Christmases (of course) as well as snow-on-Central-Park–type Christmases. Our ice cream is extra-rich (five egg yolks), and the peppermint candies nod to something whimsical while providing a contrasting crunch. And then there is the hot fudge: thick, almost chewy, rich and chocolaty hot fudge. It is supreme and necessary, and when the hot fudge is poured over this ice cream, worlds collide.

●●●● **BAKED NOTE**

The inclusion of crushed candy canes in this recipe is very retro; however, if you do not like the texture (we are well aware that some people dislike the "stick to your teeth" feel of crushed canes in ice cream), please feel free to leave them out. The ice cream is a beautiful, rich, and premium peppermint dream on its own. Also, we almost always employ a quick time-saving tip we picked up from the book *Jeni's Splendid Ice Cream at Home*: To cool the ice cream base quickly, pour it into a gallon-size zip-tight plastic bag and submerge the bag in ice water. The base should be ready for churning in 30 minutes.

INGREDIENTS

For the Pink Peppermint Ice Cream

2½ cups (600 ml) heavy cream

¾ cup (180 ml) whole milk

1 cup (200 g) granulated sugar

⅛ teaspoon kosher salt

5 large egg yolks

2 teaspoons natural peppermint extract (not mint or spearmint extract)

½ teaspoon pure vanilla extract

Red or pink food dye or gel

¾ cup (115 g) crushed candy canes, plus more for garnish

For the Hot Fudge

4 ounces (115 g) unsweetened chocolate, coarsely chopped

3 tablespoons unsalted butter, cubed

½ cup (50 g) sifted confectioners' sugar

½ cup (110 g) firmly packed dark brown sugar

¼ cup (20 g) unsweetened cocoa powder, such as Valrhona

3 tablespoons light corn syrup

½ teaspoon kosher salt

¾ cup (180 ml) heavy cream

2 teaspoons pure vanilla extract

MAKE THE PINK PEPPERMINT ICE CREAM

1 In a medium saucepan, stir together the cream, milk, ½ cup (100 g) of the sugar, and the salt. Over medium-high heat, bring the mixture to a slow, consistent simmer, just before boiling, then remove it from the heat.

2 Put the egg yolks in a large heatproof bowl. Add the remaining ½ cup (100 g) sugar and whisk the mixture until it's pale and fully combined. While whisking constantly, slowly stream in half of the cream mixture. Then, whisking constantly, transfer the egg mixture back into the medium saucepan containing the other half of the cream mixture. Cook the custard over medium-low heat, stirring constantly until it is thick enough to coat the back of a spoon (approximately 175°F/80°C), 5 to 10 minutes; do not boil. Remove from the heat and strain the mixture through a fine-mesh sieve into a medium bowl. Whisk in the peppermint extract, add the vanilla, and add food dye to reach the color you desire. Continue to whisk vigorously for a minute or two to release excess heat. Cover and refrigerate for at least 4 hours or overnight. (Alternatively, fill a large bowl with ice and a little bit of water, then pour the ice cream mixture into a smaller bowl and place that bowl directly on top of the ice; whisk the custard and turn the bowl until the mixture is completely cool. It is essential for the mixture to be completely chilled before adding it to the ice-cream maker.)

3 Pour the chilled mixture into an ice-cream maker and follow the manufacturer's directions to process, adding the crushed candy canes about 2 to 3 minutes before the ice cream is finished churning. Freeze the ice cream in an airtight container for 3 to 4 hours to freeze completely.

MAKE THE HOT FUDGE

1 Place the chocolate and butter in a heatproof bowl set over a pan of simmering water (double-boiler method, see page 19), and stir occasionally until the chocolate and butter are completely melted and combined. Do not boil or overheat the mixture; it should be lukewarm.

2 In a medium saucepan, whisk together the confectioners' sugar, brown sugar, cocoa powder, corn syrup, and salt. Stir in the cream and cook over medium-high heat until the mixture boils. Let the mixture boil for 1 minute while whisking slowly but constantly. Remove it from the heat, add the butter mixture, and whisk to combine. Transfer the sauce to a glass measuring cup with a pour spout or a serving pitcher, stir it to release excess heat, and add the vanilla. Let the mixture cool until it is just warm (it will thicken as it cools).

3 To serve, scoop ice cream into serving bowls and pour the hot fudge over it. Sprinkle with additional crushed candy canes, if you like.

HOW TO STORE

Hot fudge can be kept in an airtight container in the refrigerator for up to 4 days. Reheat (in the microwave in short bursts or on the stovetop) before serving. Leftover ice cream can be stored in the freezer in a plastic container, top covered with a layer of parchment and then sealed.

TRICOLOR CAKE

ITALIAN CHRISTMAS COOKIE CAKE

YIELD: 1 8-INCH (20-CM) THREE-LAYER CAKE • ABOUT 16 SERVINGS

ONE OF RENATO'S LIFETIME GOALS is to produce unlimited versions of and variations on his favorite Italian cookie, the tricolor (aka rainbow cookie). This is not some foolhardy quest. It is a serious, scholarly (sort of) endeavor to keep the tricolor relevant, to shelter an endangered species. While the tricolor is still a staple of most Italian American bakery cases, it has fallen on rough times. Too often the cookies are dry and tasteless. Too often they are made "somewhere else" and trucked in under the faux-homemade guise. A good tricolor cookie is moist, and the preserves should complement the almond and chocolate flavors, not drown them.

The tricolor cookies at Baked have evolved. They used to be bite-size and adorable. Currently, they are brownie-size, substantial, and addictive. Logically, at least by Renato's logic, we needed a cake version, a big, hulking slice of tricolor. Our heavenly Tricolor Cake is a tribute to tricolor super fans everywhere. The particular flavors are the same, but everything is supersized. The rich almond sponge is slightly thicker, and the chocolate component is more extreme (thanks to the combo of the chocolate crumb coat and chocolate glaze). We kept the familiar red and green colors—perfect for Christmas—but feel free to create a custom color combo to any occasion (red/white/red is perfect for Valentine's Day).

●●● **BAKED NOTE**

Pouring the glaze over the composed cake is easier than it at first appears. Our only caveats: Be prepared to work quickly (i.e., make sure your icing spatula is clean, dry, and nearby) and know that your chocolate glaze layer will only be as smooth as the crumb coat underneath. If your crumb coat is bumpy, chances are your final cake will show a few bumps as well. Regardless, it will still taste delicious.

INGREDIENTS

For the Tricolor Cake

3   cups (385 g) all-purpose flour

2   tablespoons baking powder

½   teaspoon kosher salt

12 ounces (3 sticks/340 g) unsalted butter, softened, plus more for the pans

2   cups (400 g) granulated sugar

6   large eggs

14 ounces (395 g) or 2 (7-ounce/198-g) tubes almond paste, at room temperature and coarsely chopped

1   tablespoon almond extract

¾   cup (180 ml) whole milk

Red and green food dyes or gels

For the Raspberry Filling

1   cup (320 g) raspberry preserves

2   tablespoons framboise liqueur (optional)

For the Ganache Crumb Coat

12 ounces (340 g) dark chocolate (60 to 72% cacao)

¼   cup plus 2 tablespoons (90 ml) heavy cream

2   tablespoons framboise liqueur (optional)

MAKE THE TRICOLOR CAKE

1   Preheat the oven to 325°F (165°C). Butter three 8-inch (20-cm) round cake pans, line the bottoms with parchment paper, and butter the parchment. Dust the parchment with flour and knock out the excess.

2   Sift together the flour, baking powder, and salt into a large bowl. Set aside.

3   In the bowl of a standing mixer fitted with the paddle attachment, beat the butter and sugar together on medium-high speed until light and fluffy, about 3 minutes. Add the eggs, one at a time, beating at medium speed until each is just incorporated. Scrape down the sides and bottom of the bowl. Add the almond paste and extract, and beat until combined. Again, scrape down the sides and bottom of the bowl and beat again for 10 seconds.

4   Add the flour mixture to the mixing bowl in three parts, alternating with the milk, beginning and ending with the flour mixture. Scrape down the bowl, then mix on low speed for a few more seconds.

5   Transfer one-third of the batter to a separate bowl. Add 5 to 10 drops of green food dye and fold with a rubber spatula until fully and evenly incorporated and the desired color is achieved. Add 8 to 10 drops of red food dye to the remaining two-thirds of the batter in the mixing bowl and fold with a rubber spatula until fully and evenly incorporated and desired color is achieved. (The amount of food dye is entirely up to you; we enjoy paler, less radioactive red and green layers.)

6   Divide the red batter equally into two of the prepared pans. Pour the green batter into the remaining prepared pan. Smooth the tops with an offset spatula. Bake, rotating the pans halfway through the baking time, until a toothpick inserted in the center of the cake comes out clean, 40 to 50 minutes. Transfer the pans to a wire rack and cool for 20 to 30 minutes. Turn the cakes out onto the rack, remove the parchment, and let cool completely. Once all of the layers are cool to the touch, you can start to prepare the other components of the cake in the order described below.

MAKE THE RASPBERRY FILLING

1   In a small saucepan over low heat, stir together the raspberry preserves and framboise, if using, until the mixture is uniform, warmed through, and the framboise is absorbed completely into the preserves, about 5 minutes. Set aside to cool.

INGREDIENTS (CONT.)

For the Dark Chocolate Glaze

10 ounces (285 g) dark chocolate (60 to 72% cacao), chopped (a scant 2 cups)
7 ounces (1¾ sticks/200 g) unsalted butter
1 tablespoon light corn syrup

For Décor

Red and green sprinkles

MAKE THE GANACHE CRUMB COAT

1 In a large nonreactive metal bowl, combine the chocolate and ¼ cup (60 ml) cream and set the bowl over a saucepan of simmering water (double boiler method, see page 19). Stir with a rubber spatula until the mixture is completely smooth. Remove the bowl from the pan and stir for 30 seconds to cool slightly. Whisk in the framboise, if using. The glaze should be thick (not quite as thick as hot fudge, but thick enough to coat a cake; if it is too thin it will just run off the sides) in order to get a straight, evenly glazed cake. If the mixture is thin, place the mixture in the refrigerator for about 10 minutes to thicken, stirring at least once or twice; if the mixture is too thick, add the remaining cream, a tablespoon at a time until workable.

ASSEMBLE THE CAKE

1 Place one red layer on an 8-inch (20-cm) cardboard round (or alternatively, place it on flat plate, but know that you will have to transfer the entire cake from the plate to a wire rack to glaze it). Trim the top to create a flat surface. Spread about ½ cup (155 g) of the preserve mixture into an even layer, leaving a ¼-inch (6-mm) border around the edge. Place the green layer on top of the red layer, trim the top, and spread another ½ cup (155 g) of preserves into an even layer leaving a ¼-inch (6-mm) border around the edge. With the remaining red layer, trim the top to create a smooth surface. Place the just-cut surface on top of the green layer so that the bottom of the red layer becomes the top of your cake. Refrigerate your cake for 5 minutes to set.

2 Once the ganache is spreadable, cover the cake, using the ganache like a crumb coat, making sure to use the crumb coat to fill in edges, crevices, and the space between layers. Create as smooth a cake as possible. (See photo 1) Refrigerate the cake for about 5 minutes.

MAKE THE DARK CHOCOLATE GLAZE

1 Remove your crumb-coated cake from the refrigerator and smooth out any bumps with an offset spatula. Transfer the cake to a cooling rack set atop a cookie sheet or half sheet pan lined with parchment. (See photo 2.)

2   In a large nonreactive metal bowl, combine the chocolate, butter, and corn syrup. Set the bowl over a saucepan of simmering water (double-boiler method, see page 19) and stir with a rubber spatula until the mixture is completely smooth. Remove the bowl from the pan and stir for 30 seconds to cool slightly.

3   Working quickly, pour the glaze around the rim of the cake, allowing excess glaze to run down and coat the sides of the cake (see photos 3, 4, and 5). Once you have covered the entire perimeter of the cake, work your way inward with the glaze until the entire top of the cake is covered (see photo 6). Do not worry if it looks like there is too much glaze in one spot—you can even out and scrape off excess once done pouring. After all of the glaze has been poured, use an offset spatula to smooth the top—pushing the excess glaze over the sides of the cake. Smooth the sides of the cake. Once the entire cake is completely covered in an even layer of chocolate glaze, decorate the border with sprinkles. Any leftover glaze that was caught by the cookie sheet can be gathered up and spooned into a piping bag and used to pipe a simple border along the bottom of the cake for a super-clean appearance. Transfer the cake to the refrigerator until set, about 60 minutes.

4   Remove the cake from the refrigerator and allow it to warm up for about 10 minutes. Run a chef's knife under hot water, dry it, and slice the cake with the warm knife. Serve immediately.

HOW TO STORE

The cake can be stored, covered, in the refrigerator for up to 4 days.

ORANGE PINEAPPLE WALNUT FRUITCAKE

YIELD: 1 9-BY-5-INCH (23-BY-12-CM) LOAF • ABOUT 10 SERVINGS

FRUITCAKE IS NOT A PUNCH LINE, though it is often treated like one. In fact, it's quite a tasty and versatile dessert that somehow ended up the target of countless lazy jokes (i.e., only cockroaches and fruitcake will survive a nuclear blast). This is unfair. The barrage of criticism is unwarranted. Give peace *and* fruitcake a chance.

We fancy our Orange Pineapple Walnut Fruitcake as part of the new wave. It's the Truffaut of holiday desserts. Though this recipe is vaguely reminiscent of the classic American fruitcake, studded with green and red candied fruits, this one is more cerebral. And boozier. The body is more hearty, bread-like even, and less sticky, while the pineapple is the perfect partner for the rum. The overall yet subtle vibe is tropical Christmas. While we don't imagine this will be a recipe you will make year-round— even with all of the changes it still feels very grounded in December—it is at least worth making once per year. We'd even recommend making two at once (the recipe doubles easily): one for yourself and one for an unsuspecting friend.

●●● BAKED NOTE

This is one boozy fruitcake. If you prefer a less rummy but equally tasty dessert (but why, oh why, oh *why* would you?), reduce the rum used to soak the cake to 2 tablespoons insted of ¼ cup. Do not reduce the rum in the cake itself, as it is essential to a great-tasting, lovely-textured sponge. And note, though you will want to eat the cake as soon as it comes out of the oven, you must have patience and wait a full 24 hours for the flavors to mingle properly.

INGREDIENTS

For the Fruitcake

2 oranges

1½ cups (240 g) diced dried pineapple (candied pineapple works as well)

½ cup (120 ml) good-quality dark or spiced rum

1 cup (200 g) granulated sugar

6 ounces (1½ sticks/170 g) unsalted butter, cut into ½-inch (12-mm) pieces, plus more for the pan

1½ cups (210 g) bread flour

1 teaspoon baking soda

½ teaspoon kosher salt

2 large eggs

1 large egg yolk

1 teaspoon pure vanilla extract

½ cup (50 g) toasted walnuts (see page 19), coarsely chopped

¼ cup (60 ml) good-quality dark rum

For the Glaze

1¼ cups (140 g) confectioners' sugar, sifted

2 to 3 tablespoons good-quality dark rum

MAKE THE FRUITCAKE

1 Zest the oranges; you should have approximately 3 tablespoons. Juice 1 or 2 oranges until you have approximately ⅓ cup (75 ml) juice, and reserve; use the remainder for another purpose.

2 In a medium saucepan, stir together the pineapple, ½ cup (120 ml) rum, and the orange juice. Bring to a boil over high heat, then reduce the heat to medium. Add the sugar and butter and stir until both are melted, then reduce the heat to low and simmer for about 5 minutes. The mixture should look like a thick syrup. Remove it from the stove, stir vigorously for 1 minute to release the heat, and allow to cool until lukewarm, at least 15 to 20 minutes. Set aside.

3 Preheat the oven to 325°F (165°C) and position a rack in the center. Butter a 9-by-5-inch (23-by-12-cm) loaf pan, dust it with flour, and knock out the excess flour.

4 In a medium bowl, whisk together the flour, baking soda, and salt.

5 Whisk the dry ingredients into the rum mixture. Scrape down the sides and bottom of the pan and add the reserved 3 tablespoons orange zest. Whisk for a few seconds to incorporate. Add the eggs and egg yolk, one at a time, whisking well after each addition. Scrape down the sides of the bowl and add the vanilla. Whisk until just incorporated. With a rubber spatula, fold in the walnuts and stir until combined.

6 Spoon the batter into the prepared pan and bake for 70 to 80 minutes. The loaf should be a deep golden brown and a toothpick or skewer inserted into the center of the cake should come out clean (or with a few loose crumbs).

7 Let the loaf cool in the pan for 15 minutes. Use a wooden skewer or a toothpick to poke holes all over the cake. Pour the remaining ¼ cup (60 ml) rum over the cake—don't worry if it looks like a lot of liquid; you really want the cake to get a good soaking. Let the cake cool, then cover it loosely with plastic wrap and let sit for at least 24 hours. After the 24-hour period, loosen the cake by running a small knife around the edge of the pan, then turn it out. Place it on a serving dish.

MAKE THE GLAZE

1 In a small bowl, whisk the confectioners' sugar with 2 tablespoons of the rum until smooth. If the mixture appears too thick, add another tablespoon rum or a few drops water, a little at a time, until the desired consistency is reached. Drizzle the glaze over the cake to cover the top, allowing a few rivulets to run down the sides. Allow to set for at least 10 minutes before serving.

HOW TO STORE

The fruitcake will keep, tightly wrapped, at room temperature for about 3 days.

SALTED CARAMEL CHOCOLATE CUPCAKE SHAKES

YIELD: 2 MINI (BUT RICH) MILK SHAKES

WE ARE FLABBERGASTED and mildly upset. It's not often that America lets a perfectly good holiday go virtually unnoticed. Especially a holiday that extends another holiday (Boxing Day falls the day after Christmas) and one with no real preoccupation other than eating leftovers, lounging, and shopping. Boxing Day has all the makings for a great American day, yet it is uniquely British (the day is also celebrated in Canada, Wales, and Ireland). There is no real reason we—that is, Americans—can't co-opt this holiday as one of our own. After all, it is a purely secular holiday with multiple and varied origin stories, no messy historical details to corroborate. Think of it as a respite, a vacation of sorts, from a harried Christmas. Or think of it as a holiday extension. Or just go shopping.

We're told that Boxing Day is a day of leftovers. Friends and families gather, albeit loosely, around a buffet of reheated Christmas dishes and watch TV, commiserate, and relax. If you are lucky enough to have any extra holiday cupcakes (or cake or pie), you (and your friends) are in for a special slovenly Boxing Day delight. Our Salted Caramel Chocolate Cupcake Shake is nearly a meal, and it is less cloying than it sounds. It is simply a few cupcakes blended with ice cream and milk. While the cupcakes can be day-olds (in fact, they almost work better for this purpose), do not use a lesser-quality ice cream. Use a premium brand or make your own. And remember: Cupcake shakes are all about ratios. The higher the ratio of cupcake to ice cream, the better the shake.

●●● **BAKED NOTE**

In theory, almost any cupcake-plus-ice-cream combo will work. In fact, you can replace the two cupcakes with one hefty slice of two- or three-layer cake, or even a slice of pie. The blender is your canvas. See the sidebar on page 262 for some of our favorite suggestions.

INGREDIENTS

¼ cup (60 ml) very cold whole milk, plus more as needed

3 cups (1½ pints/710 ml) salty caramel ice cream (see Baked Note)

2 frosted chocolate cupcakes (we suggest Red Wine Chocolate Cupcakes, page 117)

Whipped cream (see page 122)

Sprinkles (optional)

1 Freeze two (4-ounce/120-ml) old-fashioned glasses for at least 30 minutes.

2 Pour the milk into the blender. Add the ice cream and cupcakes and blend until thick and creamy, about 10 seconds. A good milk shake should be eaten with a spoon, so if it seems too thin, add a little more ice cream and blend again. Likewise, if the milk shake seems too thick, add a few more tablespoons of cold milk and blend again.

3 Divide the shake between the two chilled glasses, top each with whipped cream, and sprinkles if you like, and serve immediately.

OUR FAVORITE VARIATIONS

- Chocolate Mint Chip Shake: mint chip ice cream + chocolate cupcakes

- Strawberry Shortcake Shake: vanilla bean ice cream + strawberry shortcakes

- Peanut Butter Choco Bliss Shake: peanut butter ice cream + chocolate cupcakes

- Birthday Shake: vanilla ice cream + vanilla cupcakes

- Double Nut Shake: pistachio ice cream + pistachio cupcakes

- Chocolate Overload Shake: dark chocolate ice cream + chocolate cupcakes

Feel free to improvise. And, feel free to share your creations with us. We won't be content until we have tried them all.

SOURCES

Candy, Chocolate, and Other
Specialty ingredients

Bob's Red Mill
800-349-2173
www.bobsredmill.com
Beautiful bounty of specialty flours

Callebaut Chocolate
603-942-6032
www.worldwidechocolate.com

Economy Candy
212-254-1531
www.economycandy.com
Great source for bulk (like Hershey's Kisses) and hard-to-find candies

India Tree
800-369-4848
www.indiatree.com
Great resource for specialty sugars and all-natural food colorings

Jacques Torres
718-875-1269
www.mrchocolate.com

King Arthur Flour
800-827-6836
www.kingarthurflour.com

Koppers Chocolate
800-325-0026
www.kopperschocolate.com

Nielsen-Massey
800-525-7873
www.nielsen-massey.com
Great for vanilla bean paste and other extracts (and, of course, pure vanilla extract)

Saltworks
800-353-7258
www.saltworks.us
Wide variety of salts sold in bulk portions

Scharffen Berger
www.scharffenberger.com
Also available in most grocery/ specialty stores

TCHO Chocolate
415-981-0189
www.tcho.com
Addictive milk chocolate

Valrhona Chocolate
888-682-5746
www.valrhona-chocolate.com
Also available in many specialty stores

Whole Foods
512-477-4455
www.wholefoodsmarket.com
Organic foods as well as a great variety of high-grade chocolates and cheeses (often locally sourced) and nuts

Kitchen and Baking Tools and
Equipment

Brooklyn Kitchen
718-389-2982
www.thebrooklynkitchen.com
A local (nearly cult status) well-edited kitchen supply store with a staff that knows everything there is to know about cooking and baking

Crate & Barrel
800-967-6696
www.crateandbarrel.com

JB Prince
800-473-0577
www.jbprince.com

KitchenAid Appliances
800-541-6390
www.kitchenaid.com

New York Cake & Bake
800-942-2539
www.nycake.com
A fantastic resource for the New York–based baker; pans, tools, and decorating equipment

Nordic Ware
877-466-7342
www.nordicware.com
Feed your Bundt-pan obsession with the original heavy-duty creator. Nordic Ware products are also available at Williams-Sonoma stores.

Pfeil & Holing
800-247-7955
www.cakedeco.com
Decorating supplies sold in bulk

Williams-Sonoma
877-812-6235
www.williams-sonoma.com
Best resource for all of your baking and kitchen needs—including some signature Baked items and baking mixes

ACKNOWLEDGMENTS

Creating and compiling a Baked dessert book/compendium is delicious, delirious, and fun—as well as rigorous, intense, and slightly insane. It's like raising a puppy that grows very quickly. It needs a lot of attention and a lot of love and a whole lot of time. Thankfully, we were surrounded by a great group of people during this process. We would like to thank the following individuals for their support, guidance, prodding, heavy lifting, soothing thoughts, magic whispers, honest opinions, and prescription drugs:

Jessie Sheehan is a full-fledged voodoo dessert priestess. She helped develop a hefty portion of the recipes within this volume and her precision and skill are scary-good. (God bless you, Jessie, for the Blueberry Buckle recipe.)

Alison Fargis, friend and agent extraordinaire, has been working with us since we were infamous child stars. Her loyalty and guidance are a shining light. She is the Mother Teresa of agents. Hugs to the rest of the staff at Stonesong.

Much gratitude to our patient and gracious editor, Elinor Hutton. She was kind and gentle when we were frantic and manic. Her intuition was always spot-on, and (bonus) she really, really likes dessert. And much love to all of our friends at our loyal publisher, STC.

A million kudos to our brilliant photographer, Brian Kennedy. We fell hopelessly in love with each photo in this book (so much so that it was difficult to choose a cover). Brian is a great friend (we fancy him the resident Baked photographer) and sly humorist (look hard, each photo has a wicked sense of humor). We look forward to many future dessert adventures together.

THE ENTIRE CREATIVE TEAM WAS THE BOMB:
Carrie Purcell is an ace food stylist with a warm heart. She (along with her lovely assistants, Micah Morton and Cecile Dyer) treated all of our recipes with the perfect proportions of elegance and humor. Pam Morris propped the hell out of this book and we couldn't be more pleased. Ask Pam the Magician for anything and she will find it. And many thanks to Deb Wood for appropriating our endless stream of consciousness into a cohesive and beautifully designed book.

AS ALWAYS, SPECIAL THANKS TO OUR SUPER-DUPER LOVED ONES:
Sven Weidmann and Bret Hansen. We really appreciate the Herculean task of consuming multiple samples of the same recipe over and over and over again in the name of love.

A GREAT BIG SPECIAL THANKS TO SOME SUPER-SPECIAL PEOPLE—OUR DEVOTED RECIPE TESTERS AND OUR EMPLOYEES:
A well-tested cookbook is a fantastic cookbook. And we were lucky enough to have some of the most devoted testers in the country apply themselves selflessly to Baked Occasions. We could not be happier to work alongside this diligent army of chocolate and butter and sugar devotees. They are pastry warriors—wielding whisks and spatulas with precision and aplomb.

And extra-special thanks to close friend and leader of this ragtag group, Sheri Codiana. You kept us sane and wholly organized (your Excel skills are unparalleled). And perhaps the best possible compliment: Whenever we see a gay cake, we think of you. We just hope your husband doesn't mind.

Last, this book—like all of our books—is a reflection on our bakery. Our staff is our life support. Extra-special love to the tireless efforts of our current (and past and future) baking (and front-of-house) staff.

The good part: We are pleased to bring all of our testers and current kitchen employees to life for our readers via photos (a first for us). Give them a big round of applause—and if you see them on the street, don't be afraid to hug them.

Our staff, left to right: Jordan Slocum, Wendi York, Mandisa Andrews, Veronika Matunin, Melody Medina, Katie Page, Molly Marzalek-Kelly

BADASS RECIPE TESTERS

Dafna Adler

Jen Bertrand

Céline Bourbonnais

Sheri Codiana

Christine DeLorme

Kristen Fenton

Lauren Godfrey

Erin Star Hayes

Sarah Wheeler LaCombe

Susan Lester

Robyn MacDonald

Sandra Marks

Chloe McGuire

Mark Neufang

Athena Plichta

Liz Rapp

Jessie Sheehan

Judy Sogoian

Joann Tamburro

Candy Wafford

Jenn Yee

INDEX

A

Almond Butter Frosting, *91*, 92
almonds:
    Almond Glaze, 114, *115*
    Cherry Almond Crisp, *64*, 65–66
    Lebkuchen, *225*, 234–35, *241*
    Toffee Coffee Cake Surprise,
        44–47, *45*
    Traditional Linzer Cookies, *224*,
        238–39, *241*
apples: Brown Butter Apple
    Cranberry Galette, 212–15, *213*

B

Baked Alaska: Individual Baked
    Alaskas with Vanilla and Coffee
    Ice Cream, *192*, 193–94
bananas:
    Caramel-y Banana, Peanut
        Butter, and Chocolate Bread
        Pudding, 32–35, *33*
    Kitchen-Sink Dutch Baby, 61–62,
        63
berries:
    Blueberry Cake, 166, *167*
    Brown Sugar Shortcakes with
        Brown Sugar Syrup, Mixed
        Berries, and Whipped Cream,
        128–31, *129*
    Chai Spice Trifle with Mixed
        Berries, 120–23, *121*
    Nonnie's Blueberry Buckle,
        165–66, *167*
Black Forest Cupcakes, 104, *105*,
    106

Black Velvet Heart Cakes, 50–53,
    51
Blood Orange Tiramisu, 74, *75*,
    76
Bourbon Sugar, 108
bread: Cheesy Bastille Day Beer
    Bread, 144–45
Brioche, 162, *163*
    in Bread Pudding, 34–35
    Brioche Ice Cream
        Sandwiches, 161–64, *163*
Brown Butter Apple Cranberry
    Galette, 212–15, *213*
brownies:
    Milk Chocolate Malted Brownies
        with Chocolate Ganache,
        195–98, *197*
    Mini Chocolate Brownie
        Cupcakes, 178–79
    Pumpkin Swirl Cheesecake
        Chocolate Brownies, 189–90,
        191
Brown Sugar Oatmeal Whoopie
    Pies with Maple Marshmallow
    Filling, 242–43
Brown Sugar Praline Ice Cream
    Cake, 56–60, *57*
Brown Sugar Shortcakes with
    Brown Sugar Syrup, Mixed
    Berries, and Whipped Cream,
    128–31, *129*
Brutti Ma Buoni (Ugly but Good)
    Cookies, 30–31
butter, 19

Butter Whiskey Glaze, *133*, 134
Buttery Brown Sugar Bourbon
    Walnut Balls, 107–8, *109*
Buttery Pound Cake with Salty
    Caramel Glaze, 93–95
Honey Butter, 176

C

cakes:
    Baked Ultimate Birthday Cake,
        24–27, *25*
    Black Velvet Heart Cakes, 50–53,
        51
    Blueberry Cake, 166, *167*
    Brown Sugar Praline Ice Cream
        Cake, 56–60, *57*
    Buttery Pound Cake with Salty
        Caramel Glaze, 93–95
    Chocolate Rice Crispy
        "Cake" with Homemade
        Marshmallow "Icing," *160*,
        161–63
    Chocolate-Stout Bundt Cake,
        77–78
    Chocolate Texas Sheet Cake with
        Peanut Butter Frosting, 72–73
    Classic Chocolate Cake, 246–47
    Coconut Bundt Cake, 36–39, *37*
    Conversation Heart Cakes,
        50–53, *51*
    Dad's Black Cocoa Bundt with
        Butter Whiskey Glaze, 132, *133*,
        134
    Dolly's Doughnut, 36–39, *37*

Easter Coconut Sheet Cake,
    86–89, *87*
Everyone's Favorite Birthday
    Cake, 156–57
Gonzo Cake, 146–51, *147*
Hair of the Dog Cake, 28–29
Hippie Cake, 90, *91*, 92
Hot Chocolate Pudding Cake,
    135–36
Hot Milk Cake, 28–29
Italian Christmas Cookie
    Cake, 252–56, *253*
Lemon Cake, 80, *81*
Light and Lemony Jelly Roll
    with Raspberry Cream
    Filling, 79–82, *81*
The New Orleans, 56–60, *57*
Orange Buttermilk Picnic
    Cake with Chocolate Chips,
    142–43
Orange Pineapple Walnut
    Fruitcake, 257–58, *259*
Pistachio White Chocolate
    Cheesecake, 67–68, *69*
Pound Cake, 122
Purple Velvet Cake with
    Cream Cheese Frosting,
    146–51, *147*
Rainbow Icebox Cake with
    Homemade Chocolate
    Cookies, *124*, 125–27
Sour Cream Cake with
    Chocolate Cream Cheese
    Frosting, 156–57

St. Patrick's Drunk Bundt Cake, 77–78

Strawberry Supreme Cake, 100–103, *101*

Toffee Coffee Cake Surprise, 44–47, *45*

Tricolor Cake, 252–56, *253*

Ultralemony Lemon Bundt Cake with Almond Glaze, 113–14, *115*

Vanilla Bean Angel Food Cake with Milk Chocolate Glaze, 54–55

Vegan Chocolate Cake, 90, *91*, 92

Very Vanilla Sprinkle Cake, 24–27, *25*

Wintermint Cake, 244–48, *245*

Campfire Cookies, *224*, 237, *241*

caramel:

Caramel Candy Popcorn Balls, 96, *97*, 98

Caramel-y Banana, Peanut Butter, and Chocolate Bread Pudding, 32–35, *33*

Salted Caramel Chocolate Cupcake Shakes, 260, *261*, 262

Salted Caramel Soufflé, 158, *159*, 160

Salty Caramel Glaze, 94–95

Sweet and Salty Caramel Sauce, 58

Chai Spice Trifle with Mixed Berries, 120–23, *121*

cheese:

Cheesy Bastille Day Beer Bread, 144–45

Mega Easter Pie, 84–85

Cherry Almond Crisp, *64*, 65–66

Chinese Five-Spice Sesame Scones, *40*, 41–42

chocolate, 19–20

Black Forest Cupcakes, 104, *105*, 106

Black Velvet Heart Cakes, 50–53, *51*

Blood Orange Tiramisu, 74, *75*, 76

Campfire Cookies, *224*, 237, *241*

Caramel-y Banana, Peanut Butter, and Chocolate Bread Pudding, 32–35, *33*

Chocolate Chip Hush Puppies, 168, *169*, 170

Chocolate Cinnamon Chipotle Sugar Cookies, 204–7, *205*

Chocolate Cookie Crust, 68, *69*

Chocolate Cream Cheese Frosting, 156–57

Chocolate Espresso Tapioca Pudding with Kahlúa Whipped Cream, 220–21

Chocolate Glaze, *116*, 118, 235

Chocolate Pop Tarts with Peanut Butter and Jam Filling, 199–202, *201*

Chocolate Rice Crispy "Cake" with Homemade Marshmallow "Icing," 160, 161–63

Chocolate-Stout Bundt Cake, 77–78

Chocolate Texas Sheet Cake, 72–73

Classic Chocolate Cake, 246–47

Dad's Black Cocoa Bundt with Butter Whiskey Glaze, 132, *133*, 134

Dark Chocolate Coconut Filling, 38

Dark Chocolate Glaze, *253*, 255–56

Dolly's Doughnut, 36–39, *37*

Exceedingly Chocolaty Crinkles, *225*, 230, *241*

Frozen Swiss Chocolate Pie, 172, *173*, 174

Fudge Topping, *139*, 140–41

Hippie Cake, 90, *91*, 92

Hot Chocolate Pudding Cake, 135–36

Hot Fudge, 250

Kitchen-Sink Dutch Baby, 61–62, *63*

Lebkuchen, *225*, 234–35, *241*

Milk Chocolate Glaze, 55

Milk Chocolate Malted Brownies with Chocolate Ganache, 195–98, *197*

Mini Chocolate Brownie Cupcakes, 178–79

Nanaimo Ice Cream Bars, 138–41, *139*

Nutella Chip Cookies, 48–49

Old-School Oatmeal Chocolate Chip Cookies, 110, *111*, 113

Orange Buttermilk Picnic Cake with Chocolate Chips, 142–43

Peanut Butter Blossoms, *225*, 228, *241*

Peppermint Chocolate Chip Meringues, *224*, 232, *241*

Peppermint Chocolate Ganache, 246–47

Pistachio–Chocolate Chip Meringue Cookies, 30–31

Pumpkin Swirl Cheesecake Chocolate Brownies, 189–90, *191*

Rainbow Icebox Cake with Homemade Chocolate Cookies, *124*, 125–27

Red Wine Chocolate Cupcakes with Chocolate Glaze, *116*, 117–18

Salted Caramel Chocolate Cupcake Shakes, 260, *261*, 262

Toffee Coffee Cake Surprise, 44–47, *45*

Vegan Chocolate Cake, 90, *91*, 92

Wintermint Cake, 244–48, *245*

Cinnamon Topping, 166

cocoa powder, 19, 21

Cocoa Frosting, *201*, 202

Cocoa Pretzel Crust, *139*, 140

Dad's Black Cocoa Bundt with Butter Whiskey Glaze, 132, *133*, 134

coconut:

Coconut Bundt Cake, 36–39, *37*

Dolly's Doughnut, 36–39, *37*

Easter Coconut Sheet Cake, 86–89, *87*

Conversation Heart Cakes, 50–53, *51*

cookies:

Brown Sugar Oatmeal Whoopie Pies with Maple Marshmallow Filling, 242–43

Brutti Ma Buoni (Ugly but Good) Cookies, 30–31

Buttery Brown Sugar Bourbon Walnut Balls, 107–8, *109*

Campfire Cookies, *224*, 237, *241*

Chocolate Cinnamon Chipotle
Sugar Cookies, 204–7, *205*
Chocolate Cookies, 126
Date Squares, *224–25*, 240, *241*
Derby Cookies, 107–8, *109*
Election Palmiers, 208–11, *209*
Exceedingly Chocolaty Crinkles,
225, 230, *241*
Gingersnaps with Lemon Sugar,
224, 229, *241*
Lebkuchen, *225*, 234–35, *241*
Mae's Crescent Cookies, *225*,
236, *241*
Nanaimo Ice Cream Bars,
138–41, *139*
Nutella Chip Cookies, 48–49
Old-School Oatmeal Chocolate
Chip Cookies, 110, *111*, 113
Peanut Butter Blossoms, *225*,
228, *241*
Peanut Butter Butterscotch
Cookies, *225*, 233, *241*
Peppermint Chocolate Chip
Meringues, *224*, 232, *241*
Pistachio–Chocolate Chip
Meringue Cookies, 30–31
S Cookies, *225*, 227, *241*
Spicy Mini Elephant Ears,
208–11, *209*
Traditional Linzer Cookies, *224*,
238–39, *241*
Whipped Shortbread, *225*, 231,
241
Cream Cheese Frosting, 148
Chocolate, 156–57
Vanilla, 52–53

cupcakes:
Black Forest Cupcakes, 104, *105*,
106
Individual Baked Alaskas with
Vanilla and Coffee Ice Cream,
192, 193–94
Mini Chocolate Brownie
Cupcakes, 178–79
Red Wine Chocolate Cupcakes
with Chocolate Glaze, *116*,
117–18
Salted Caramel Chocolate
Cupcake Shakes, 260, *261*, 262

D

Dad's Black Cocoa Bundt with
Butter Whiskey Glaze, 132, *133*,
134
Date Squares, *224–25*, 240, *241*
Derby Cookies, 107–8, *109*
Dolly's Doughnut, 36–39, *37*

E

Easter Coconut Sheet Cake, 86–89,
87
Egg Wash, 164
Election Palmiers, 208–11, *209*
equipment, 15–19

F

fillings:
Cherry Filling, 66
Cherry-Kirsch Filling, 106
Dark Chocolate Coconut Filling,
38
Filler Icing, *205*, 206–7
Frozen Swiss Chocolate Filling,
173, 174

Maple Marshmallow Filling, 243
Peanut Butter and Jam Filling,
199–202, *201*
Pistachio White Chocolate
Cream Cheese Filling, 68, *69*
Raspberry Cream Filling, 80, *81*,
82
Raspberry Filling, *253*, 254
Spiced Apple Filling, *213*, 214
Strawberry Whipped-Cream
Filling, 103
Sweet Potato Filling, 218
frostings:
Almond Butter Frosting, *91*, 92
Black Forest Cupcakes, *105*, 106
Broiled Frosting, 29
Chocolate Cream Cheese
Frosting, 156–57
Cocoa Frosting, *201*, 202
Coconut Frosting, *87*, 88–89, *89*
Cream Cheese Frosting, 148
Peanut Butter Frosting, 73
Peppermint Buttercream, 245,
246
Vanilla Cream Cheese Frosting,
52–53
Vanilla Frosting, 102
Very Vanilla Frosting, 26
Frozen Swiss Chocolate Pie, 172,
173, 174

G

galette:
Brown Butter Apple Cranberry
Galette, 212–15, *213*
ganache:
Chocolate Ganache, 195–98, *197*
Ganache Crumb Coat, 254–55

Peppermint Chocolate Ganache,
246–47
gels, 20–21
Gingerbread Spices, 234–35
Gingersnap Crust, *216*, 217–18
Gingersnaps with Lemon Sugar,
224, 229, *241*
glazes:
Almond Glaze, 114, *115*
Butter Whiskey Glaze, *133*, 134
Chocolate Glaze, *116*, 118, 235
Dark Chocolate Glaze, *253*,
255–56
Milk Chocolate Glaze, 55
Rum Glaze, 258, *259*
Salty Caramel Glaze, 94–95
Simple Coconut Glaze, 39
Whiskey-Baileys Glaze, 78
Gonzo Cake, 146–51, *147*

H

Hair of the Dog Cake, 28–29
ham: Mega Easter Pie, 84–85
Heavenly Meringue, *216*, 218, 219
Hippie Cake, 90, *91*, 92
Honey Butter, 176
hush puppies: Chocolate Chip
Hush Puppies, 168, *169*, 170

I

ice cream:
Brioche Ice Cream Sandwiches,
161–64, *163*
Brown Sugar Praline Ice Cream
Cake, 56–60, *57*
Individual Baked Alaskas with
Vanilla and Coffee Ice Cream,
192, 193–94

Nanaimo Ice Cream Bars, 138–41, *139*

Pink Peppermint Ice Cream with Homemade Hot Fudge, 249–50, *251*

Salted Caramel Chocolate Cupcake Shakes, 260, *261*, 262

icings:

Filler Icing, *205*, 206–7

Homemade Marshmallow "Icing," *181*, 182–83

Royal Icing, 196, *197*, 198, *205*, 206–7

Italian Christmas Cookie Cake, 252–56, *253*

K

Kahlúa Whipped Cream, 221

Kitchen-Sink Dutch Baby, 61–62, *63*

L

Lebkuchen, *225*, 234–35, *241*

Lemon Bundt Cake with Almond Glaze, 113–14, *115*

Lemon Cake, 80, *81*

Lemon Sugar, 229

Linzer Cookies, *224*, 238–39, *241*

M

Mae's Crescent Cookies, *225*, 236, *241*

Maple Marshmallow Filling, 243

maple syrup, 21

Mega Easter Pie, 84–85

meringues:

Baked Alaska Meringue, *192*, 194

Heavenly Meringue, *216*, 218, 219

Peppermint Chocolate Chip Meringues, *224*, 232, *241*

Pistachio–Chocolate Chip Meringue Cookies, 30–31

muffins: Peanut Butter and Jelly Crumb Morning Muffins, 186, *187*, 188

N

Nanaimo Ice Cream Bars, 138–41, *139*

New Orleans, The, 56–60, *57*

Nonnie's Blueberry Buckle, 165–66, 167

Nutella Chip Cookies, 48–49

nuts, toasting, 19

O

oats:

Brown Sugar Oatmeal Whoopie Pies with Maple Marshmallow Filling, 242–43

Crumb Mixture, *224–25*, 240, *241*

Old-School Oatmeal Chocolate Chip Cookies, 110, *111*, 113

Orange Buttermilk Picnic Cake with Chocolate Chips, 142–43

Orange Pancakes with Honey Butter, 175–76, *177*

Orange Pineapple Walnut Fruitcake, 257–58, *259*

P

pancakes:

Kitchen-Sink Dutch Baby, 61–62, *63*

Orange Pancakes with Honey Butter, 175–76, 177

peanut butter:

Caramel-y Banana, Peanut Butter, and Chocolate Bread Pudding, 32–35, *33*

Chocolate Pop Tarts with Peanut Butter and Jam Filling, 199–202, *201*

Peanut Butter and Jelly Crumb Morning Muffins, 186, *187*, 188

Peanut Butter Blossoms, *225*, 228, *241*

Peanut Butter Butterscotch Cookies, *225*, 233, *241*

Peanut Butter Frosting, 73

pecans:

Pralines, 58

Whipped Shortbread, *225*, 231, *241*

Peppermint Buttercream, *245*, 246

Peppermint Chocolate Chip Meringues, *224*, 232, *241*

Peppermint Chocolate Ganache, 246–47

Peppermint Ice Cream with Homemade Hot Fudge, 249–50, *251*

pie crust:

Chocolate Cookie Crust, 68, *69*

Cocoa Pretzel Crust, *139*, 140

Frozen Swiss Chocolate Pie, 172, *173*, 174

Gingersnap Crust, *216*, 217–18

Mega Easter Pie, 84–85

Pistachio–Chocolate Chip Meringue Cookies, 30–31

Pistachio White Chocolate Cheesecake, 67–68, *69*

Pound Cake, 122

Pralines, 58

Pretzel Crust, Cocoa, *139*, 140

puddings:

Blood Orange Tiramisu, 74, *75*, 76

Caramel-y Banana, Peanut Butter, and Chocolate Bread Pudding, 32–35, *33*

Chocolate Espresso Tapioca Pudding with Kahlúa Whipped Cream, 220–21

Hot Chocolate Pudding Cake, 135–36

Pumpkin Swirl Cheesecake Chocolate Brownies, 189–90, *191*

purple yam/ube powder, 21

Purple Velvet Cake with Cream Cheese Frosting, 146–51, *147*

substituting sweet potatoes for, 149

R

Rainbow Icebox Cake with Homemade Chocolate Cookies, *124*, 125–27

Raspberry Cream Filling, 80, *81*, 82

Red Wine Chocolate Cupcakes with Chocolate Glaze, *116*, 117–18

Royal Icing, 196, *197*, 198, *205*, 206–7

rum:

Glaze, 258, *259*

Hair of the Dog Cake, 28–29

Lebkuchen, 225, 234–35, *241*

Rum Syrup, 122

S

Salted Caramel Chocolate Cupcake Shakes, 260, *261*, 262

Salted Caramel Soufflé, 158, *159*, 160

salt/sea salt, 21

sauces:

Hot Fudge, 250

Sweet and Salty Caramel Sauce, 58

scones: Chinese Five-Spice Sesame Scones, *40*, 41–42

S Cookies, *225*, 227, *241*

shakes: Salted Caramel Chocolate Cupcake Shakes, 260, *261*, 262

shortcakes: Brown Sugar Shortcakes with Brown Sugar Syrup, Mixed Berries, and Whipped Cream, 128–31, *129*

Soufflé, Salted Caramel, 158, *159*, 160

Sour Cream Cake with Chocolate Cream Cheese Frosting, 156–57

St. Patrick's Drunk Bundt Cake, 77–78

Strawberry Supreme Cake, 100–103, *101*

Strawberry Whipped-Cream Filling, 103

sweet potatoes:

substituting for yam powder, 149

Sweet Potato Tart with Gingersnap Crust and Heavenly Meringue, *216*, 217–19

syrups:

Brown Sugar Syrup and Berries, *129*, 130–31

Lemon Syrup, 114, *115*

Orange Syrup, 143

Rum Syrup, 122

T

tarts:

Chocolate Pop Tarts with Peanut Butter and Jam Filling, 199–202, *201*

Sweet Potato Tart with Gingersnap Crust and Heavenly Meringue, *216*, 217–19

techniques:

double boiler, 19

folding, 19

sifting, 19

tiramisu: Blood Orange Tiramisu, 74, *75*, 76

Toffee Coffee Cake Surprise, 44–47, *45*

toppings:

Chocolate Topping, 136

Cinnamon Topping, 166

Crisp Topping, 66

Crumb, *187*, 188

Fudge Topping, *139*, 140–41

Tricolor Cake, 252–56, *253*

trifle: Chai Spice Trifle with Mixed Berries, 120–23, *121*

V

Vanilla Bean Angel Food Cake with Milk Chocolate Glaze, 54–55

vanilla bean paste, 21

Vanilla Bourbon Sugar, 108

Vanilla Cream Cheese Frosting, 52–53

Vanilla Frosting, 102

Vegan Chocolate Cake, 90, *91*, 92

Very Vanilla Sprinkle Cake, 24–27, *25*

W

walnuts:

Buttery Brown Sugar Bourbon Walnut Balls, 107–8, *109*

Cocoa Pretzel Crust, *139*, 140

Mae's Crescent Cookies, *225*, 236, *241*

Mini Chocolate Brownie Cupcakes, 178–79

Orange Pineapple Walnut Fruitcake, 257–58, *259*

Walnut Crust, *173*, 174

Whipped Cream, 122

Brown Sugar, *129*, 131

Kahlúa, 221

Rainbow, 126

Rum-Flavored, 29

Strawberry Filling, 103

Whipped Shortbread, *225*, 231, *241*

whiskey:

Butter Whiskey Glaze, *133*, 134

Whiskey-Baileys Glaze, 78

white chocolate: Pistachio White Chocolate Cheesecake, 67–68, *69*

Wintermint Cake, 244–48, *245*